Dr Bonnie VandeSteeg lives . ⎯⎯ ⎯⎯ ⎯⎯ ⎯⎯ ⎯⎯ ut is a regular visitor to Badenoch and Strathspey. She ⎯⎯ a teacher for over 30 years and taught many subjects in a range of educational institutions, including English as a Foreign Language in adult education, economics for the Open University and, latterly, A-level philosophy and anthropology in a London sixth form college. Her anthropology studies and research were sandwiched between these work commitments. Retirement has brought time to devote to writing and campaigning in London on issues discussed in her book, such as land use, the environment, housing and local community involvement, and improving community participation in local decision-making. She also continues her hill-walking and climbing interests and is an active member of a number of mountaineering clubs, including the Strathspey Mountain Club.

LAND FOR WHAT? WHAT? LAND FOR WHOM?

*Senses of Place and Conflict
in the Scottish Highlands*

Bonnie VandeSteeg

STORMY
PETREL

First published in 2021 by Stormy Petrel

Cover illustrations by Nick Hayes

Map © Ashworth Maps and Interpretation Ltd 2020.
Contains Ordnance Survey data © Crown copyright and database
right 2020. Ordnance Survey licence number 100040965,
Cairngorms National Park Authority.

landforwhatlandforwhom.org
landforwhatlandforwhom@gmail.com

This book is based on research conducted predominantly between
1999 and 2000, with some updates in more
recent years. With respect to some situations, views and
information may have changed. The author welcomes
updates sent via the above email address.

ISBN: 978–1–838–22500–1
ePub ISBN: 978–1–838–22501–8

A catalogue record for this book is available
from the British Library

Text designed and typeset in Warnock by Patty Rennie

Printed and bound in the UK by The Lavenham Press Ltd,
who can be contacted by emailing enquiries@lavenhamgroup.co.uk

*This book is dedicated to the members of the Strathspey
Mountain Club, past, present and future. Thank you for
sharing the Scottish Hills with me, giving me your time, thoughts
and ideas, and friendship. In particular, I would like to thank
Robert Waterson who not only got me up Munros and Corbetts
and introduced me to important tea and coffee shops, but
who served as one of my main sounding boards both
during my research and up to his death in 2018.*

Members of the club have climbed, walked, cycled, ran, driven, camped, hostelled, bivvied, bothied, chatted, laughed, drank, partied, danced, photographed, sunbathed, dreamt of, mapped out, plotted, planned, talked about, but most of all, members have done just two things: shared and enjoyed their love of mountains for 40 years.

*Victoria Fuller: President
in her address at the celebration of the
40th anniversary of the club in October 2013*

Contents

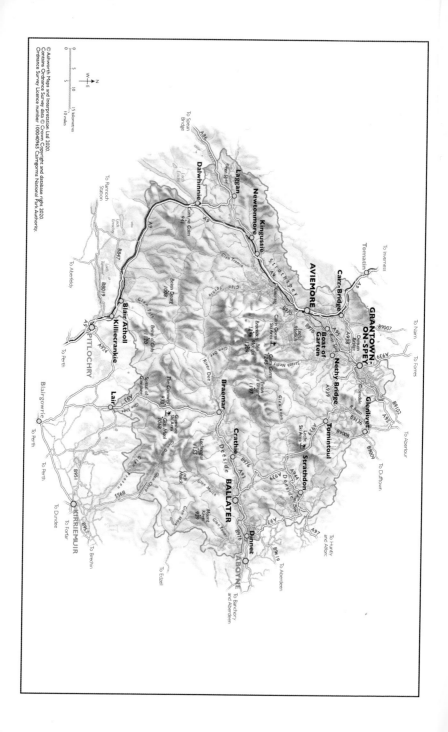

Introduction

The Cairngorms region of Scotland is many things: a place of beauty and a source of inspiration; a challenging and hostile environment in which one can test one's skills; the home of many rare and fragile species; somewhere to have fun whizzing down a slope on skis or walking with friends; and importantly for many, a place in which to make a living and raise a family. Like all places, it is made up of people and their activities, history and memories, situated within a particular physical environment. In addition, the place is shaped by forces beyond its geographical boundaries: the political, economic and social forces of the wider world. 'People's lives are neither global or local – they are glocal' (Eriksen 2001: 302).

I spent one year in the Cairngorms, from 1999 to 2000, as part of my research for my anthropology doctorate. I have continued to visit the area regularly because of the attachments I made both to the physical place and to the people. Anthropologists have a special relationship to place. They traditionally focus on one, spending months or even years getting to know everything they can about it. The aim, however, is to do more than understand it, it is to see what one place can tell us about bigger issues (Eriksen: 2001). My aim was to look at conflicts between three main views on how land should be used: livelihood, recreation and conservation.

Similar themes are found all over the world. In the western USA, environmentalists and Native Americans regularly clash with mining and resource industries. One of the first such conflicts

1

was over the building of the Glen Canyon Dam on the Colorado River in the 1960s. The arguments of those who opposed the plan on the grounds that flooding the canyon was equivalent to destroying the most sacred and beautiful of religious monuments were eventually overruled by people's need for energy and water. More recently there have been battles over the building of an oil pipeline through the sacred ground of Standing Rock as well as protests against fracking in many western states. Again, the needs of people for jobs and resources to maintain the American lifestyle are pitted against those who would like to see more of the West kept as wilderness, both for recreation and ecological reasons. In Africa, conservationists and their supporters in a hostile environment struggle to do anything to save endangered species such as the elephant. Local farmers fighting to survive in difficult conditions made worse by climate change have no sympathy for the elephants and other wildlife that come on to their land and destroy their crops (Neumann). Meanwhile, people tempted by the huge sums offered on the illegal market for ivory are driving the species to extinction. The old growth forests of eastern Poland saw protesters come from all over the continent to try to stop the government and logging companies from harvesting some of the few remaining truly old trees in all of Europe.

In Britain, protesters turn out in their thousands to challenge fracking. The industry claims that fracking is necessary to meet Britain's energy needs whilst those against argue that fracking contributes to climate change destroys valued environments. Britain also has a long history of fighting for access to land for recreation. The Kinder Scout mass trespass of 1932 challenged the right of landowners to restrict access to those who came as their guests for grouse-shooting. Though legislation has been passed opening up the countryside, walkers still feel that landowners have too much power in deciding when and where they can walk. Conflicts over grouse moors have come to the fore yet again in recent years. This time it is the grouse moor owners who are under attack. It is not just a question of gaining access but whether they should exist at all. Those supporting grouse moors use the jobs and liveli-hood argument, similar to that used elsewhere. In addition, there is a cultural clash. Many struggles over land are often between those who live and work on the land and people who are seen as coming from outside the area and therefore lacking in under-standing of the needs and traditions of locals.

This book documents conflicts over land use in the Cairn-gorms of Scotland. The year 1999–2000 was an exciting and controversial time. Debates raged over the proposed funicular railway and the plans for the National Park. Similar to others all over the world, the conflicts appeared on the surface to be between those who sought to develop the area and those who were critical of such development. These were often framed in terms of 'locals' and 'outsiders', with the 'outsiders' often repre-sented as big powerful organisations such as the Royal Society for the Protection of Birds (RSPB) or Scottish Natural Heritage (SNH). My aim was to look beneath the surface in order to see what created and then fuelled the different sides in the debates. By doing this I was able to understand that the land-use conflicts were much more complex than they are characterised to be. And, there is much potential for finding common ground.

Looking back, since both the funicular (now named the moun-tain railway) and the National Park have come to pass, it might be tempting to think that the conflicts have died down. However, in the Cairngorms, like elsewhere, debates around how we use land, who benefits from it and who makes decisions are as alive as ever. There is much at stake with the ever-increasing threat to the planet that is climate change as well as the need to ensure a satisfactory standard of living for all.

Land conflict in Scotland

The Highlands of Scotland have seen many bitter conflicts over land use, very similar to the conflicts documented by anthropologists elsewhere in the world, that is to say clashes between livelihood, recreation and conservation interests. The proposed super-quarry on the Isle of Harris is one example in which locals were split, with both sides supported by different groups from the rest of Scotland. Issues such as wind farms, hydro schemes and the building of hill tracks on wild land continue to polarise different sections of both local communities and the rest of the country.

The Highlands have a long history of economic and social injustice, in line with the experiences of other colonised people. The power of the landowners, either English or in close association with the English ruling class, transformed the Highlands from a society based on the clans, cattle and arable farming to one in which people were 'cleared' from the land to make way for sheep and deer (Hunter: 1976). The land that visitors so admire today is not so much empty as emptied (Short: 1991: 75). The Highlands have since been considered a deprived area and are the target of much European Union (EU) and other development funding.

Meanwhile, the explosion of interest in outdoor recreation and the growing concern and appreciation of wild places has made the Highlands a prime tourist destination. It is one of the few places in Britain where people can come close to having a wilderness experience, complete with the feeling of expanse and solitude, far from the trappings of the urban world (McCarthy: 1998: 1). People come to 'do the Munros' (climb 282 peaks over 3,000 feet), go on long-distance backpack trips, kayaking or mountain biking, or just enjoy a quiet picnic by a remote loch. A number of organisations have sprung up to provide the full range of outdoor activities available and outdoor shops and businesses have become a pillar of many local economies.

In addition, there has also been growing concern about protecting fragile ecosystems and habitats. The Highlands, because of its 'empty' character has become a focus for various projects to preserve habitats or restore ecosystems that have been destroyed by centuries of deforestation (Smout: 1992). It has, therefore, been the target for many directives and protection measures. A key way in which biodiversity policies have been carried out is through the buying-up of land by conservation organisations, including the RSPB, the Scottish Wildlife Trust (SWT), the Woodland Trust, the National Trust for Scotland (NTS) and the John Muir Trust (JMT). Other land is managed by government organisations such as Scottish Natural Heritage (SNH) and the Forestry Commission.

The scene is set for potential conflict. The long-term residents of the Highlands dependent on farming and sheep, the sporting estate, fishing, and now increasingly tourism, have an obvious interest in developing and diversifying the Highlands economy. Anything that will create jobs and enhance development is encouraged, such as the current spread of wind farms across the Highlands. These are not just to meet energy needs of the locals but to generate energy to be exported, as well as to create jobs. The Clearances have not been forgotten and the goal is to increase the population of the Highlands, not to keep it empty. The multiplying effects of North Sea oil have significantly contributed to economic development and Inverness, the capital of the Highlands, is now one of the fastest-growing cities in Britain. There is a need for more housing and infrastructure. Inverness has been transformed in recent years as developers build huge retail parks and housing estates on land sold to them by crofters. There is a general attitude, expressed most forcibly by politicians in the Highland Council and the Highlands and Islands Enterprise (HIE) that development and economic growth are necessary to overcome the underdevelopment caused by the Clearances and depopulation. Some of the aims are: to develop an innovative, productive and internationally competitive business base with resilient and resourceful communities that are empowered, capable and inclusive, and to encourage a growing population, particularly through the attraction of more economically active young people. (http://www.hie.co.uk/about-hie/our-priorities/default.html)

How to go about doing this is a matter of intense debate as those with different interests including sporting estates, agriculture, energy, fishing, technology, creative industries and tourism compete for recognition and financial support.

The situation has been further complicated by the relatively recent arrival of other powerful interests: outdoor recreation and conservation. It appears on the surface that the goals of these are in conflict with the local development goals. Outdoor enthusiasts want to maintain the wild character of the landscape, using their organisations (for example Mountaineering Scotland, the Ramblers Association, Cairngorms Campaign) to lobby against projects involving hydroelectricity and wind farms. Conservation organisations object to the number of sheep and deer as well as obstacles to tree regeneration projects, and therefore come into direct conflict with crofters, farmers and sporting estates. The fact that those who promote outdoor recreation or conservation are often not native Highlanders exacerbates the situation and echoes of the English and southern Scottish-instigated Clearances can be heard. The popularity of the Scottish Nationalist Party demonstrates the widespread antagonism towards the influence of people and institutions south of the border. And for many in the Highlands, that border is much further north than England, stretching well into Perthshire and therefore placing the cities of the Central Belt on the 'other' side.

Resentment against those who seek to promote outdoor recreation and conservation values is often expressed in the political arena. One example of this was the formation of 'People Too' in 2001 by Kirsty Macleod. Macleod was from a crofting family on the Isle of Coll, but was raised largely elsewhere, her family spending a large part of their time in Canada. She was married to the owner of Glen Roy estate, consisting of 7,500 acres near Spean Bridge, between Fort William and Inverness. The aims of the organisation were explicitly to challenge 'environmental people' who are 'getting unchallenged media coverage' and have too much influence on government policy (Maxwell: 2001). In particular, they opposed the RSPB. 'It is an organisation with so much influence at government and SNH level, and there is a growing feeling that this is simply not right. There is a feeling about the RSPB that if the choice is people or birds, then birds would always get the priority' (quoted in Maxwell: 2001).

More recently sporting estates are fighting back against attempts by critics to ban grouse moors both in Scotland, and in England and Wales. They have launched a well-funded campaign called 'You forgot the birds' (https://youforgotthebirds.com/) aimed primarily at the RSPB.

Land conflict in Strathspey

Strathspey, on the northern side of the Cairngorms, is an especially suitable research site to examine environmental conflict. According to Lambert (2001), referring to the possibility of the area being designated as a National Park:

> The last century has pointed out the importance of nature conservation and recreation as land uses in the Cairngorms area, but time has not solved the question of balance between them, nor how to achieve this balance along with a strengthening of the economic prosperity of the region, without which any future designation would not be sustainable in the long-run (p. 271).

Two major issues were sources of conflict during the period of fieldwork 1999–2000. One was the building of the funicular (later known as the mountain railway) and the other was the debate over making the area part of Scotland's second National Park. Both conflicts involved a number of interest groups that were represented by various organisations and spokespeople. The funicular debate was largely between local business interests and conservation and recreation interests, which were often represented by organisations based outside the local area. Local business interests, especially those associated with the skiing industry, were adamant that the funicular was vital for the economic prosperity of the area. Conservationists were concerned about the fragility of the habitat on the top of the Cairngorm plateau. They argued that a funicular would make it easier for people to access the plateau and therefore cause destruction of habitats and rare species. The conservationists were joined by hill-walkers and climbers who did not want to see the hills overrun by tourists who could just step out at the top and be in a serious mountain environment.

The National Park debate included similar players. The Cairngorm Partnership was set up by the Scottish Executive in order to prepare the way for the new park, as a way of facilitating the identified interest groups working together. Membership of this organisation and its various committees was based clearly on interest groups, referred to as stakeholders. The committees reflected the interest groups that have been identified in other conflicts: local livelihood interests (sporting estates, farmers, businesses), recreation (skiing, hill-walking and climbing, cycling and kayaking) and conservation (RSPB, Badenoch and Strathspey Conservation Group). The debate around the National Park had many of the same themes as the funicular debate. Local economic interests were concerned that National Park status would prevent development. Conservation and recreation interests were both in favour of the park but often for different reasons. Hill-walkers and climbers, mountain bikers and kayakers were keen to control development as well as ensuring access for their respective sports. Conservationists focussed more on biodiversity and habitat concerns. They were keen to discourage human intrusion whether that be from developers or from those engaged in various leisure pursuits.

The situation in the Highlands, therefore, mirrors the situation elsewhere in the world, with local economic and social concerns in conflict with the interests of 'outside' conservation and recreation interests. The issue appears to be one of conflicts between different interest groups that are impossible to resolve. Anthropologists have made an important contribution to understanding land-use conflict, often by revealing the negative side of conservation and giving a voice to groups who are socially, economically and/or politically marginalised. However, this then seems to belittle the concerns of environmentalists (Benav: 2018, Dowie: 2009, West: 2007). The way the problem has been posed, in terms of a choice between environment and local livelihood, makes it difficult to see a way forwards (Brechin, Wilshusen, Fortwangler and West: 2003).

CHAPTER ONE

A New Place

Arriving in the Cairngorms as an anthropologist was a strange experience. I had visited the area as a hill-walker and mountaineer many times in the past. This time was different; I felt as if I were entering a new place. A place differs depending on your purpose for being there and, most importantly, what activities you are involved in. I spent a lot of time as a hill-walker and mountaineer over the course of the fieldwork but this time I was also an anthropologist, there for research purposes, with the aim of understanding the place from a variety of views, inhabiting it as others would.

The A9 winds its way to the Highlands from the Central Belt cities of Glasgow and Edinburgh. Though the high hills can be seen from as far away as Stirling on a good day, it is only after Perth that one feels that one is 'getting there'. The road starts to climb gradually until the border of the Highlands is reached at Drumochter Pass, a rather desolate place that doesn't invite lingering. The hills on other side are rather drab – brown the dominant colour. The Drumochter Hills on the east side of the pass are probably the most easily accessible Munros (hills over 3,000 feet) and are also considered amongst the most boring. However, if you stop and peer behind the road-side hills and up the glens to the west, you can get a glimpse of the enormity of what lies behind: endless remote landscape to be explored. The signs about road closures testify that at this point drivers will often encounter snow in winter. This is also the border of Badenoch and Strathspey, the Highland district, which is home to the Cairngorm Mountain region and was the original entry point to the new National Park on its southern side. When I first drove this road, the park was not yet a reality, and the debate around it would dominate my stay.

Badenoch and Strathspey, where I was to make my home for the next year, spreads diagonally from south-east to north-east on either side of the A9, following the course of the River Spey from Laggan in the south-east close to the river's source, to Grantown-on-Spey in the north-east. The whole area is often referred to by visitors as simply the Cairngorms and this is reflected in the fact that the National Park, despite covering many other mountain areas, is named the Cairngorm National Park. This name is in fact a nickname, as the mountain region itself is the 'Am Monadh' or the 'red hill-range', distinguishing them from 'Am Monadh Liath' or 'grey hill-range' (Watson: 1992: 1) and there is just one single peak known as Cairn Gorm. The name is also somewhat misleading because it is used more by visitors than residents to refer to both the 'high' and 'low' ground. However, the Cairngorm massif itself is ringed by population centres on the low ground or straths (valleys) with their own names and identities, meaning both are seen as part of the Cairngorms.

Coming up the A9 one comes first to Dalwinnie. Despite being the home to a distillery, the village seems somehow apart from the main tourist centres of the region. Residents have lobbied for years to get a tourist service area built in order to entice the A9 traffic off the road. Further on I passed the exits to Laggan, Newtonmore and then Kingussie, off to the left of the highway, nestled under the Am Monadh Liath. Laggan is a tiny community, over ten miles further to the west from the next major population centres. These two communities are officially part of Badenoch. Both villages, though popular with visitors, have a long history of settlement with established populations. However, though these villages and their hills have managed to attract their own dedicated clientele, the average visitor will continue north, the Cairngorm massif (Am Monadh) now visible to the right, drawing the attention of the visitor with considerably more power than its less flashy cousins.

Guidebook descriptions of the area invariably involve terms such as 'wild' or 'wilderness' (for example Watson: 1992, McCarthy: 1998). Apart from a few rough hill tracks, no roads cut across the Cairngorm massif. It stretches for thirty kilometres east and west, and twenty-five kilometres north and south. At this point on the A9, it is the hills above Glenfeshie as well as the Cairntoul plateau that one can see. The most popular hills for the average visitor won't be visible until arrival in Aviemore.

Aviemore was also my destination. I pulled off the A9 and drove towards the village. However, like many other visitors, I didn't head for Aviemore itself, instead turning right just before, entering the village at the sign saying 'Glenmore and Cairngorm', to head up what is commonly called the ski road. I was immediately in an extensive forest, such different surroundings to the bare hills I had been driving through up the A9. This forest is justly famous for its native Scots pines. There are a number of tracks that eventually emerge out of the forest and onto the Cairngorm hills themselves, passing popular beauty spots such as Loch an Eilien (Loch of the Island). As the road is the one most frequented by tourists, there is a wide variety of attractions there, from clay pigeon shooting and fishing, to ski rental and souvenir shops. I first passed Inverdruie, a village in its own right and part of the Rothiemurchus Estate, which has been in the Grant family for generations. The current Grants, John and Philippa, have continued the family tradition of encouraging tourism and preserving one of the last remnants of the Caledonian forest in Scotland. They have used this, as well as the fact that the land is not particularly suitable for the traditional pursuits of farming and shooting, to develop a range of tourist-orientated money-making activities. In fact, Rothiemurchus has been a tourist destination since the last century when tourists first began to visit the Highlands. In addition to ski, outdoor and tourist shops and a major hotel complex, Inverdruie has a small number of residents whose houses are tucked away in the pine forest. Since that time, Rothiemurchus and the Grants have been embroiled in controversy over their proposed 'new town'– Campus Mor – which is to be built across the Spey River from Aviemore on land owned by the Grants.

Further up the road, I entered Glenmore, owned mainly by the Forestry Commission. I was now in the heart of the Cairngorms, where the vast majority of visitors are concentrated. It was a glorious day – not all that common as I would find out – and the views of the hills were magnificent. Soon on the right I saw Loch Morlich. Cars were in the lay-by here, taking classic photos of the loch with the Northern Corries (steep, rocky amphitheatres) of the Cairngorms as a backdrop. There were a number of wind-surfers out from the small watersports centre on the east side of the loch. Just past the loch by the dry ski slope, and opposite the turn-off for the national mountaineering centre Glenmore Lodge, I turned into Glenmore campsite. The campsite is owned by the Forestry Commission, which also has a visitor centre and hosts various businesses such as the Glenmore Cafe and dry ski slope and a youth hostel on either side of the road. This was to be my home for the next three weeks.

The campsite wasn't crowded because it was towards the end of the season, so I was able to select a prime site with an uninter-rupted view of the Northern Corries. It is these craggy cliffs that add drama to the rounded hills of the Cairngorms. They are the prime destination for winter climbing. The two corries, or 'coires', Coire an t-Sneachda and Coire an Lochain, are sliced through with gullies that lead the climber from the base to the top of the Cairngorm plateau. This was the one part of the area that I knew well. I had been on several winter climbing courses at Glenmore Lodge, the national outdoor centre, and I then came back to climb with friends most winters.

Arriving now in summer, it was the first time I had actually seen these hills without snow; not quite as spectacular but still beautiful and I was keen to get up there. Days were still long so I pitched my tent, sorted my rucksack and drove further up the road to the ski area car park. The car park is several hundred metres above Glenmore and therefore popular with walkers who are keen to save a bit of time and effort getting into the hills.

At 600 metres the ski car park is the main focus of outdoor activities in the area. The northern rim of the Cairngorm plateau has the most visitors; this is where I spent most of my high-ground time. The corries of the northern edge are divided into two recreational uses. Coire Cas, beneath Cairn Gorm itself, has been developed as a major ski centre. Coire an t-Sneachda and Coire an Lochain are two of the most popular winter climbing venues in Scotland. All three corries are owned by Highlands and Islands Enterprise who then lease the ski area to the Cairngorm Chairlift Company, later renamed Cairn Gorm Mountain Ltd since the replacement of the chairlift with the funicular mountain railway. Management of the ski area has changed hands several times and there is now talk of a community buy-out, especially in light of the ongoing problems with the mountain railway itself, which was out of action for the 2018–2019 and 2019–2020 seasons.

The height of the ski car park makes the high hills very accessible for climbers and walkers, both in summer and winter. In 1999 the mountain railway was not yet built, and though approved, it was still a source of controversy both locally and nationally. Instead, there was a chairlift that took both skiers and walkers up to the top station, just below the actual peak named Cairn Gorm. In winter, many climbers wanting to make the forty-five-minute walk-in even shorter, would take the chairlift up to the middle station and cut over the ridge into Coire an t-Sneachda. Walkers could cut off several hundred metres of ascent by taking the chairlift up.

However, most serious hill-walkers would walk from the car park itself, heading off with the climbers towards the Northern Corries and then cutting off from the valley path up on to one of several ridges that lead onto the immense Cairn Gorm plateau itself. From there, the destinations would be the peak of Cairn Gorm, other Munros on the rim of the plateau or the second highest peak in Scotland after Ben Nevis: Ben Macdhui. The Cairngorm plateau is the only subarctic terrain in Britain, resembling Iceland and Greenland in some respects. It is six kilometres across the plateau from the northern edge and its corries to Ben Macdhui. The featureless terrain can be a serious test of one's navigation abilities. What makes this walk even more dangerous is that the Cairngorm plateau is like a giant table, cut off from the other hill-groups by sharp drops. It is these qualities, together with its accessibility, that give it its reputation for having one of the busiest Mountain Rescue Teams.

Calling myself a serious hill-walker, I eschewed the chairlift and set off from the car park in the direction of the Northern Corries. The path was well marked, though a bit muddy. I soon came across someone who was busy actually constructing a path, laying flat stones like a jigsaw puzzle. He said that they had to put in such a path as the quantity of walkers all year round was causing considerable erosion. I walked past Coire an t-Sneachda and then headed up the ridge dividing it from Coire an Lochain. Being my first day of fieldwork I was not yet hill-fit and I huffed and puffed up to the plateau to be met by the most spectacular view. Looking from south-east to south-west, I could see miles of hills, many over 3,000 feet, divided by glens and lochs and begging to be explored. Braeriach and Cairn Toul lie to the west of the Cairngorm plateau, divided by a deep pass called the Lairig Ghru. It is possible to walk from the north side of the Cairngorms to Deeside on the south side. To the east of Braerich lies Glen Einich, yet another ridge of hills topped by Carn Ban Mor and then a final drop to Glenfeshie, with another north–south hill track route. From the south-eastern edge of the plateau, you can look straight down at the dramatic 4.8 kilometre-long Loch A'an (or Avon), the source of the River A'an, which can be followed eastwards for many miles before reaching the road that cuts down from Badenoch and Strathspey to Deeside. Ben Avon and

Beinn a Bhuird are two other major peaks that lie far on the other side of the River Avon and are usually accessed from Deeside. Most of these I would explore over the course of the year.

I carried on around the rim of the Northern Corries and then headed up to the top of Cairn Gorm itself. The summit is dominated by a weather station, a perfect location to record some of the more extreme weather in Britain; wind speeds of over a hundred miles an hour are not uncommon. Today, being a weekday at the end of the summer season, I had the place to myself. It is the summit that in many respects marks the contrast between the wilderness of the Cairngorm plateau, site of numerous accidents, and the built-up environment of the ski area. Ironically, many people have perished a few hundred metres from so-called civilisation itself. The path down from the summit is like a staircase, designed to ensure that those tourists who have taken the chairlift to the top of the ski station will not get lost as they 'bag' the easiest Munro in Scotland. However, this was in 1999, before the mountain railway had been built. Now tourists are forbidden to leave the parameter fence around the top station with its new Ptarmigan restaurant and visitor centre. In theory, then, no one who has taken the railway up can actually go on to climb Cairn Gorm. This was all part of the deal that was made with Scottish Natural Heritage before they would give their approval to what was then called the funicular. The old Ptarmigan restaurant, a distinctive bubble, was much loved and there were various ideas about what to do with it. In the end, Clive Freshwater, long-time owner of Loch Insh activity centre bought the relic.

I carried on down through the ski area. The contrast couldn't be more striking. The slopes were littered with various skiing paraphernalia – the chairlift itself and various tows – plus the snow fences designed to keep snow in the ski area rather than being blown away by the frequent winds. This area changed with the building of the mountain railway; the main chairlift was removed and in 2019, with the funicular out of action, there was only a poma lift to the top. I was walking down the tracks that later would be ski runs. I could see Aviemore in the distance, or rather I could see the high-rise Hilton hotel sticking out, some would say like a sore thumb, from the surrounding forest. Without wanting to make prejudiced comments on aesthetics, I couldn't help agree that the ski area was ugly, a view shared by both visitors and locals. The discussion around what to do about this eyesore was to dominate my stay in the area. Whilst some argued for the ski area to be dismantled and 'returned to nature', others supported the upgrading of the ski area, with the funicular being the key to this process.

It is not surprising that skiing is a major focus of local concern. In addition to the ski area itself, there is a whole range of businesses that cater to snow sports, from organisations offering to plan school trips to shops selling ski and snowboarding gear. Skiing on the Cairngorms was first introduced by a Norwegian in the 1960s. As a result, many skiers from all over Britain gravitated to the area, getting jobs as ski instructors and/or setting up ski related businesses. Many local children went on to become top international skiers. However, the weather in recent years has meant that the future of skiing has been uncertain.

Global capitalism has had an effect on the skiing industry. It is difficult to predict exactly what will happen in the future, but cheaper foreign travel is changing the demand for holidays in Scotland. More and more people are going to the Alps rather than Scotland for their skiing. The increased availability of cheap travel abroad has been blamed by some for the general difficulties of the Scottish tourist industry. But climate change is also blamed for the economic woes of the ski industry. Snow conditions have become increasingly unreliable and two Scottish ski areas closed down in 2004. The industry is desperately struggling to adapt to the changing nature of the market, experimenting with different ways of attracting tourists, such as the development of mountain biking areas. These changes are very much in evidence in the Cairngorms area, which is very much in flux, economically, politically and socially.

As a result, many now look to other outdoor activities to maintain the health of the local economy. The debate over the building of the funicular was often posed in terms of whether skiing could actually continue to sustain the economy. The hill-walkers' lobby has had a powerful spokesperson in Cameron McNeish, who lives in Newtonmore. He was editor of *The Great Outdoors*, as well as a film-maker who has been behind many of the mountaineering programmes on television. In a regular column he stressed the income generated from non-skiing outdoor recreation. According to the Ramblers Association, which McNeish became president of during my stay, visitors involved in hill-walking and climbing contribute £438 million to the Scottish economy, including £150 million to the Highlands (McCall: 2002).

Apart from those directly employed in outdoor recreation, it is difficult to calculate how many others have set up businesses such as bed-and-breakfasts to cater to the outdoor tourists. There are a number of outdoor centres, including Glenmore Lodge, the prestigious national sports centre. Many independent mountaineers, kayakers and climbers have been attracted to the area because of the chance to engage whole-heartedly in their chosen sport. They either attach themselves to a centre or work freelance.

Walking down through the ski area with the strath below, one becomes fully aware that there are in fact two worlds, often referred to locally (in the newspaper and public meetings) as the 'high' and the 'low' ground. Many who live and work in the strath, have never been on the Cairngorm plateau, and many who spend days on the plateau, stop in the low ground only long enough to stock up on provisions. Yet, the fate of both is intimately linked.

Branching out

I was determined to get to know aspects of the area that would be completely different from the hill-walking and mountaineering activities that were so familiar to me. Land ownership and the sporting estate are key issues in debates on land use in Scotland. I therefore needed to find a way of participating in the activity of shooting. I didn't really want to do any shooting myself but I wanted to get as close as possible to those who did. Since a sporting estate would be difficult to get access to, I decided to start immediately looking into the possibilities. I proceeded to investigate the various estates that ringed Aviemore and the other settlements. These are for the most part outside the Cairngorm hills themselves. Cairn Gorm mountain and the ski area are owned by Highland and Islands Enterprise Board. Along the ski road, or Glenmore corridor, Rothiemurchus is owned by the Grants and their main interest is tourism rather than shooting; I needed to venture elsewhere. The result of this venturing would be the discovery of both the traditional landowner and the conservation landowner.

My first port-of-call was Glenfeshie. To get there I needed to drive south from Aviemore and then through the small village of Kincraig and over the Spey as it flowed out of Loch Insh and then over to Feshiebridge. Following the course of the Feshie River I arrived in Glenfeshie, a beautiful long glen with hills rising up on either side and the Feshie River running through. When the Glenfeshie Estate came up for sale in the late 1990s, a consortium of conservation organisations, with support from land reform groups, tried to buy this 'wilderness gem' in order to reduce deer numbers and facilitate regeneration of the remnants of native woodlands. However, Klaus Helmersen, a wealthy Dane, was able to bid more money – and that sealed the deal. This fuelled much resentment on a national level and forced the landowner to make some efforts to reduce deer numbers, but the estate was still managed mainly for stalking. Helmersen's stint as a Scottish laird did not last long and in 2002 he sold the estate secretly to another Dane, Flemming Skouboe. This caused an uproar in the Scottish Parliament, reinforcing moves to pass the land reform bill that would make it obligatory to first offer any land to the

community to buy. (www.heraldscotland.com/news/12246194.
secret-sale-of-glenfeshie-estate-criticised-by-land-reformers/).
It was all change again in 2006 when another Dane, Anders
Povlsen purchased the estate and turned it into a conservation
showpiece. He has gone on to become the largest landowner in
Scotland with eleven estates totalling 221,000 acres.

At the time of my visit in 1999 Glenfeshie was still very much
a sporting estate. The owner visited regularly but left the day-
to-day management in the hands of the factor, an employee who
has overall responsibility for the estate. My first visit there proved
unfruitful in terms of my aim. (About a month later I would be
back as a grouse-beater). I saw the white-washed cottages of
the estate workers and passed the farm of Donnie Ross whose
anti-conservation letters I would soon be reading in the local
paper. I also met up with three hill-walkers who showed me my
first bothy before they headed up the glen. But there were no
Tweeded gentlemen out shooting and so I pushed on to look
elsewhere.

On my way back to Aviemore, I stopped at Alvie Estate, owned
by Jamie Williamson. This estate differs from Rothiemurchus in
that it has more sporting clients but, like Rothiemurchus, the
owner has diversified into a range of business interests including
a quarry, forestry consultancy and a caravan park. Both John
Grant of Rothiemurchus and Williamson are very active in the
community, involving themselves in public debates and committees. Williamson was also President of the Scottish Landowners
Federation at the time of research. I had no luck with my
queries about my 'participant observation' but was told to try at
Kinveachy, a very large estate which fans out north of Aviemore.
My investigation of Kinveachy brought me into contact with
another distinct part of the region.

*

Kinveachy, the name used by locals, is officially part of Strathspey
Estate, itself just one part of Lord Seafield's 95,814 acres, which

also includes holdings to the north at Cullen on the Moray Firth. He is the sixth biggest private landowner in Scotland. It has been in the same hands for thirteen generations. The owner lives on the northern part of his estate and I was told by employees that he rarely came to Kinveachy. At the time of my research, it was an important sporting estate for both stag and grouse-shooting. Heading north through Aviemore and then through the small village of Carrbridge nestled in the forest, you come again to the A9 trunk road and the landscape opens up into the Dulnain River Valley. This is where the Kinveachy deer tend to congregate, by the river, up on the bare hills above or in the forest on the edge of the valley. 'The Burma Road', an old hill track and official Right of Way, follows the River Dulnain for several miles before turning north-east and winding its way through Alvie Estate to join the A9 just south of Aviemore. It is a popular walking and mountain biking route, one of the few parts of Kinveachy that was used regularly for activities other than shooting. Deer could also be found in the extensive Kinveachy forest, where guests shot from towers rather than stalking the deer. The grouse moors extended from the Dulnain up to Slochd Summit, cut in half by the A9 trunk road.

Following the River Spey, you enter a very different landscape. Cattle farms are spread all along the Spey and along the continuation of the Dulnain east of Carrbridge to Grantown. Some of these farms are still owned by Kinveachy and leased to farmers. Other farmers have been able to purchase their farms. Reavack estate borders Kinveachy in this part of the Spey Valley. This estate was broken up several years ago and many farmers were given the opportunity to buy their farms. Farming has been declining for decades, dependent on grants and subsidies. However, as was seen during the outbreak of foot-and-mouth disease, the farmers have an influence far beyond their numbers because of their long-term link to the land. They are the only group whose families have lived in the area for many generations and therefore hold the status of 'natives'. There is much overlap between the farming community and the sporting estates, not only because the farming land is often owned by the estates but because both estate workers and farmers are considered to be part of the traditional occupations on the land.

Driving north of Aviemore, following the Spey, one enters a pleasant open valley. The hills are much smaller and the view is dominated by farmland and woods. The Cairngorms are still in the distance but cease to be the main focus. One gets more of a sense of the land being a place where people work rather than a tourist attraction. Grantown-on-Spey is the main centre of this part of the region. Though it would like to have a larger share of the area's tourist trade, it has more of an identity as a business and administrative hub. It is also the nearest town to some of best salmon fishing and is home to a smoke house owned by Ian Anderson, lead singer of Jethro Tull. It has one of the area's two high schools (the other is in Kingussie) and one sign that it is more than a tourist town is the fact that it has regular problems with vandalism and 'loitering' young people. From Grantown, the road splits in three. One road heads south over the eastern edge of the Cairngorms to Deeside and the southern Cairngorms, one goes straight north to Forres and Nairn on the Moray coast, and the other follows the Spey into whisky country and Aberdeenshire. However, Grantown marks the end of my fieldwork site. It also gave me my first major breakthrough in my research. It was here that I met Frank Law, the Sporting Estate Manager for Kinveachy. His office was just outside Grantown on the Spey. Later I would hear him referred to as the jogging gamekeeper but at this point he represented the first real contact with a world that was completely foreign to me. He couldn't promise any deer-stalking but would I like to get paid for doing some grouse-beating? My perseverance paid off! This was to prove to be the beginning of a major part of my research, providing not just data on the sporting estate, but spawning many more contacts and sources, which I would follow up over the course of the year.

Move to town

One morning I woke in my tent to a particularly wet and cold day. I decided that I needed a proper breakfast and drove into Aviemore. At the entrance to the village, just past the tourist office, I was enticed into Harkai's Fish Restaurant by the offer of £1.99 breakfasts. I noticed the sign on the door that said: waitress/waiter wanted. I had worked as a waitress on various occasions before embarking on a career as a teacher. The restaurant was very appealing – cozy and inviting. Also, it would be a place where I could meet the locals as well as earning some money to help support my unfunded research. I inquired and was immediately hired. I started the next morning, serving breakfast to the Harley Davidson rally participants. Fortunately, my waitressing skills came back quickly as I somehow managed to cope with the queue of hungry bikers, equally tempted by the cheap breakfasts. I was also fortunate to have co-workers such as fourteen-year-old Craig who taught me the ropes and I was able to make a good hot chocolate beyond my skills. I had always come for the outdoor activities but Aviemore has long been the destination of more conventional tourists – hen and stag weekends, business conventions and in this case the Harley Davidson gathering. The owners of the restaurant were both from Hungary, John Harkai having come as a refugee to Britain after the Hungarian uprising in 1956. He started in the fish and chip business down in Yorkshire and then moved to Aviemore, seeing the potential for increased tourism with the new ski development in the 1960s. I was now seeing a different aspect of the place, not as a tourist but as someone who was making a living out of the tourists. I had now moved from the high to the low ground – a place where people live, work and raise their children. It was a long way from the Cairngorm plateau and an equally long way from the closed world of the sporting estate.

It was now the end of September. It might have started out being fun – the anthropologist living out of a tent – but after almost a month it was beginning to lose its novelty. Now that I was busy with my grouse-beating, waitressing and following up research contacts, it was time to move into town. Aviemore is the only place you are likely to encounter a traffic jam, primarily in tourist season, usually in front of Tesco where a pedestrian crossing forces cars to stop frequently. This was Aviemore's only supermarket – a second one just opened recently, an Aldi – and it was the one place where everyone, both visitor and resident, was likely to come at some point in the week, often every day. The north end of Aviemore contains a number of major housing developments, many for tourists but also modest dwellings, including some council housing, for lower-income families. This is where I took up residence for my fieldwork year. North of Aviemore, you are soon back in open country, with forests, small farms and a few houses dotted about, built in a position to capture a good view of the northern edge of the Cairngorms. Since then, two major housing developments have encroached on this open countryside.

One of the key features of Badenoch and Strathspey is the variety of the people who have been attracted to the area over the years. This migration reveals much about what is going on economically and politically outside the area as well as in the area itself. There has been wave after wave of immigration, starting with the railway workers in the nineteenth century and then the loggers up until World War II. The next wave included immigrants from Scandinavia and Austria who established Scotland's first ski industry in the 1960s. The economic development that ensued attracted an array of people from Scottish cities looking for jobs and a better environment in which to raise children. And in more recent years, with the general expansion of the outdoor industry, many others have followed the skiers, including mountaineers, kayakers and mountain bikers. They have spawned a host of new businesses with general outdoor shops and mountain bike sales and rentals proving to be more profitable than those who cater to skiers only.

The area has also been a major destination for those seeking to flee the urban areas. Many of these people are retired, but fit and active. They turn their energies to doing things in the community and are present on many committees and active in clubs and associations such as the Tennis Club, the Provosts (an association for retired professionals), a film club, a local history society and walking clubs such as the Ramblers and the Strathspey Mountain Club.

The area must also be situated in the context of global capitalism. North Sea oil has had an enormous impact on Aberdeen but repercussions have been felt much further afield. With the expansion of Inverness, just thirty miles north of Aviemore, Badenoch and Strathspey is increasingly being seen as a commuting suburb. Many oil workers' families have also chosen to live in Badenoch and Strathspey, as a convenient and quiet place to raise children whilst the men are off working on the rigs. As Inverness and its environs become more of an economic, political and cultural centre, land in the area has become more valuable. Rothiemurchus and Kinveachy estates have both been selling parts of their estates for new housing developments and there is pressure from other property developers for more land on which to build. In addition, with the revolution in communication systems and greater mobility of capital, the Inverness area, with its low-wage economy, has become attractive to business, just as are many countries in the developing world. Aviemore has a range of businesses, not all geared to tourism (www.visitaviemore. com/business/). However, efforts to diversify employment have not all been successful. A call centre established on the basis of a contract with HSBC had to close in 2012 when the company moved their business elsewhere, with a loss of eighty-five jobs. However, in 2018 planning permission was given to build affordable homes, creating more jobs in the building trade – a common source of employment in the region.

Many people choose the area as a base for either working from home, or for frequent business trips. I met one man who travelled regularly as an environmental consultant for the oil industry and then did the rest of his work from home. That meant he could live in a place that he liked because of its outdoor attractions rather than having to be based in a city office. Another woman raises her children and commutes to work in Inverness whilst her husband travels the world as an engineer for the oil industry.

A walk on the 'wild' side

I was now well into the second month of research. Most of my time had been spent on Kinveachy Estate, settling into the town and continuing with my hill-walking explorations. I was now a regular reader of the local paper, the *Badenoch and Strathspey Herald*, commonly known as the *Strathy*. I noticed a meeting of the local chapter of the John Muir Trust. Jamie Williamson was to be the guest speaker. I also met members of the Badenoch and Strathspey Conservation Group (BSCG), such as Roy Turnbull. I came across his name almost every week in the letters page of the *Strathy*; he is a keen opponent of Donnie, whose house I had passed the month before on Glenfeshie. He was arguing passionately for landowners to stop managing the land for sport and let it return to a state of wildness. One of the main problems was the number of red deer. Abernethy Estate was mentioned as an example of what could be done. This was the estate owned by the RSPB and had often been the target of abuse by the keepers and stalkers I had come across on Kinveachy. This meeting prompted me to explore what would turn out to be a large network of conservation organisations, landowners, businesses, and individuals.

RSPB's Abernethy is an ex-sporting estate, previously owned by Liverpool shipping magnates. It is a very large estate, extending from the forest to high up on the north-eastern side of Cairn Gorm. Its main aims are to protect species such as the endangered capercaillie and black cock, as well as promoting the growth of native trees. In addition, it is home to the famous

Osprey Centre, which is used by the RSPB both to educate the public and protect this popular bird of prey. The nearest villages are the Boat of Garten and Nethy Bridge. Both villages are popular with visitors and are known for having a very high percentage of holiday homes.

I wanted to participate in the activities of the RSPB. Fortunately, an opportunity came along when I was invited by a fellow waitress, Ailsa, to go to a public meeting hosted by another RSPB reserve at Insh Marshes. Ailsa was a zoology student from Kingussie who was working at the restaurant to save for her plans to do wildlife volunteer work in Australia. Kingussie, together with Newtonmore, are the main centres of the Badenoch part of Badenoch and Strathspey. They are located further upstream as the Spey flows to its source in the hills to the south-west of the Cairngorms. Insh Marshes is to the north-east of Kingussie, just past the turn-off to Glenfeshie. It is an important site for birds because it is here that the Spey enters a flood plain. During the winter months, the plain floods and becomes home to many species of wintering birds, including hundreds of whooper swans. The warden of Insh Marshes, Tom Prescott, was to become one of my most helpful and interesting contacts.

The purpose of the meeting was to make links with the surrounding communities such as Kingussie and Kincraig. Together with a representative of the RSPB from Inverness, he was trying to stress how the reserve was concerned with listening to the views of the local community and how the management of the reserve was compatible with other interests such as grazing and economic livelihood. They were both clearly concerned about the RSPB having a negative public image in the local area. It seemed that this was largely due to the reputation of Abernethy. Tom welcomed me and said he would be happy to have me do some volunteering on his reserve. Ailsa and I were then invited to come back and have a look at the hen harriers' roost, and so began my association with Insh Marshes, which provided not only data for my research but friendship with some remarkable people. It was, in many ways, so similar to my time at Kinveachy, despite the fact that they are considered to be the polar opposites when it comes to land management.

The significant role played by conservation interests is also indicated by the presence of wildlife tourism companies such as Speyside Wildlife, a Scottish Natural Heritage office and a ranger educational programme for both visitors and schools. As a result, a number of people have come to the area to work in conservation-related occupations, on the reserves as wardens, as rangers or wildlife guides.

A place of conflict: local politics in a national context

I experienced local politics through the local paper and public meetings. The paper and the meetings covered all of Badenoch and Strathspey, from Grantown in the north-east, Carrbridge in the north, along the Spey to Aviemore, Kincraig, Kingussie, Newtonmore, and even Laggan, a small outlier village almost half-way to Spean Bridge and Fort William in the west of Scotland. In some respects, the local paper created its own space, one full of controversy and conflict. The letters page was dominated by attacks and counter-attacks, primarily between those who were either pro-development or pro-conservation and recreation. The same names kept appearing and gave the impression of a very divided community. A similar theme was played out in public meetings. As the area was about to become a National Park, the focus of the meetings tended to be on the impact of this on local development. It soon became apparent that at the level of local politics battle lines had been drawn between local development interests and the conservation and recreational interests of so-called incomers and outsiders. I was to find that this was a much too simplistic analysis.

Like other parts of Scotland, Badenoch and Strathspey has been affected by the growth of Scottish nationalism. We have seen how unusually great numbers of incomers have transformed the area. This has led to resentment, as elsewhere, but the situation is complicated by the fact that the definition of incomer is being continually redefined. As there are very few real natives, local and incomer is a relative term, based on how long one has been in the area. Bill Wilkie, who came to Aviemore to work in the railway before the war, told me in an interview that he still doesn't consider himself a local. Many of those who came in the 1960s in the wake of the growth of the ski industry see themselves as local, whereas the more recent arrivals in the general outdoor industry are still considered to be incomers. This resentment is often directed at the English, but often it is against those from the urban areas of Scotland as well. There is some sense of Gaelic identity, but it is relatively insignificant compared to the west of Scotland. Still, the resurgence of nationalism and the interest in heritage has had an impact on the area.

Landowners such as John Williamson and John Grant were regularly heard of at public meetings, testimony to the key role they play in local politics. The different landowners use their public presence and local involvement as a way of showing the success of the current system of land ownership, both economically and environmentally. The national debate, with the new Scottish Parliament as a focus, has meant that the activities of landowners have come under greater public scrutiny. On Kinveachy, there was recently a plan for the community to buy-out some local woods that the estate was going to sell to a logging company. Debates about land reform on a national level are clearly linked with land issues at a local level.

Questions to answer

These first months provided the focus for the research. In many cases, people seemed to be familiar only with certain parts of the area. Moreover, even when they did inhabit the same physical space, they seemed to perceive that space differently, as if different groups inhabited parallel worlds or places. I wanted to understand the relationship between these individual senses of place and the public conflicts over land use I had seen in the paper and in public meetings. I wanted to go behind the scenes of what were very public battles in order to understand how these conflicts came about. By understanding the meanings, motivations, emotional attachments, perceptions and attitudes, the sense of place of the different groups involved, how they are formed into interest groups and why these interest groups then clash so bitterly, I hoped to offer some possible ways out of the impasse created by the divisions between conservation, recreation and livelihood approaches to the environment.

CHAPTER TWO

Sense of Place
and Mountaineering

Activities: Planning, Anticipating, Preparing, Walking,
Climbing, Pacing, Munro-bagging, Navigating, Surviving,
Looking for Affordances, Having an Epic, Learning Skills,
Bonding, Sharing, Remembering

My eyes are drawn upwards to the skyline; it is the first thing a visitor notices coming over the Drumochter Pass from the south: the hills, the Cairngorms. It is not a particularly remarkable mountain range seen from this angle; no dramatic precipices, no pointed, snow-capped peaks. There is no viewpoint to pull into as there is in Glencoe, complete with bag-piper, from which the visitor can see the hills from the perspective of the tourist gaze (Urry: 1990) and take the obligatory picture. One has to go further, at the very least turning off the A9 and then again, resisting the temptations of the shops of Aviemore, and head up Glenmore. Here the Cairngorms reveal a more dramatic face. One of the best views is from the Glenmore campsite. This is where I came on my first day. I drove to the very edge of the site and pitched my tent so that I could sit and have an uninterrupted view of the rocky buttresses and ridges of the Northern Corries. And today the view was especially appealing, the hills outlined by a perfectly blue sky; the kind of view you are more likely to see in a tourist brochure than in reality.

The view from Glenmore is what attracts many people to this campsite. Sandra and Tommy have been coming with their caravan for years, always pitching in the same spot. Sandra says she 'never gets enough of the view'. They are apologetic, however. As they have got older they do not go out walking in the hills like they used to. The view may be an attraction, but that is only the preamble to what many believe really counts – not just looking, but going into the hills. As soon as you see them there is a 'stretching towards' (Merleau-Ponty: 1962) and then, as for Nan Shepherd, a desire to 'go into the mountain' (Peacock: 2017).

It is not enough just to sit there looking, especially on a day like today. Once I have settled into my new home, I set off, moving through the view that I had been looking at. The terms of my engagement have changed. I am no longer looking at a landscape painting. I am moving through that painting. Not only has the scene become three dimensional, I am immersed in it – both physically and mentally.

Within a few hours I have reached the top and the view has changed; I am now looking back down at the campsite. It is not the same as looking up. Walking through the landscape to get to this point has changed the quality of the visual experience. The Victorian artist and critic John Ruskin said that to appreciate beauty, you have to do more than just look at it (quoted in De Botton 2002). Ruskin painted it. Others move through it.

People who come to the Cairngorms for the purpose of immersing themselves in the hill environment form a sense of place. They engage in a range of hill experiences – summer and winter hill-walking, rock-climbing and ice-climbing – and what these activites all have in common is an intense engagement with the natural environment. This engagement is characterised by an interaction between the subjective, the individual's own perceptions, desires and feelings, and the objective, the physical 'affordances' (what the place has to offer) and the constraints of the environment. This does not mean that the sense of place is 'mapped on to' (Ingold: 1996: 140), the physical environment but rather that it emerges out of the activity itself, binding together the person and the place. The detail of this interaction between the person and the physical place illustrates the incredible complexity of the interweaving of the objective and subjective that a sense of place entails.

Preparing, anticipating and preparing

Something of value is on the roads and hills and thousands set off each Saturday to find it. Each one sees it differently. I have only described what I have found (Borthwick: 1983).

The question of why people go into the hills in the first place is the subject of extensive literature, often written by mountaineers themselves, analysing the many motivations and going well beyond Mallory's reply – 'Because it's there' (Bartlett: 1993, Noyce: 1954, Macfarlane: 2003, Alvarez: 1988, Simpson: 1988, 1993, 2003, Rose and Douglas: 1999, Wilson ed.: 1973). Wacquant, in his study of boxing, is aware of the many complex sociocultural factors that might push people towards a potentially dangerous and often uncomfortable activity. However, he argues that what is interesting is to understand the experience itself and how boxers live that experience. By understanding what is involved in the experience, we will be better placed to answer the question: why?

The people I met, whose experiences make up the substance of my research, began their preparation long before they went into the hills. Armed with aspirations born from past experiences of themselves or others, maps and guidebooks, hours are spent in planning a trip to the hills. My desire to do a winter ascent of Tower Ridge on Ben Nevis was partially motivated by reading Bill Murray's account of his epic climb just before he went off to fight in World War II. Others may be influenced by the idea of a popular challenge, such as doing all the Scottish 4,000ers or all the Munros. The process of planning and preparing reveals much about what people think is important in their interaction with the hills. Which aspect of the variety of hill experiences they select indicates which aspect of the place they value. This decision is determined partly by subjective reactions to past experience and preferences, and partly by physical factors such as weather and season.

John's Weekend

John, in his early forties, is a deputy head at a London college. Though he has been a hill-walker for many years, it is only in the past ten that he has become involved in serious mountaineering: summer and winter climbing rather than 'just' hill-walking. Unfortunately, living in London means that he cannot indulge what he refers to as his craving very often. He is typical of many London-based mountaineers who have to balance their other life commitments with their 'need' to get to the mountains. Not many are willing to go to the lengths that Mick Fowler did when he was a tax inspector in London – drive overnight on Friday to the far north of Scotland every weekend in winter (Fowler: 1995). However, John occasionally showed his willingness to go to similar lengths. When the opportunity arose for John to climb in Scotland one weekend in December, he booked his flight, despite the fact that he had a job interview on Monday morning. With only two days, John was intent on making the most of it. Friday evening was spent planning. He had arrived with clear aims.

I definitely want to do some winter climbing and it has to be good – something challenging. I have checked the forecast on the internet – including the avalanche and climbing conditions, and it looks good – fairly low risk of avalanche and reasonable snow conditions. I am a little bit worried about my fitness. I know I want to do something in the Northern Corries – it is near here, an easy walk-in, reliable conditions and some easier-graded routes. But we could do that on Sunday, when I don't have so much time. Tomorrow we could try another area.

The guidebooks were consulted and the decision was made to go over to Torridon in the north-west and do the traverse of Ben Alligin, which includes the difficult 'Horns of Alligin'. This ridge had several stars in the guidebook and would be challenging in snow conditions because of the 'horns', but not too challenging – only a grade I, the easiest route that is still classed as a 'climb' rather than a 'walk'. It would be a relatively safe route as it wasn't a gully climb, so there was no danger of avalanche. It would be a short enough day and even if we were going slower than the guidebook time, there were escape routes. A final reason for choosing this objective had to do with what Torridon was: a new area for John – not too far away and in a spectacular setting – with contrast between sea and hills and made famous by Mick Fowler's legendary weekend trips from London. John's decision emerged from a combination of factors, ones that I observed in many other planning situations: the role of guidebooks and classification systems, the desire for challenge with careful management of risk and the appeal of places with historical, cultural and aesthetic value. All of these involve a combination of objective and subjective factors.

Munro tables and guide books

Summer hill-walking refers to walking at any time of the year when there is no significant snow cover. This season stretches from spring to autumn but this can be affected by late or early snowfall. Scotland's mountains have been categorised and given names, according to height. A Munro (named after the man who first drew up the table) is the name given to all hills over 3,000 feet and these have formed a focal point for walkers. The appeal of the

Munros is obvious. They give a goal to one's walking: to arrive at the top. As they are the highest mountains in Scotland they tend to be the most challenging and interesting. There are 282 of them scattered all across the Scottish Highlands so they are a way of exploring both well-known and more obscure parts of Scotland. The people I met during my research, most of whom came from within the area, had a variety of reasons for 'doing Munros'. They liked the challenge and the sense of achievement, but also found it a way of organising their walking. They particularly liked the way it encouraged them to go places that they normally wouldn't go. For Victoria, a long-term member of the Strathspey Mountain Club and on her third round of the Munros, it is much more. 'I love the Munros but it is not about why I do the Munros, that is only what my heart feels. It is my delight in their beauty, my struggle to be part of them, my strength to be amongst them, my challenge to leave a little of me on them and my constant need to be with them. For them to be a part of my life, it is my freedom, my joy.'

Some of the Munros require enormous logistic organisation. This does not mean that people do not have the clear objective of doing all the Munros: several members of the Strathspey Mountain Club, such as Victoria, have done them more than once and Douglas, a local farm worker, is on his fifth round. However, more narrowly focussed 'Munro-baggers' certainly exist. They are characterised by a lack of interest in doing hills twice, or by different routes, and by a certain sense of urgency to get the tick in order to move on to the next one.

Munros are not just a cultural phenomenon (Lorimer: 2000). Though the practice of 'doing Munros' is something people have invented, it emerges out of the physical features of the land. When walking through the hills there are really only two options: follow the ridges up to the top or follow the valleys or glens around the bottoms of the hills. The latter is the preserve of the long-distance walker. For the hill-walker, it is the ridges that draw them upwards until they can go no further. Johnson

(1987) argues that we shape our reality by 'the contours of our spatial and temporal orientation and the forms of our interactions with objects' (p. xix). We have a sense of 'up-down' because it is an imaginative structure that has emerged from our bodily experience. In the context of hill-walking, this sense of 'up-down' structures our destination. However, the 3,000-foot cut-off point is clearly an arbitrary cultural imposition. There has been talk of changing to the metric system, but this has provoked outrage. 'Doing the Munros' would not be the same.

Anne has been doing her Munros for several years, ever since she and her husband George moved up to the area after retiring from work in Edinburgh. She is an active member of the Strathspey Mountain Club. She loves this new life: 'I feel like I am where I belong'. The Munros are a way of 'organising and focussing' her newly discovered passion for the hills. She has a map on her kitchen wall and when she completes a hill, she colours in the triangle and fills in the date. She had done about half when I arrived and I joined her on a number of Munro trips.

Some Munros are more coveted than others. The very rounded hills of Drumochter Pass are 'boring'. On the other hand, the In Pin (The Inaccessible Pinnacle), perched high on the Cuillin Ridge on the Isle of Skye, is one of the most anticipated objectives. It is a shark's fin of rock, standing out even amongst the scores of pinnacles on the ridge, easily recognised from a number of vantage points. To do this Munro requires climbing skills, a skill most Munroists do not have. Therefore, Anne asked a friend, Richard, a young Sheffield climber living temporarily on Skye, to take her up, with George. The planning began. Anne has a number of books that outline the routes of ascent to the base of the In Pin. Using the map, she worked out the route to take. The Munro guidebooks have become a key aspect of any planning – a way of working out the most convenient way to the top (Lorimer: 2000). However, for Anne, the guidebooks are only one part of the route-planning process and she prefers to rely more on her own reading of the map and on advice from people who

have done the hill before. The logistics became more complicated because Richard planned to do a climb further down the
ridge before meeting them. She had to work out the timings,
not an easy thing with the rocky terrain of the Cuillin. The days
were long in May, but she still had to make sure that all could be
accomplished before dark – a descent off the Cuillin in the dark
is a dangerous proposition. The result was a successful ascent –
with a hug for Richard and a bottle of whisky. The ascent of the In
Pin was a product, then, of the existence of the Munro Tables and
the use of guidebooks, but its challenging and aesthetic aspects
could be considered objective qualities of the hill itself (Brady:
2003).

Classification of climbs:
aesthetics and management of risk

Planning for climbers also involves classification systems as presented in the guidebooks put together largely by the British and
Scottish Mountaineering Councils. There are different grading
systems in other countries. The British system is distinct because
of the fact that climbs in Britain demand that the climber place
their own protection as they ascend. There are no bolts pre-
placed. This is known as traditional or 'trad' climbing. Sport climbing, with pre-placed bolts, is becoming more common, but it is
still seen as what they do on the Continent rather than in Britain.

Early climbers did not have such aids and would instead
choose their routes by examining the rock face, looking for
gullies, grooves, chimneys and cracks that would afford them
a way up. Today, these original routes have been codified into
guidebooks, given names, grades (difficulty) and a star rating
(quality). However, these are firmly based on the experiences
of the first climbers. Some argue that you can ignore the guidebooks and others seek their own new routes in the blank places,
but most people use the guidebooks to choose routes because

these routes do exist 'on the ground'. And it matters which route you choose, partly because climbers claim that some routes are actually better than others, but most importantly in order to match one's skill to the route. The grading of rock-climbs is very complicated. There is one overall grade that refers to the difficulty of the climbing as well as the amount of protection available and the degree of exposure. In addition, each pitch of a climb is given a numerical technical grade, which refers only to the difficulty of the climbing.

The grading system (summer):
climbing grades from easiest to most difficult

Difficult
Very Difficult
Severe
Hard Severe (4a, 4b)
Very Severe (4c)
Hard Very Severe (5a)
E1 (5a–5b)
E2 (5b–5c)
Continuing to E9/10

The grading system in winter goes from I to X. However, guidebooks have begun to divide each grade into subdivisions, as for summer rock-climbing.

Like Munroists, climbers will also have tick lists of climbs they want to do. These will be influenced by the star system, assigning stars to routes that have gone down in history as being 'good' routes, often referred to as classics. A rating of zero stars means that the route is of limited interest – vegetated, loose rock, lack of a good 'line', whereas three stars indicates a classic. There is also a history behind the classics, these routes have normally first been taken by climbers that have now become famous. The importance of tradition is illustrated by the 'chock stone debate' in the

Peak District over whether two climbers should have removed a large rock from the chimney of a three-star route. Two climbers returned to replace the chock stone, arguing on the climbing websites that this was how the route had traditionally been done.

The following entry from a Cairngorms guidebook is an example of what a climber would be confronting:

Description of route with technical grade for each pitch

The Magic Crack 105m HVS (Hard Very Severe) ***
An excellent route with a unique finger crack.
Start at a deep left-facing corner by a huge beak of rock.

1. 35 m 4c   Climb the corner and the broad brunt rib above to a platform and a large spike belay.

2. 25 m 5a   Climb the rib a short way, then take the thin clean crack on the right. This leads into corners which run up to below the deep corner of The Genie (another route).

3. 45 m 5a   Move up right and climb the superb finger crack. Cross an overlap and climb the cracked wall above to easier ground.

The three stars would immediately attract attention. The description of the climb makes it sound like an interesting 'line', with the finger cracks, corners, ribs and walls. However, the HVS grading would deter many people as this is higher than the grade climbed by the average climber. If the climber did feel capable of doing such a climb, the next words to consider would be 'finger crack'. This is a style of climbing that not everyone is suited to. I asked Ed, a very focussed climber who visits Scotland regularly from Surrey, to explain how he went about selecting what climb to do.

The stars drag your eyes to the route in the guidebook. You genuinely think it will be a better route. A better climb is one that has a line to follow – obvious features or the rock, like cracks, corners or arêtes. The line is obvious on a good route – the rock leads you there. It is not broken but continuous. You don't want to find it suddenly disappearing where you have to start walking. Often a route is not liked because it is contrived. Or, a good route could have a lot of variety, many different types of climbing rolled into one – a crack, a traverse, an arête with a variety of types of holds. It is also the situation you are in – the exposure or the view. When you don't get out climbing that much – maybe a dozen trips a year, you may not get back to a particular crag again so you want to do the classic climbs. I also choose a route based on personal climbing preference, like if you prefer slabs, cracks or corners. You also have to understand guidebook speak. I want a route that will give me a challenge but not too much of a challenge. So I choose a grade that I think I can do but then I read the description and watch out for words like 'strenuous' and 'sustained'. Though the grading can be a bit arbitrary – sometimes a route gets a star and I don't know why or else the climb seems over or undergraded, but then that is so subjective – so it is a dialectic between you and the rock.

The factors affecting the choice are incredibly complex. Ed, who has a high level of both body and mental confidence, continually aims to push the grade. Therefore, when he goes rock-climbing he would prefer not to do anything below a 'Very Severe'. John, on the other hand, lacking Ed's confidence and skill, will be happy to lead a 'Severe'. On the whole, people choose objectives that they think will match their skills but still provide a challenge. If it is too easy, then the climb will seem disappointing. Csikszentmihalyi (1998) calls this combination – of the maximum risk that fits one skill – as essential for creating 'flow', the total involvement in what one is doing. He argues that it is this feeling of flow that leads to the optimal experience. Happiness does not come whilst in flow but only afterwards, upon reflection. The climber knows that an objective must be chosen that will give some sense of risk, but a controlled risk, one that he/she feels they are able to deal with. 'The evolution of self-reflective consciousness has allowed our race to "toy" with feelings, to fake or manipulate feelings in ways that no other animal can' (1998: p. 17). The climber knows what emotions lie in wait on the climb and upon completion of the climb. The objective is chosen with this in mind.

Mountaineering culture and history

Objectives are often determined by stories and memories. Sometimes these are personal stories and other times it is the collective memory as preserved in mountaineering literature and guidebooks. Stuart is training to be a full-time mountaineering instructor. He is immersed in a mountaineering environment, both in terms of the physical experience itself and as part of a tradition. He never tires of talking about climbing whether it be of details, of routes he has done, advice on which Goretex jacket is best, or stories of famous climbs. He continues to seek out new places as part of expanding his knowledge of the hills and gaining experience for his instructor's assessment. He was up in Scotland, from his home in the Peak District, in order to prepare for his winter Mountain Leader Assessment. He wanted to go to a new area to practice navigation somewhere that he wouldn't know very well. The south side of the Cairngorms is very remote – requiring many miles of walking up a Land Rover track before even getting to the base of the main hills – Beinn a Bhuird and Ben Avon. This seemed a suitable destination. But what clinched the decision was reading about a place called the 'secret howff'.

The 'secret howff' of Beinn a Bhuird is a mystery that has miraculously been guarded for thirty years, the best kept secret in the history of Scottish mountaineering. The howff's location today is still tantalising those who know of its existence, but who have not been admitted to the word-of-mouth freemasonry which maintains its seclusion' (Brown and Mitchell: 1997: 126).

I found out about its location whilst grouse-beating on Glenfeshie Estate. I got talking to someone and mentioned the 'howff' and for some reason he felt I was worthy of learning its location. So the trip was on!

The adventure

Despite the close relationship between prior knowledge from past experience, stories, guidebooks and maps to the physical reality, the experience of this reality is distinct. According to Lorimer and Lund (2003), though guidebooks may to an extent regulate behaviour, they are subjected to improvisation in practice. As the philosopher David Hume says, the idea can never be as powerful as the sensation itself (1972). Nevertheless, the planning, the preparing and the anticipating have a crucial role to play. These subjective factors – humans' classification and organising dispositions and the use of history and stories as a way of giving meaning to places in our imagination – are combined with the objective affordances and limitations of the actual physical land as well as our own bodies.

Moving through place: the body, the ground, space and time

Where does it all start? Muscles tense and leg a pillar, holding the body upright between earth and sky. The other a pendulum, swinging from behind. Heel touches down. The whole weight of the body rolls forward onto the balls of the foot. The big toe pushes off, and the delicately balanced weight of the body shifts again. The legs reverse position. It starts with a step and then another that add up like taps on a drum to a rhythm of walking (Solnit: 2001: 3).

According to Merleau-Ponty (1962), our meanings originate in what he calls the body-subject. The body is the source of 'prereflective cogito'. In other words, without the body, 'we would be impossible'. And it is the movement of the body in the world that gives meaning. The body is what situates us in the world (1962; 135–136).

Moreover, it is the bodily activity within an environment that unifies the physical, the mental and the cultural into a seamless whole (Ingold: 2000). Therefore, when discussing people's experience of walking it is impossible to distinguish between the physical effects, our thoughts, and the cultural influences. So the walk or climb begins with the whole person, who will be further transformed in the course of the new experience as a result of the interaction of the active person and the environment.

Walking and climbing are very different types of movement. The first thing you notice as you start walking is the physical effort. The mental image gained from the map cannot tell you what it is like to be *in* the land. You set off on your planned route. You are heading 'towards' something. Sometimes you can see the objective.

As John approached Kinlochewe, the village at the foot of the Torridon hills, it began to get light. He caught sight of these distinctive hills and then, when he saw Ben Alligin, he let out a gasp. It seemed so steep with a rocky skyline of peaks and pinnacles – and with the snow on top and the loch below, the scene was amazing. John kept saying: 'Oh, yes!' He had a good view of the Alligin 'horns' – they did look a challenge, and the ridge itself looked enormous but according to the guidebook, it should only take six hours. The view of the objective affected our pace. We walked with excitement, with anticipation and with some anxiety. What would it be like? The 'walk-in' is the time to focus the thoughts. The physical movement helps to alleviate the mental anxiety. With a less worrying objective, the beginning of the walk is more relaxing. The paths are better lower down and it is more obvious where you have to go so you don't have to concentrate too much. This is the time for chatting. The body is in the background. It was during the first parts of walks that I did most of my interviewing.

However, it is also in the first stages of the walk that one measures oneself against others in terms of fitness and walking speed. The group soon divides into people with different paces. Paces are related to the level of physical fitness and to what seems to be each person's own personal rhythm. I thought I would have no trouble keeping up with the sixty- and seventy-year-olds in my first Strathspey Mountain Club outing. However, I was soon struggling. It can be a source of conflict in the group as there is such a difference in walking speeds. Stuart was incapable of walking slower than six kilometres per hour, even when going uphill. So as the gradient steepens, concentration is focussed on the movement of one's body and how it is responding to the gradient. Initially, it would seem that walking speed is limited by physical capability, but there are other factors affecting one's pace. John set a fast pace on this walk-in because he knew daylight was limited. But John has also walked quickly for competitive reasons. He and his friend Andy had an unspoken contest going on throughout the sixteen-mile walk-out from a backpacking trip in the southern Cairngorms. They both admitted that their pace gradually increased because of a silent competition between them. One would speed up and the other one would match him and then move a little ahead, causing the other one to move more quickly. The result was a frantic pace. Andy said that when he got to the car park he had to keep walking around in circles because his legs wouldn't stop. Meanwhile, I was left miles behind, not being able to compete!

The environment itself begins to play a more obvious role in shaping the experience: as the terrain becomes more challenging, the walker needs to adapt. The gradient affects not only how fast one walks, but how one walks. This can be seen in the way trainee mountain instructors are taught to measure distance. Counting one's paces may be counting abstractions, but these abstractions are generated through certain kinds of embodied and emplaced experience (Lorimer and Lund: 2003). From looking at the abstraction of counting paces, it is possible to understand the underlying experience of movement. Stuart explained how it works.

> Pacing is a way of measuring how far you have travelled. You first need to know how many double paces you take to go 100 metres on a normal flat surface such as a dirt track or good path. However, as soon as the terrain becomes more varied and steeper, with rocks and bumps, clumps of heather, bog and rocky steps, then the pacing has to be adjusted. This is not something that is picked up quickly. It only comes with experience and focus.

I found that you have to be incredibly aware of how your body is moving, in particular how big or small your step is. So when walking through a bog you may take a bigger than average step but when moving up very steep and/or rocky ground the steps become smaller. As you move, you count. Normally I take seventy double paces for 100 metres. But if I move up very steep ground I will take a step and count one, another step and count two and then call the next step two as well. Both the body and mind are totally involved in this process, 'reading the ground with your body' (Lorimer and Lund: 2003) as well as allowing the ground to dictate how the body moves.

Climbing involves a different way of moving. Lewis (2000) argues that climbing leads to an unmediated relationship with the physical environment (p. 59). All human activity involves 'being in the world' (Ingold: 2000) but climbing is a distinct type of relationship with the world. Lewis says that it 'usurps the pre-eminence of cognitive expression' (p. 71). This means that conscious thought does not dominate. I would argue that cognition doesn't disappear, but shifts. According to John Petts, a sports psychologist I interviewed:

> Climbers are particularly prone to a hemispheric shift because in other sports the consequences aren't so great, but in climbing they are so serious. The climber has to switch from left to right. When we have a complete shift to the right we are not aware of ourselves. There is a change in perception. Things slow down. We are not aware of time; there is less distinction between reality and fantasy, time and space.

This supports Csikszentimihalyi who characterises climbing as a 'flow experience' (Csikszentimihalyi: 1997). Flow refers to the holistic sensation present when we act with total involvement. We experience it as a unifying flowing from one moment to the next in which we are in control of our actions, and in which there is little distinction between self and environment; between stimulus and response; or between past, present and future.

The movement of climbing is obviously different from walking. However, there are some similarities. Walkers become more focussed on the activity itself, with little room for other thoughts when the terrain becomes awkward and lack of concentration could lead to a slip or a fall. With climbing, the terrain is immediately awkward and lack of concentration in this case could lead to much more serious injury or even death. The climber therefore moves with more precision, carefully thinking about where to place hands and feet. The movement itself might appear almost instinctual, the result of having made similar moves before and just knowing what to do (Merleau-Ponty: 1962) The body 'is the fabric into which all objects are woven, and it is, at least in the relation to the perceived world, the general instrument of my "comprehension"' (1962: 235).

The climber does not make a move without studying the rock, looking for where he or she will place the hands and feet as well as thinking about how these holds will be used exactly by the appendages, what affordances the rock face provides. Stuart would sometimes take over fifteen minutes to make a hard move. He will not move upwards until he knows what move he will make. Ed commented after taking considerable time to make a move: 'you look and look and don't know how you are going to do it, and then you figure it out and you just do it. It is like finding the right combination to a lock.'

The climber may bring a certain skill, the result of past experience, and a certain mental attitude (for example confidence, positive feelings about the climb), but once he or she puts the first hand and foot on the rock face, the climber must move with the affordances of that rock. Though there may be different ways of 'doing a move', depending on the physical characteristics and skills of the climber, there are not infinite variations. That dependence on the environment creates a distinctive relationship that does appear 'to unite body and world' more intimately than many other activities (Lewis: 2000).

Time and space

The activities of hill-walking and climbing invoke particular senses of time and space. Time, like pacing, can be crucial for survival. Therefore, it is not simply an abstraction but is based on calculations of how much you can achieve before dark. Time is therefore measured on the basis of distance you have walked. This is not all that different from how we use time at work – where do I have to be by a certain time? What do I need to have accomplished? John and I decided to cut short our route by the early afternoon. We had taken much longer than anticipated and would not complete the route in the daylight left. We took advantage of the escape route that the terrain afforded, after having offered nothing but obstacles such as extreme winds and difficult snow conditions up until then.

Though the mountaineer is limited by the relationship between time and distance, time still takes on characteristics that are distinct from normal urban life. There is no looking at the watch when you want to have a break or eat. That decision is taken by the body as well as by the environment. Tops are places people stop to eat, a reward for the effort, though you might also stop at the base of a steep climb for a drink of water and an energy snack. You don't need to look at a watch to know that it is getting dark and that you need to hurry. As with the counting of paces, time is an abstraction that is nevertheless directly related to the physical movement through the environment and the pace of the sun through the sky.

Many climbers have commented on the perception that time disappears whilst climbing: 'You get to the top of the climb and look at your watch and you can't believe you've been on the route for so long' and 'Time goes so quickly when you're climbing.' John commented on the difficulty of saying how long it took us. He couldn't remember what time we'd started so he had to guess. Was it two or was it four hours? 'It's difficult to keep track of the time because you are so focussed on what you are doing.'

Unlike walking, time has no relationship to distance. The winter climbing routes in the Northern Corries on Cairn Gorm are only 450 feet in length, yet one climb took John several hours to get up. Duration of ascent depends on so many factors such as how long you may have to wait for others, your own skill at setting up stances and managing the rope and of course the difficulty of the climb relative to one's skill. Stuart once took two hours to lead just one part of a winter climb because he was at the limit of his ability.

Space also takes on particular qualities due to the nature of the activity. When starting the walk, it is common to take a photo, showing the peak that you are going to climb in the background. It always seems so far. It is said it is best not to keep looking at how far you have to go, but just to walk. And this is of course essential if the ground is awkward. There is no space left for looking up and ahead; you are just negotiating the ground beneath your feet. One of the most infuriating aspects of space is the false summits – when you think you have arrived at the top, but then see that the real top is still further. The weather also affects the sense of space. A clear day will evoke feelings of infinite space – seeing forever – whilst a day with little visibility makes you feel claustrophobic. If you are walking at night, distances and sizes are totally distorted. Stuart got lost once whilst out practising 'night navigation'. He came upon a lake that he was convinced was the one he was camping by. But as he got closer he realised that it was a totally different size. 'Things can appear much larger and further than they actually are.' A whiteout can be equally disorientating. 'You cannot even tell whether the ground is going up or down.' And then, when you get back to the start, you cannot believe where you have been. After returning from our winter walk to Ciste Dubh in Kintail, Anne kept turning around and saying: 'I can't believe we were all the way up there.'

Climbing also gives you a particular sense of space. Being on vertical rock, high above the ground is not a common occurrence for human beings. The first experience of this 'void' can be overwhelming. You have put your body in a specific relation to the world that is not part of your previous bodily experience. Gradually, however, as with other activities, the body orientates itself in the world and situates itself and learns to feel at home. John describes the experience: 'You look up at the rock face or snow gully and it seems so steep. But when you are on it, what was once a blank rock face is transformed into something that you can be on, even feel comfortable on. You have entered another world, but one that, with the right skill, you can belong in.' Some people grow to love the sense of 'exposure' – the word climbers use for parts of the climb that have especially sharp drops, the feeling of space all around you. Others never quite get used to it, but admit that the exposed parts of the climb are the most exhilarating. Often the sense of exposure does not enter the conscious part of the body until the move has been made. As Ed says, 'I get so involved in the climb that I do not even notice the drop below'. People learn to cope with exposure.

A person's activities are the source of new meanings (Merleau-Ponty: 1962). As the novice climber has more experience with the vertical environment, what was once called fear of heights is transformed into exposure. Exposure can be dealt with; it can be fun and exhilarating. So, a new meaning has now been consciously articulated. As Ed put it: 'The climb is exposed, not the person is scared'. 'Multi-pitch' climbs can be exposed and therefore potentially terrifying because they involve going up several rope lengths in stages. The person leading proceeds up the rock face whilst the 'second' remains on what is often a very small ledge or stance, just big enough for the feet, and 'belays' (feeds out the rope through a safety device as the leader moves up the rock, ready to hold a fall) the leader. The leader may take some time to climb the pitch, which gives the second ample opportunity to become aware of the drop below. Ed explains how his fear of heights got transformed:

I went on my first multi-pitch, something where I had to hang around on miniscule ledges, waiting for the leader to do the next pitch. When I finally got to the top, I swore that I would never do it again. My Thai boxing matches would never frighten me again – they're nothing in comparison!

Now he seems completely unfazed by the drops.

Climbing has a distinctive way of dividing up space. The walker sees space in terms of many kilometres and several thousand feet or metres of ascent and descent, spread over the day. The climber's day moves through space in shorter chunks. There is first the walk-in, which is ideally kept to a minimum because the longer you take to walk to the climb, the less time you have for the climb. After the climb, there is the walk-out, which is also kept to a minimum, because depending on how the climb goes and the time of year, it might have to be done in the dark. The main space for the day's activity is the actual route on the rock or on the ice or snow. That route becomes the climber's space for the duration of the climb. The climber moves up the climb in distinct sections, called pitches. As with the pacing and measuring of distance, the length of pitches is an abstraction, a human inscription on the rock, but they relate to the length of the rope you are using and the affordances of the rock for places to stop. Therefore, there is a clear link between the abstraction and the physical reality. The lead climber moves up the rock or ice, placing protection (bits of metal that can be slotted into the rock) and clipping the rope such that if he or she should fall, the length of the fall will be limited by how far above the protection one is. The lead climber moves up until he or she reaches a suitable stance, defined as any place that affords places to attach oneself to the rock. At this point, the climber 'brings up' the second, who is tied on to the other end of the rope and who has been belaying on the ground. Stances are indicated in guidebooks, but these are selected because they have real physical aspects that make them places where you can stop. Getting to a stance is a relief for the leader as the danger of death is temporarily over. This is especially true if you are 'swapping leads' and it is now the turn of your partner to be at the 'sharp end of the rope'. So, stances are special spaces, havens of relative security where you can let yourself go, as long as you have overcome your fear of heights as in the case of Ed.

The pitch itself is also divided up according to affordances – what the rock provides. The basic division is between places where you are able to rest relatively comfortably and those parts where you just have to keep moving because you would not have the strength to hang on if you had to stop. The hardest in a sequence of moves on a pitch is called the 'crux' and is therefore a significant space as it is at this point that you most risk falling. Another special space is the top, for different reasons. 'Topping out' marks the end of climbing space. You have now returned to where you feel totally safe.

A climb involves a set of movements through space and each move is classified in the climber's perception according to the degree of safety afforded. This will be different for different climbers depending on skill and experience, as with the variations of response to exposure. Your mental state can play a large part in deciding what is a safe space and what is a dangerous space. Jim Perrin (1997), a well-known climbing writer, once described how his perceptions of the rock changed whilst climbing under the influence of cocaine and when the effect of the cocaine wore off. He had been climbing fluidly without fear, but then part way up, that situation changed and the last part of the climb was a frightening experience. Alex Honnold is an extreme example of how fear is relative. He has soloed (without any rope protection) up huge vertical rock faces in places like Yosemite and his ability to focus completely on the climbing means that his fear is pushed to the back of his mind. However, there is a limit to how one's mental state can affect the perception of safety. It is still an interaction between the inner state of the person, their subjective perceptions and the objectivity of the rock. Though people have now climbed rock that was once considered impossible, there are still many rock faces that really are.

Attending to place and evolving skills:
surviving and asesthetic appreciation

Moving through a place simultaneously involves 'attending to place'. Attention to place means that the whole person is engaged with the environment, using all the senses, skills and aesthetic appreciation in that engagement. The particular activity that one is doing will determine the nature of that engagement (Ingold: 2001). The walker and climber will 'attend' to their surroundings in different ways because they are moving in different ways through that environment. In addition, how one attends will depend to a certain extent on features of the physical environment. Though people can perceive danger when it isn't there, with mountaineering there are frequently 'right' and 'wrong' ways of attending or rather 'skilled' and 'unskilled' ways. If you get it wrong, there will be physical consequences: getting lost, slipping or even death. It is the element of real, physical danger in the environment that is part of the attraction of the sport, especially with climbing (Macfarlane: 2003, Simpson: 1994, 1997).

Wacquant's study of boxing in Chicago has many parallels with walking and especially climbing. According to Wacquant (1995), the successful practice of the sport is dependent on both physical and mental skill. In addition, it is a 'strategic and interactive contest' (p. 11). In the case of boxing, the contest is with another human being and with the walker/climber it is with the environment. For both boxing and mountaineering, the possibility of physical injury if one does not have sufficient 'embodied competence' provides the underlying conditions of the activity.

As with boxers, mountaineers deliberately engage in activities that they know will give them both a mental and physical challenge and necessarily involve some degree of suffering. The following quote from Jim Perrin illustrates how the mountaineer deliberately immerses him/herself in a hostile environment, where they have no choice but to be completely attentive to the environment with all their being:

> I used to go out looking for epics at one time. When the weather was bad, the snow coming down and a wind rattling the windows I'd thrust out of the door and set off into the Carneddau, seeking the whiteout, the wind-howled slopes streamed with snow. I would brace my shoulders and pump fists and head pugilistic (my emphasis) against the gusts until I was up there on the whale-roll of the great ridges with the snow-pall obliterating all stored sense of place (quoted in Ament: 1999: p. 57).

Seeing the Micro: Looking for Affordances

When setting off, the eyes are first drawn to where one is going, looking up and to the distance. As the terrain roughens, the eyes are focussed downwards on where to place one's feet. The shape of the rocks is particularly noticeable, as the walker has to make sure that he or she places their foot on a flattish surface so as not to twist an ankle. As the walker struggles up a steep slope, all that is seen is what the foot is on. There is no time to stop and study the rocks, but the different shapes, colours and textures are noticed because of the need to keep oneself moving successfully up the slope with no slips or loss of balance. The degree to which one can look around depends on one's fitness and general agility, that is to say, skill. Stuart says that he does not need to pay that much attention because as he moves easily over the rough terrain, mistakes are automatically rectified. He does not mind the odd fall. When coming down through frosty grass, he slipped several times in a few hundred yards. Others are more concerned to stay upright at all times and therefore have to keep their eyes more carefully focussed on each step.

The climber has an extremely narrow focus, but as with walking, the range of the focus can change depending on what one can safely cope with. To move upwards on the rock one needs to find 'holds' on which to place hands and feet. This involves scanning the rock, even before you set off. The climber looks to see what the rock affords and then makes the moves accordingly. What to a non-climber appears to be a blank face of rock, has for the climber, a wealth of possibilities. Again, the ability to see depends on experience. A novice climber will often comment 'there's nothing here', where the more skilled climber can see affordances in the slightest protrusion. Of course, this is linked to the ability to use the tiny bump or edge. The novice will not see because they do not have the skill or confidence to use these features. There is, thus, a close relationship between seeing and skill. Once one is encouraged to put the tip of one's rock boot on that small bump and the climber succeeds in moving, then he or she has developed their skill, which will lead to seeing more affordances in the future.

The characteristics of the body will also affect what one sees as a potential hold or series of holds. The rock face, far from being a blank face, is complex terrain. There is often an accepted general route up that face, as discussed above, but how it's done can vary. Climbers talk about what kind of climbing they are best at and what kind of rock features they like. For example, Ed is able to make the most of chimneys and cracks. On one occasion he remarked on the fact that his climbing partner had taken ages to lead up one section, which he then seconded up easily. He asked what had taken so long and it transpired that his partner had not used the crack at all and had just moved up the face, which was a bit 'thin', meaning there was nothing obvious to use as a hold. When asked why she hadn't used the crack, she replied that she hadn't seen how it could be used. Ed used such incidences to support a Freudian theory of climbing that he had heard about: men prefer cracks and chimneys and women enjoy face and slab climbing. This is an example of the way climbers can see their hobby as a metaphor for other aspects of life, something that has been taken up in reverse in books devoted to improving climbing performance. For example, Ilgner (2003) describes his Rock Warrior's Way which 'seeks to develop an adventurous, vigorous, deliberate approach to climbing. Initially it breaks down the habitual and self-limiting mental framework we bring into climbing and into life in general' (p. xxvii). By working on developing 'attention' in his or her 'normal' life, the climber can then transfer this skill to climbing. And, by expanding this awareness in climbing, the climber will reap the benefits in everyday life.

The character of the walker's or climber's visual perception is revealed in a more pronounced way when safety and security in the environment are the main focus of attention. In both cases, the visual perception and skill are intertwined and put to the test in action.

Surviving: Perception and Technical Skill

Imagine being on the top of the Cairngorm plateau in winter with a howling wind and poor conditions to the extent that visibility is reduced to a few feet ahead. There are steep drops to the left with many gullies cutting into the plateau such that to keep a perfectly straight course would mean stepping into one and falling hundreds of feet. The only tools to ensure safety here are map, compass and skill.

We were comfortably settled into our snow hole high above Loch A'an on the plateau. As we were on a winter Mountain Leadership training course, we could not stay settled for long. After dinner, we put all our gear back on and ventured out into the darkness and blizzard conditions. We were excited to go out with our instructor Steve who had received the Golden Head Torch Award on several occasions because of his apparent enjoyment of night navigation, often returning late with his groups. Our aim was to practice our navigation with map and compass, taking turns to lead a leg. Setting off on a compass bearing into a dark, white nothingness was at first scary. I couldn't imagine being up there on my own. But soon it was exhilarating. We realised that we could identify where we were on the map. On we went, no longer frightened, partly because we trusted ourselves to find the way, but also because we had Steve with us. Several hours later we returned safely to our snow hole.

Skill is an essential component of both walking and climbing as we learn to 'see' our environment. However, in the most extreme situations, the walker and climber will augment their skills through the use of tools. The walker will use map and compass and the climber will protect the climb by placing protection and using a rope. Ingold (2000) calls this technical skill, rather than technology, because the tools used are under the control of the mountaineer.

For the walker or climber, survival does indeed depend on combining their perception with the skilful use of their tools.

The compass can be contrasted with GPS systems. The GPS represents a technology that actually separates people from the land they are moving through. The map and compass do not detract from relating to the land; the walker is continually matching map to the ground. The GPS changes that relationship; it becomes a technical relationship in which the device on its own takes control. I have witnessed several incidents where the GPS user became lost, unable to relocate because they had no sense of the land around them. Coupled with the fact that the GPS relies on batteries that can run out, the use of the GPS may cause more problems for the Cairngorm Mountain Rescue Team than it solves. This is why many people I know in the Strathspey Mountain Club still rely heavily on map and compass. They may have a GPS in their rucksack but only as a back-up. And if they do use the new programs available for phones, they will still keep up their map and compass skills.

However, some from my London- and Essex-based club have fully converted to the GPS. We have had many arguments about its use. For the converts, they will hold it in their hands at all times, even when it is obvious where to go. I experienced the consequences of a walker's GPS addiction when one member of our club was supposed to be practicing for his Mountain Leader assessment (for which the GPS is not to be used). I took his GPS out of his hand and said I would put it away. He responded with uncharacteristic violence, fighting me to get it back. The others were shocked, and when he got it back, he himself was astounded by his reaction. Ever since, his GPS has been known as 'the precious'; his reaction was not dissimilar to that of Gollum when deprived of the ring.

Climbers also have to rely on their skill. The challenge of the activity is that the climber is the one who places their own gear on the climb and manages the rope. It is their own skilful use of these tools that ensures their safety. There is no external system to trust. Many British climbers mistrust the continental system of preplacing bolts on the climb. This in-situ protection must be carefully examined before it is used and trainee instructors are taught how to check on the safety of this equipment.

The main danger faced by walkers is that of getting lost. In the hills of Scotland, especially in winter, losing your way can have life-threatening consequences. According to Steve, a Glenmore Lodge instructor, the Cairngorm plateau has been the scene of many serious incidents caused by navigation errors. Much of their work at the Lodge involves training people to navigate in both winter and summer conditions. Although they will now teach people how to use a GPS, it is still the map and compass that are the essential tools. People use different methods to find the way, depending on the conditions. If visibility is good, then one can usually see where one is going. Walkers will orientate themselves by following the paths and making their way in the direction of the objective. To a certain extent this will involve the use of the map. Ingold distinguishes between two types of moving from point to point.

To use a map is to navigate by means of it: that is to plot a course from one location to another in *space*. Way-finding, by contrast, is a matter of moving from one *place* to another in a region (2000: 219).

Strangers to a place are navigators; inhabitants of a place are way-finders. Way-finding is seen as 'a skilled performance in which the traveller, whose powers and perceptions have been fine-tuned through experience, "feels his way" towards his goal, continually adjusts his movements in response to an ongoing perceptual monitoring of his surroundings' (2000: 220). Ingold stresses that the terrain is variegated and therefore the way-finder cannot just rely on instincts. The only way to 'hold a course in such an environment' is to 'be attentive at all times to what is going on around you' (2000: 223).

When examining the method of navigation used by mountaineers, it must be kept in mind that they can be both navigators and way-finders. As will be discussed in Chapter Four, stalkers and keepers on the sporting estates do not use maps at all and

would fit the description of Ingold's way-finding local but mountaineers all use maps to a lesser or greater degree. The extent to
which they use them will be affected by how often the person
has been over a particular terrain, the weather conditions and his
or her skill. However, even in circumstances where the mountaineer is totally reliant on the map, their attention and response
to the environment fits closely to Ingold's depiction of the local
way-finder.

The person who has been over a terrain many times, and who
has excellent visibility, will use the map the least. In this case,
as a result of past experience, the visitor has become in some
senses a local. A mountaineer from Edinburgh is likely to know
the terrain around Cairngorm better than many actual locals.
One of the most regular objectives of mountaineers is to do
winter climbs in the Northern Corries. On 'topping out', they
need to find their way back down. In good visibility, they make
their way down by looking for familiar landmarks. However, in
poor visibility, both the newcomer and the most experienced
mountaineer, will rely on map and compass to get them off the
mountain. The latter may have less need to carefully study the
map because he or she is already familiar with what the ground
along the route should look like. The newcomer will decide on
the best route to follow and then look at the map in order to 'see'
what features to expect along the chosen route. Will the ground
go up or down and how steeply? Are there any 'catch' features
(for example an unexpected steep incline) to indicate that one
has gone too far or strayed off route?

Even the most experienced local will get the map out and
use the compass to check what they think is the right route in
conditions of extremely poor visibility. Once located on the map,
the compass provides both the direction of travel and a means
of measuring distance. Anyone going into the hills is advised to
learn how to use the map and compass to navigate. On training
courses people learn how to take a bearing and then walk on a
bearing. Skilled use of the map and compass are essential for

survival in the hill environment. In the most extreme cases, they become the eyes through which you see; without them you would be blind.

*

John and Douglas had topped out on a winter climb to near whiteout conditions with a howling wind. Douglas, a local, and John, a visitor, both went through the same procedures. They sheltered themselves from the wind as much as possible and took their maps and compasses out of their rucksacks. They took a bearing for the direction of travel, ensuring that they 'aimed off' slightly in order to avoid walking straight over the drop. They also used the markings on the compass to measure the distance so that they could pace the distance as a way of knowing what features to expect at a particular time. The route is divided into stages or 'legs' according to changes in direction. They study the route on the map. They set off, compass in hand pointing in the direction of travel. They pace the distance of the first leg. At the same time they are noticing what is happening to the slope. They expect it to first go down steeply and then descend more gradually. This is seen on the map but also known by Douglas through experience. With this combination of pacing, compass bearing and noting of the features, they arrive at what they are confident is the beginning of the next leg, where they turn slightly to the left and now head up hill. They will know they have gone too far on the first bearing if they start going steeply up hill. Their pacing brings them successfully to at a flat area and they set the new bearing and repeat the procedure. When they arrive at a large boulder, a familiar landmark to those who know the Cairngorm plateau, they know they have found the correct ridge. But again, even Douglas does not rely completely on past experience to choose the correct direction. He checks where he thinks he should be going with the map and compass. They set off down the ridge and are soon beneath the cloud line, able to 'see' where they are going without the map. They now rely on familiar landmarks and make their way easily back down to the car park.

Gell (1985) distinguishes between maps that are subjective, indexical, and those that are objective, non-indexical. He criticises Bourdieu for arguing that locals are able to move from point to point on the basis of 'practical', indexical knowledge as opposed to 'Cartesian space' that is based on non-indexical knowledge (Gell: 1985). He argues that anyone, whether a local or a visitor, will use non-indexical knowledge, whether that be in the mind, for the local, or on the map, for the outsider. In the above example we have seen that both local and outsider are relying on the map as well as the existence-objective points that match up to the map. According to Gell:

> We are obliged at all times to locate our bodies in relation to external co-ordinates which are unaffected as we move about, and it is in relation to these co-ordinates that we entertain token-indexical beliefs as to our current location in space, and the location of other places relative to ourselves (p. 279).

Without going so far as to support Gell's assertion that we use external co-ordinates 'at all times', it is clear from the above example that external co-ordinates exist and are used. By using the map and compass to position themselves, John and Douglas were able to match up the map and the ground at all times. If they had not, they could have made a life-threatening mistake. If they had made a tiny error, they could have walked off the edge just to their left or else veered off to the right and ended up missing the crucial descend ridge. In winter, when you cannot actually see the edge, this is a real danger. Therefore, in the case of navigation in extreme conditions, the mountaineer is relying on the existence of Cartesian space as well as using Ingold's way-finding techniques to move safely from one point to another.

'Seeing' in the case of mountain navigation involves a more general spatial awareness. One cannot see things in two dimensions as one would a landscape painting, but must learn through experience to perceive the land in three dimensions. With walking it is the shape of the land. Trainee mountain instructors learn about taking bearings and walking to the bearing, but as seen in the example of Douglas and John, the 'lay of the land' or the 'features' must fit with where you think you are on the map. As part of his practice for the Mountain Leader assessment, Andy, John's mountaineering friend from London, would sit in one place with his map in hand. He would look at the tiniest features on the map and try and locate them on the ground. Features included ring contours, re-entries and even a particular contour line on the slope. There is a continual movement from the two-dimensional map to the three-dimensional ground. It is the over-reliance on the compass that causes some people to fail their assessment according to one trainer. Those who develop the skill of navigation to a fine art are those who can interchange the map for the ground instantaneously.

In rock-climbing, spatial awareness is also important. Part of moving safely up the rock face involves the placing of protection. A climber must learn to see the affordances the rock provides for placing nuts, hexes and camming devices in the features of the rock.

As with seeing holds, the novice also takes time to be able to see opportunities to place protection. When Douglas first simulated leading, placing protection as he went, he missed a number of opportunities. He just didn't notice them. I went up beside him and immediately saw what he didn't. This is another skill that evolves through experience. With greater participation in the activity, skill increases and one becomes more aware of what affordances are there. And this is no abstract exercise; the ability to find protection could mean the difference between life and death, just as the skill of navigation can mean survival when walking. The rope is used in conjunction with the protection as a means of moving safely up the rock. A number of skills are involved: tying on correctly, belaying, clipping in and setting up stances. Many climbers comment that this rope work is as much part of climbing as the actual climbing. People attend courses more to learn about this rope work than they do to learn how to climb.

However, mental training is also important to climbing. The ability to climb a route safely involves having the right mental attitude and self-confidence. A route that should be well within one's grade can become impossible if the confidence is not there. Confidence affects the movement of the body. You may hug the rock and not see crucial holds or you may be too tense, sapping your strength. One experienced climber gave advice to his son: even if you are not confident, climb as if you are confident. You will soon be climbing well and this will then give you real confidence. Ed describes one of his experiences:

> I was climbing a route that I thought was a V Dif (Very Difficult). It should have been easy, but I wasn't finding it easy. Since I thought I should be able to do this, I carried on and completed the climb. Afterwards, I looked in the guidebook and realised I had been on the wrong route – an HVS (Hard Very Severe) rather than a V Dif! So thinking that I was on an easy route affected my attitude.

Appreciating the view: the aesthetic aspect of perception

Once the objective of the walk has been obtained – reaching the top of the Munro or the top of the climb – then seeing broadens out from a micro to a macro perspective and a different kind of seeing comes into play. Now that survival is no longer at the forefront, the mountaineer is free to see aesthetically. It is at this time that the view becomes important. There is no doubt that the appreciation of the view from the top of a mountain is to a certain extent socially constructed. Much has been written about how appreciation of the mountain 'view' changed remarkably in the nineteenth century (Pepper: 1996, Solnit: 2001, Urry: 1990). Samuel Johnson's description of the Scottish Highlands is often quoted: 'Matter incapable of form or usefulness: dismissed by nature from her care, quickened only with the power of useless vegetation.' (in Smout: 1992: 23)

Mountains went from being ugly places of terror to places of sublime beauty. 'Sublimity' is a concept used particularly with reference to mountain landscapes where there is a quality of wildness. According to Edmund Burke, sublime places evoke an impression of power greater than humans (De Botton: 2002).

It is no coincidence that the Western attraction to sublime landscapes developed at precisely the moment when traditional beliefs began to wane. It is as if these landscapes allowed travellers to experience transcendental feelings that they no longer felt in cities and the cultivated countryside. The landscapes offered an emotional connection to a greater power, even as they freed them of the need to subscribe to the less plausible claims of biblical texts and organised religions (De Botton: 2002: 171).

Others argue that there is something more universal about humans' attraction to mountain views. Work in environmental psychology suggests that people prefer natural landscapes to urban ones, and that they produce more positive physiological effects (Cave: 1998).

Some of my experience suggests that an appreciation of a view comes out spontaneously and does not necessarily require cultural learning. Without fail, arrival at the top will evoke non-linguistic exclamations from people. The way people just look up, see the view for the first time and gasp. Or the way walkers or climbers will take time at the top just to sit and immerse themselves in the vastness of their surroundings. Chris Bonnington, on descending from Everest, said 'I sat down every few paces, beyond thought, and just absorbed the mountains around me' (quoted in Ament: p. 108) and Stuart, despite focussing on climbing, said 'You spend all the time focussed on the rock and you turn around and see the view. It's great.'

Other evidence supports the argument that an appreciation of dramatic mountain landscapes is not just transmitted via culture (Brady: 2003). This comes from the experience of local people who have taken up walking. The stereotype is often that those who are engaged with the land in a practical sense will not appreciate the 'useless' beauty of the hills. However, Strathspey Mountain Club members Gordon, Douglas and Isobel, all from farming backgrounds, recounted their emotional reactions to their first encounter with the uninhabited Scottish landscapes. The general feeling was of being 'overwhelmed by the views'. Indeed, it was the 'amazing views' that motivated them to take up hill-walking. Isobel, like Nan Shepherd, still remembers her first glimpse of Loch Avon, hidden down in a cleft over the back of Cairn Gorm – a view that can only be seen once you have gone well beyond the ski cark park and 'into the mountain'. Douglas had been down the Lairig Ghru before but it was getting to the top of the hill that grabbed him: 'I had never seen anything like it.'

However, other data supports the idea that how one responds to the views depends on cultural ideas of what beauty is. Alan, a founding member of the Strathspey Mountain Club, told me that some of the stark, bare, deforested landscape so appreciated for its beauty and wildness by some appear to him as 'desolation'. He himself greatly enjoys hill-walking, having completed all his Munros; the beauty of the views is certainly part of his enjoyment. However, because of his extensive knowledge of the environmental and social history of the area, he also perceives the damage that has been done to the landscape as a result of human activity and the emptying of the land by the Clearances. He is well aware that this landscape is not wilderness at all, but the result of destruction.

The nature of people's appreciation of the landscape develops out of their engagement with a particular environment. There may or may not be an innate sense of beauty. However, views can become beautiful as a result of experiences. Appreciation of a mountain view on the part of the mountaineer must be examined in relation to the activity they are engaged in. People do not have a predisposition to appreciate the view; it develops out of the experiences they have of such a view.

We overlook certain places because nothing has ever prompted us to conceive of them as worthy of appreciation, or because some unfortunate but stray association has turned us against them' (De Botton 2002: 192).

Isobel, Douglas and Gordon may have the innate potential to appreciate a view but it is only by engaging in the activity of hill-walking that the potential is realized.

The questions to this answer, then, are: what is it in the activity of mountaineering that develops an aesthetic appreciation of the mountains? And what is the specific nature of that appreciation? According to Yi-Fu Tuan (1974), the appreciation of scenery is fleeting unless one's eyes are kept on the view for other reasons. This is supported by Ruskin (De Botton: 2002). Part of appreciating beauty is to possess it. Many people try and possess mountain scenery by photographs. For those who are on the tour bus and just look at the view from the lay-by, they look, probably show fleeting appreciation and then try to prolong this by taking a photo. Ruskin finds this totally inadequate. The only way to possess beauty properly is to understand it. According to him, this is done through drawing or trying to describe in writing what one has seen. De Botton (2002) summarises Ruskin's opinion:

> True possession of a scene is a matter of making a conscious effort to notice elements and understand their construction. We can see beauty well enough just by opening our eyes, but how long this beauty survives in memory depends on how intentionally we have apprehended it (De Botton: 225).

Mountaineers may not draw or write about the mountains whilst they are on the top (though the mountain literature, poetry and art done by mountaineers is extensive). Instead, because they have moved through the landscape and have been forced to focus on a variety of details, they have developed a different kind of understanding that is not 'fleeting'. Maurice Bloch in his study of the Zafimaniry in Madagascar (1995) found that people also liked to look at views. They would regularly stop at vantage points and comment on the view. They emphasise the clarity, list the hills and mountains in sight and the villages that still stand on them. The people at Zafimaniry tested Bloch on his knowledge. According to Bloch, their aesthetic appreciation of the view was bound-up with other aspects of their lives – the fact that clarity is a central value of their society and that for so much of the time they cannot see because of the mist. In addition, what is important to the people is that they have made a mark on the land, so if they can see that there are villages on the mountain-tops, then they have transcended their own impermanent nature and become part of the land.

There are many parallels with walkers and climbers. One of the main things to do with the view is to identify peaks. There is an element of showing off. If you can name the peaks, it is a sign that you know them well and are experienced. Rather than taking a photo, it is a way to possess beauty by showing you understand, that you know. Robert, a life-time walker and another Strathspey Mountain Club member, stopped regularly on our walk up the Hills of Cromdale, east of the road linking Strathspey to Deeside. These are not particularly high, but they afford spectacular views over to the whole Cairngorm area. Robert had not seen them from this angle before. He first tried to identify all the peaks just by looking, but then had to get out the map. The others had left us behind, but he didn't want to continue until he had identified each one.

People also identify peaks because they have been there and have a memory and a story or because they may want to go to there in future and are visualising what the walk would be like. I stood with Douglas on top of Aonach Mor, a Munro near Fort William, and we could see as far as Skye in one direction and across all the mountains back towards Aviemore. He proceeded to recount in great detail, pointing to various peaks as he talked, an adventure he had had with Gordon, his main walking companion in the Strathspey Mountain Club, which involved walking an incredible distance over many of the peaks we could see in front of us. Then he turned to face the Isle of Skye in the west and tried to identify the peaks where he would be going that May when he attempted the Cuillin Ridge traverse. These examples illustrate how looking at the view within the context of the mountaineering sense of place can lead to a Ruskin-approved appreciation and knowledge of the hills.

Attention, skill and the environment: the experience of snow

The above discussion has focussed mainly on visual perception. However, when walking and climbing, all the senses are being used to some degree. Lewis (2000) stresses the importance of touch in climbing. Climbers describe and rate rock according to its texture: rough and grippy or smooth, polished and potentially lethal. Walkers will also use other senses to make many decisions. The feel of the wind, the amount of precipitation and the temperature are crucial when deciding what to wear or even whether to carry on with the walk. Clothes and equipment can make a huge difference and to some extent have transformed the walking experience (Michaels: 2000) but they only go so far in protecting people from the elements. Wind can transform a walk from an easy day out to a nightmare, battering both the body and mind.

In order to show how all the senses and cognitive faculties are used, together with skill in a particular environment, I use the following extract from my field notes, which describes the experience of a group under instruction from Glenmore Lodge for the Winter Mountain Leadership Award.

The focus was very much on the immediate area around us. There were only a couple of times that we could see any 'views' and then there were not any comments. People were too focussed on what they were doing. In fact it was the snow that dominated all of our senses – everything from its structure, to types of snow – windslab, melt-freeze, snow crystals, for the real initiates, how hard the snow was for making a snow bollard or ice axe belay, or how hard it was to dig our snowholes and whether it would drip or not. And of course, crucial was the avalanche risk, digging pits to see the snow profile and the likelihood of the layer coming off. The character of the snow made all the difference to every aspect of being in the hills in winter – crampons or not – how hard it is to walk, the speed, the pacing. Then there was the snow in your eyes, the famous white-out where everything looks up as the ground merges into the sky. As Shaun, one of the instructors, said when we were digging the snowhole: 'it puts you face to face with the snow, living in it and with it.' It protected us from the elements, provided a sleeping place, storage space, shelves for candles – it was amazing how it could be moulded to suit our human needs. Yet, if we don't understand it, adapt or retreat, it can also kill. Steve, another instructor, insisted upon going out for a night navigation exercise in blizzard conditions even though it wasn't strictly necessary. He said he just likes 'being out in it, immersed in the snow, completely dependent on map and compass.'

This extract brings together many of the points made so far in this chapter. Firstly, the mountaineer is completely embedded in the snow environment. By being and acting in this environment, the mountaineer is bringing forth particular perceptions and skills. Your eyes have to see snow in a certain way – for the affordances it offers for moving on or living in it as well as for the potential danger. You also use other senses. Because you cannot trust your sight, you use your map and compass as your eyes and then you navigate by feeling the terrain beneath your feet. Because your visual sense cannot give you accurate information about distance or even slope, you have to sense the slope of the ground as you walk. Your body tells you if you are going up – you find it harder going, your steps get closer together. Touch is also vital when assessing for avalanche danger. When you walk you feel the texture of the snow – is it hard so that you remain on top, or is there a layer of soft snow that you go through on to a harder surface – a potential avalanche situation on certain slope gradients? When you dig your avalanche pit you thrust your fist or ice axe point into the layers of snow that have been revealed. If your fist goes in easily to a layer on top of a layer where even your ice axe point went in, then you know that there is an avalanche risk on that slope. Aesthetic appreciation of the environment is completely related to the activities in snow. By having the opportunity to spend time in this white environment, people develop an appreciation of it aesthetically.

Retrospective enjoyment: mountaineering in the pub

It is through my relation to 'things' that I know myself; inner perception follows afterwards' (Merleau-Ponty 1962: 383).

Mountaineers devote a significant amount of time to thinking about the meaning of the experience, whether that be informally in the pub or in mountaineering writing. Because of the embodied nature of the activity, reflection and self-examination take place after the experience. All mountaineers agree that their activities provide them with sheer enjoyment, or happiness.

There are many ways of finding those moments of delight, which come from a sense of complete harmony with wild surroundings. Some of us seek them through the mastery of difficult terrain or stormy seas, by quickening our awareness in contrast with the elements (Shipton: 1970: 278).

71

Csikszentmihalyi (1998) argues that the most intense happiness comes from being involved in flow activities, such as dancing, creating art and climbing. In these cases we only become aware of this happiness after the experience. Happiness is closely linked to a sense of achievement. You feel happy because you have achieved something difficult. Ed the climber coined the term 'retrospective enjoyment'. After his initial fright, and his vow never to do it again, he soon tried climbing again. He said it took him a while, but he reached the stage of 'retrospective enjoyment'. Now he spends a large part of his time planning his next climbing trips. He still measures the scariness of the climb by how long (and how many pints!) it takes him to say how great the experience was. The happiness derived from climbing and hill-walking goes beyond enjoyment of the experience itself. Retrospective enjoyment arises also because of the sense of accomplishment that one feels having overcome the challenges. A veteran of the first successful expedition to Everest quotes Nietzsche to support his analysis of why people climb.

'We will be stronger than fear, greater than danger, we will master both of them because we know that every conquest is a step to perfection (quoted in Noyce: 1950: 134). And Noyce (1950) himself says: 'There is discipline and concentration demanded by the effort to climb high, to see much. This discipline is all of a piece with the Nietzschean theory that suffering, itself bad, may be productive of good.' (p. 130).

The sense of accomplishment that one feels after overcoming a serious challenge features strongly amongst the mountaineers I encountered in the field.

Having an epic

Mountaineers have a particular way of talking about those experiences that they find the most memorable, that give the most retrospective enjoyment – they are elevated to the category of 'epic'. Different climbers tried to define 'epic'. Ed said that it was when you were 'subjectively terrified but objectively enjoying yourself' – meaning that looking back this would seem a good experience. Another said it was when the challenge you had chosen 'came closer to the limit than you planned'.

On the descent from Ben Alligin, John talked about the hill experiences he remembers most. They tended to be ones that did not go according to plan and where difficulties were encountered. He remembers a time when driving from London in the college minibus; his group didn't arrive until 3 a.m. and then had a very long walk the next day, getting to the campsite at 5.30 p.m., just as it was getting dark. They had been working on navigation so his mind was tired as well as his body. He remembers cooking a meal and then going to bed at 6.30 p.m. and not waking until eight the next morning. He said it was the best night's sleep he ever had. The next day he made a mistake in finding the top of a hill; though he eventually found it, he then had to make a steep descent on which he fell and gashed his leg. He still has this scar, which reminds him of this 'brilliant weekend'. Sometimes John seems to deliberately instigate an epic. Friends recall the time John walked them all across Dartmoor, knowing full well that they would have to walk back in the dark. Or the time he encouraged his friends to descend via a difficult scramble rather than taking the path with only one hour of daylight left. He recalls one scene, which always reminds him of why he loves mountaineering. He remembers the 'buzz' in the Claichag Inn in Glencoe one February weekend. Climbing conditions were good and he described the scene as groups of climbers came in over the course of the evening, straight from their climb, still wearing their harnesses, with ice screws and ice axes dangling. The talk was excited and as John says, 'They'd had an epic'. John felt part of this scene as he and his climbing partner Barry had just returned themselves from a long, difficult ridge traverse.

'Having an epic' can be analysed in terms of flow. An epic has to combine challenge with skill. Too much challenge and it could end in disaster, but if one has survived an epic, then you feel as though you have just the right skill to match the challenge. Stuart and another trainee instructor, Rosie, had such an epic that it kept them talking for days. Stuart's first words on arrival back were, 'We had an epic!', which set the scene for the story to come. They had been busy practising navigation for their Winter Mountain Leader Assessment. They had decided to take a day off from that and do what they most enjoyed – climbing, as the conditions were so good. They went over the back of the Cairngorm plateau and descended to Loch Avon to do a grade V climb, a challenge for both of them. It took them longer than expected and they 'topped out' on the plateau just as it was getting dark. They still had to get themselves back across the plateau and find a safe way off, a navigational nightmare, as the plateau is ringed with steep cliffs. To add to their problems, the wind had picked up considerably and had reached gale force. Stuart describes them crawling across the plateau, periodically digging in their ice axes to hold them down. At the same time, they had to take compass bearings. In the end, they made it and Stuart was 'full of it'. Not only had he done a difficult winter climb, but he had put his navigation skills to a serious test and survived. During the experience itself, you are too focussed to be happy (Csikszentmihalyi: 1998). In fact, you are in a great deal of discomfort if not terrified. It is only when you know you have survived, that you feel that you are happy, that you can relax and appreciate what you have achieved.

It is difficult to convey what an epic is to non-climbers. Many of the climbers I met expressed frustration that they couldn't share their adventures with their friends. Ed says that he has given up trying to tell his friends about his climbing experiences. He said they 'just glaze over'. And even if they are willing to listen, they just don't understand why people find these activities at all enjoyable. According to Wacquant (1995), such experiences cannot be 'captured and conveyed linguistically to outsiders' (p. 10). The climber can really only tell the story of an epic to another climber. It is only by participating in the activity that you can appreciate its value for your life. Again, there are parallels with boxing: in spite of all the pain, suffering and ruthless exploitation it entails, of which fighters are painfully cognizant, boxing can infuse their lives with a sense of value, excitement and accomplishment (p. 9).

Many climbers recount how the impact of a climbing trip will spill over to other aspects of their lives, giving them confidence and an identity. In some ways the experience could be compared to that of participating in a ritual or a performance. According to Schieffelin (1985, 1998), 'rituals achieve some kind of social and psychological transformation, which happens in the course of the performance, making present realities vivid enough to beguile, amuse or terrify' (1998: 194). This is because there is a juxtaposition of the 'ordinary and non-ordinary' (Hughes-Freedland: 1998: 2). And, you cannot dictate the meaning of the ritual by looking at content; it emerges out of the interaction between performer and audience. In climbing, the meaning would emerge out of the interaction with the environment. Though climbing may involve conformity to the rules of the ritual, it is an activity that is done 'in comparison to other, usually more quotidian activities (Bell: 1992: 74). According to Lewis (2000): 'As an extreme experience, climbing becomes a kind of corporeal subversive politics, ripe with possibility for renewal that feeds back into private and social life, inflecting it with new horizons for human embodied agency.' (p. 65).

John blames his good climbing weekend in Scotland for his getting a job that turned out to be less than ideal. When he flew back down to London and went more or less straight to the interview, he was still 'buzzing from the weekend' which he thinks made him appear very dynamic and capable at the job interview.

Phil Bartlett (1993), in a book devoted to exploring the reasons why people climb, argues that what makes climbing experiences so special is that they are contrasted with normal life.

Given the pace and scale of recent changes and the contrasting slowness of genetic change within ourselves, modern life must be missing something. Mountaineering is one way to redress the balance. You feel caught in a system that controls your life and eats away at your self-respect; climb a rock face and feel gloriously renewed, confident that you can still 'do'. In all this, mountaineering is an escape from a world that seems one-sided (p. 97).

Many climbers talk about the importance of climbing in their lives. For Jamie, a City insurance executive and a new father, there is little opportunity to go climbing. But he says he can't give it up completely. He says his wife understands; she knows that it is the 'only thing in my life that gives me a sense of accomplishment'. Jason, a sixteen-year-old climber says: 'It gives me something to channel my energies into, something to focus on. I don't know what I'd do if I didn't have climbing.'

In addition to gaining a sense of personal identity and achievement, climbing and hill-walking also link people with each other and the land itself. Again, we can make a comparison with ritual. Bloch (1989) describes physical rituals as a way of constructing an identity, a place in the social group. Gow (1995) argues that stories told about the land are expressions of kinship. We have already seen that, for mountaineers looking at a view, their memories are infused not only with the places they went, but with the people they shared the experiences with. Once you have experienced 'an epic' with someone, a bond has been formed. Any memory of place or experience, mingles with the memories of the people you shared that experience with. As a result of that bond, you will go on to have more experiences together, further strengthening the ties of climbing kinship. This often extends to other climbers that you have never met to the point that people often refer to the climbing community. This climbing bond was described eloquently in a book actually called *The Bond* (Simon McCartney: 2016). Decades after his epic climbs in Alaska with his partner Jack Roberts, Simon recalls with amazing accuracy the special relationship not just with Jack but with all the other climbers on the mountain that in the end saved their lives.

*

Returning to our car and driving back the way we came, heading south down the A9, we may take a moment to pull into the viewpoint to look back. The view, the place, is the same, but our sense of it is somehow different, just as we are different. It is not just an abstract view, but a place to care about. A sense of place has been embedded in both body and mind, becoming part of who we are (Harrison: 2000) and establishing a bond (Hay: 2002).

> When you give yourself to places, those places give you yourself back; you come to know them with the invisible crops of memories and associations that will be waiting for you when you come back. (Solnit: 2002: 13)

The activity of mountaineering is characterised by an intensity of experience, imprinted on the whole being and unlikely to be replicated in other parts of life. Though there is considerable variation in the sense of place of different mountaineers – demonstrated by the comparison between hill-walkers and climbers – they have all developed an attachment to the kind of environment that has enabled them to have whatever kind of mountaineering experience they prefer. In other words, they want a place to have the features that are conducive to the pursuit of their passion. In the Cairngorms, this has implications for their stance on development of the area. Though there are many disagreements amongst mountaineers themselves over how accessible the hills should be, on the whole they would like the Cairngorms to retain its wild character, where they can be challenged physically and mentally, develop skills, appreciate the beauty of the landscape and generally enjoy themselves. This sense of place is in many ways relative. It exists in contrast to the places they have come from. In other words, what they notice, appreciate and love about the hill environment are the qualities that mark it off from the urban environment of their normal lives. Even though they do not live permanently in the area, their often epic adventures have created a sense of belonging, at least to the high ground of the Cairngorms. Therefore, they feel that they have a part to play in determining its future.

In this chapter we have seen how the sense of place of walkers and climbers emerges out of the activity, a synthesis of the subjective and the objective. In particular, we have focussed on the physical attributes of the land. However, the activity of mountaineering also has a social aspect, The next chapter will build on the points made in this chapter, about the importance of the interaction of the person with a physical environment, but will highlight the social aspect of the land that is part of the bringing forth of a sense of place.

CHAPTER THREE

Sense of Place and Conservation

Activities: Watching, Looking, Scanning, Seeing, Focussing,
Hearing, Listening, Listing, Classifying, Naming, Noticing,
Enjoying, Loving, Caring, Counting, Capturing, Consuming

John and Ross were working for the RSPB at Insh Marshes. Pete was a birding guide for Speyside Wildlife. Andy, a client of Pete's, was an amateur, birding only in his spare time. They would proudly admit to being 'birders', a name that implies not just a hobby but a passion. They use the term 'birder' and 'birding', as opposed to 'birdwatching' for a reason; the activity involves so many more ways of seeing than just watching. Birds are a central feature of any place they find themselves. John's house was full of bird books. He had a telescope set up in his window and would leap up to have a look at the slightest sign of anything. No matter where he is or what he is doing (often driving!) his senses are open to birds. Andy admits that he is obsessive and that birding is addictive. He spent twenty hours a week on his patch of ground near his home in Cheshire, observing and monitoring the bird life there. He has a lot of friends that are also birders and they socialise together. He also has a passion for books about birds. He thinks about birds all the time and his wife knows that given the choice he might prefer to go birding than spend time with her! This interest in birds of the feathered variety elicits many sexual innuendoes from non-birders, a source of some irritation for the serious birder (Cocker: 2001).

In Britain, birds have a special status for many people, much more so than in other countries (Cocker: 2001, Franklin: 1999). This is reflected in the one million plus members of the RSPB and the take-up of birding holidays. However, this interest is not new. Whether it be birds or other flora and fauna, observing and 'collecting' (literally or metaphorically) is a pastime that can be traced back to the eighteenth century. According to Thomas (1983: p. 271), 'Equipped with a pocket guide to the Linnean classification and a portable press for drying plants, they roamed the fields and woods in search of new discoveries. Natural history had become fashionable amongst the middle class and nowhere more so than in the British Isles, especially England.

This chapter uses the activity of birding to explore how people come to develop a sense of place that is tuned-in to the wonders of the natural world. As with mountaineering, the activity involves an intense interaction of the body and mind with aspects of the physical world, taking place within a social environment. Whilst still recognising the importance of the sensuous experience of place, here we focus more on the social and cultural processes at work as well as how the popularity of birding has contributed to the emergence of conservation as a feature of the wider economic and political context. With the increase in leisure time, standard of living and ironically the car, more and more people have the opportunity to spend time observing and learning about flora and fauna. The interest has been fuelled by the plethora of nature programmes on TV (Franklin: 1999) and people's love of nature, augmented by their experiences (Milton: 2002) in particular of birds, has motivated them to form groups and organisations to protect what they perceive to be a most precious component of any place. Conservation as an issue is firmly on the political agenda and conservation organisations, helped by the fact that they have become major landowners, are now key players in local, national and international politics. As a result of the economic and political significance of conservation, many who start out as amateur birders find careers, either working directly for organisations on reserves, like John and Ross, or as birding guides like Pete. What begins as an activity of the individual within a social group has an impact far beyond that group.

Most of my research took place on the RSPB reserve at Insh Marshes. According to the RSPB website: 'The Insh Marshes covers ten square kilometres of the River Spey floodplain between Kingussie and Kincraig in Badenoch and Strathspey. It is said to be one of the most important wetland areas in Europe, supporting populations of breeding waders including curlew, lapwing, redshank and snipe'. This floodplain is ever-changing, making every visit different. After extensive rain or snowmelt, the whole marsh is covered in water and locals can kayak around it. Other times, cattle graze on the succulent grasses. But always there were birds.

Birding: tuning in to the activity

John talked about being 'tuned into birds'. 'It's like a channel frequency you have never turned on, but once you do you can't turn it off!' It's not something that can be explained – it is an awareness that is learned by doing, a form of 'non-linguistic' knowledge' (Bloch: 1991: 186). There are a variety of stories of the first 'tuning in'. Many people are introduced to the activity through friends and family. Ross first learned to be aware of birds and other species as he grew up on Alvie, one of the local estates, where his father was the farm manager. Pete, from England, first started birding with his father when he was ten. He left it for twenty years and then came back to it as an escape from work. Birding exists on another 'time plane' from his daily routine. You need to be in a position to be still, to look and observe. This decision to change pace has to be consciously made. Ross's background meant that he already lived a lifestyle that involved working and being part of the natural environment, although this was from a traditional land management perspective. The decision to take up a trainee warden position was a step away from that tradition but one that had been nurtured through an interest in birdlife and cautious family support.

Sometimes such a change in lifestyle is forced upon people and provides the opportunity for them to begin to notice birds. John had always climbed trees and played in the woods in his native Yorkshire. He had also shot birds when he was fourteen or fifteen and had an interest in falconry. But it was only when he was on long-term convalescence that he really became interested. Because he had nothing else to do, he spent his time birding, and became aware of the amazing variety of birds. This is similar to the experience of Michael Fiennes described in his book *Snow Geese* (2003). His trip to follow the snow geese was the result of a fascination developed during a long convalescence. Several people I met had taken it up as a retirement activity – something that they now had the time to do that also did not require them to be in the peak of physical fitness.

My contacts remarked on the social composition of birders. During a day out with a group of birders on an organised tour, there was only one woman in twelve, and she was part of a birding couple. This was my experience throughout my fieldwork and is supported by Cocker's comprehensive study of birders (2001). When I discussed this issue with people they offered a few ideas. John said that especially with the photography, it is like an extension of the hunting role that men had. Some said it was related to 'the male thing about collecting'. Birding is very much about collecting species. But in the eighteenth century, both men and women were mentioned as having an interest in natural history. (Thomas: 1983), which can be seen in the number of female nature writers (Anderson: 1991).

However, John said that in his experience birding cut across class boundaries; it is no longer the preserve of the middle class. (Cocker: 2001). I found no evidence to the contrary. Conservation managers tended to have some education but for some, like Tom Prescott, the warden at Insh Marshes, it had been in a different field, in his case engineering. Some, like Ross, had a traditional rural background. Others came from the urban areas. Amongst the amateur birders, there were a variety of occupations. For example, in the course of my birding on one day I met a builder, a small business owner and a white-collar worker in a tax office.

It is difficult to pin down exactly what social factors or characteristics have pushed people towards birding. The environment provides the affordances and then a complex combination of factors influence whether the affordance is taken up. My aim is rather to explore the sense of place that develops once the initial contact has been made, focussing on what there is in the activity of birding itself that pulls people in.

Eyes and 'bins':
seeing, looking, watching, focussing, scanning

The activity of birding brings out the fact that there are endless ways of using the eyes, just as there are many ways of walking (Edensor: 2000, Ingold: 2001). The aim of the birder on the most general level is to see the bird. This is not as straightforward as would first appear but involves different levels of skills. The first is that of seeing that a bird is there at all. When I went out to try and see the hen harriers roosting on Insh Marshes with Ross, John and some of the other volunteers, the others had all seen them and I couldn't see anything! They seemed to have the skill to notice the slightest difference in colour from the surroundings or the tiniest movement. This is a skill that requires you to look. Dick Balharry (1937–2015), a resident of Newtonmore, had decades of experience working in conservation. He first learned his skills, as a trainee gamekeeper and then understalker on a sporting estate. He said that he learned how to see and hear the animals from the head stalker. If he couldn't see something that the stalker could see, he was told, 'You're not looking hard enough'.

Looking involves another activity which people call 'scanning'. In order to look you need to know where to look. As they already possess a certain amount of knowledge about the habits of particular birds, the birders have an idea of the kind of places the birds might be found. In the case of the hen harriers, the Insh Marsh volunteers knew the birds would nest near the ground and could sometimes be found on fence posts. The aim of scanning is to find the type of area where the birds might be and then to further scan to see if a bird was there. Sometimes, when looking for anything, the birder would do a general scan just to see what he or she could pick up.

The most advanced skill in seeing is recognising what Pete calls the GISS of a bird. This is a term taken from the US Air Force and stands for the General Impression of Size and Shape. This could be something like recognising the wing. John told me how to group raptors into broad-, long- and short-winged. But it is more than this. Some of the better birders can tell a bird by just getting a sense of the way it moves, even at a distance so far away that the colour and wing size are undetectable.

Once a bird has been located, the birder will focus on the bird, either with the binoculars or the telescope. It is this technology that enables the birder to actually be a birdwatcher. The birders would delight in observing the details of the bird, its colouring, its movements and actions. The relationship between watcher and bird is both practical and embodied, where the watcher is totally immersed in the bird's environment. However, as Michael (1991) points out, our experiences of nature are not totally pure. For example, in photography, the camera is placed between observer and object (Urry and Macnaghten: 1991). Michael shows how even the most mundane technologies, walking boots, reshape the affordances of nature by expanding the range of possible actions available to the body. In many respects, binoculars have given birth to the activity of modern birding by considerably 'expanding the range of possibilities'. According to Cocker (2001): 'They convert life into something else, something almost abstract, something purer, clearer, usually more beautiful and almost always something you'd never really seen that way before (2001:33): Two Insh Marsh volunteers said they have had nightmares about going on a birding holiday and forgetting their 'bins'.

In addition, binoculars and telescopes create a 'hierarchy of seeing'. Though birders still get pleasure out of identifying a bird at a distance, the most intense satisfaction is obtained when one can get a close-up of the bird, studying the details of its look and its activities. When out with Pete and his group, there was a discussion as to whether or not identifying a bird from a distance actually counts as having seen a bird. Some people do not even consider that they have seen the bird unless they have had a good look at it. Others may still add the bird to their list but note the inferior circumstances in their notebook, with the idea of aiming to see the bird again closer up.

The intervention of technology has been taken to extremes in the Osprey Centre on the RSPB Abernethy Reserve. There are TV cameras focussed on the osprey nest so that you can see inside it on the TV screens. When male capercaillie are in lekking – preparing for breeding – the only way you can watch is by seeing the birds on a TV link or waiting your turn to go into a specially designed building and see through the telescope. The aim is to protect the birds. Many birders would not count this technologically mediated viewing as authentic and would search out a real sighting (Boyle: 2003).

The following example, from my field notes, illustrates the way birding involves a hierarchy of seeing:

Andrew had come up from London for the express purpose of seeing some of the birds typical to the area. We went to the Osprey Centre and he was very disappointed. He didn't feel that he had 'seen' the birds at all. The use of bins and telescope may be acceptable but this had gone 'too far'. Ross and John told me of another osprey nest that most people didn't know about and gave more 'satisfying' watching. I took Andrew there. He later said that that was one of the best birding moments of his trip – the thrill of seeing the osprey fly in over the loch towards the island where its nest was and then watch it as it fed its young.

Binoculars are an acceptable tool because they are an extension of oneself, similar to the way many mountaineers will use a compass but not GPS. Though there is some variety in what might happen in the televised osprey nest, going out and finding your own nest, with the uncertainty of what will be going on and whether or not the bird will even be there, is superior birding.

Listening and hearing

Vision is not the only sense used. As birders become more skilled, it is the aural that becomes tuned-in. The better birders can identify a bird by its call alone. Seeing the bird is still the aim, but if you can hear a bird first, one at least knows the bird is there and can start looking. Roz, one of the volunteers at Insh Marshes, has a number of bird tapes at home and listens to them so that she can learn to recognise the calls. I found this an incredibly difficult skill to learn. I remember the satisfaction when I learned to recognise the call of a curlew. It took several outings with others before I was able to identify the call whilst on my own. As with seeing, you have to learn to hear. In other words, this education of the senses needs to be guided.

In his article 'The Climbing Body', Lewis (1991) argues that climbing is an activity that gives agency to the body and provides an unmediated relationship with the world, something that is impossible in our urban bodies. Though he refers to movement and touch, a similar case could be made for the heightened awareness of the visual and the aural in birding. He quotes Merleau-Ponty: 'My body is the seat or rather the very actuality of expression. (It) is the fabric into which all objects are woven, and it is, at least in relation to the perceived world, the general instrument of my "comprehension". (1962: 235).

Like climbers, birders use the visual and aural aspects of their body to bring the world into themselves. As we have discussed, being a birder involves bird awareness, a tuning in; it is not something that can then be tuned out. This awareness has been woven into the body.

The sense of place of the birder is thus based on a way of being in place, with eyes and ears, and a way of learning place, the development of the skills that allow you to enhance your perception. The being in place and learning also involve the development of stillness. Whereas Lewis's climbing body is active in terms of body movement, the birder's body might appear passive, but it is the stillness that allows for the activities of looking and listening so that one can see and hear. This is why the birding body can be contrasted with the urban body in the same way as the climbing body can be. In everyday urban life, we are not still (Lopez: 1999) and if anything we try and tune out the world. We are bombarded with things such that we retreat into our own intellectual or psychic self (Lewis: 2000). Birding involves the opposite; you open yourself up to the world, at least a certain part of it.

My time birding changed my own way of being in nature. As a mountaineer, I was constantly on the move, with the occasional rest stop. If climbing, when not leading myself and focussed completely on the rock, I was belaying and focussed on the person leading. With birding I had to learn to just sit or stand in one place for long periods of time. It is amazing what you can notice if you just remain still, looking and listening.

Classification and the birding list

Despite the importance of the body and the senses to the activity of birding, like any other human activity it also involves the mind and cultural and social influences. Firstly, although there is an opening of awareness, there is also a closing-down. This is because to see and hear birds you have to not see and hear other things. This requires your mind to make choices about where to direct the senses. I found in my own experience that I could not do serious birding at the same time as kayaking or walking and climbing. If I was looking for birds, I had to stop walking and often cease to notice the general scenery around me. So, engaging in the activity of birding involves a selection of what the environment makes available to the senses.

The other mental aspect of birding is the universal tendency to organise and classify the data received by the senses, though there is no one system for doing this.

All observation of the natural world involves the use of mental categories with which we, the observers, classify and order the otherwise incomprehensible mass of phenomena around us; and it is notorious that, once these categories have been learned, it is very difficult for us to see the world in any other way. The prevailing system of classification takes possession of us, shaping our perception and thereby our behaviour (Thomas: 1983: 52).

Classification within birding is based on the now traditional scientific method for classifying (Lynch and Woolgar: 1990). Natural scientists developed methods of classification that were based on structure. Previously, animals and plants were classified according to their relationship with man, for example edible and inedible, or wild and tame, or according to character. With the new system, species are classified according to their own attributes, even if these have been selected by humans (Franklin: 1999, Thomas: 1983).

Against this long-established tendency of men to see animals and plants as mere symbols of themselves, we should place the search for new and more objective principles of classification which dominated the scientific botany and zoology of the early modern period. What is notable about their work is that they tried increasingly to group plants not alphabetically or according to their human uses, but by relation to their structural character-istics (Thomas: 1982: 65).

Birders use the birding list to classify birds, which is only partially based on an abstract structure. The way they compile their lists arises out of the needs of their activity: to record the sightings of birds in various contexts. Chris, based at Insh Marshes, had worked for Scottish Natural Heritage, the official government conservation body on the Shetlands, for almost ten years. He has several 'lists': a life list, a garden list, a country list and he often makes a day list. He puts all the information in a notebook, something I was told by everyone that I had to get, and then transfers the information on to the computer. In these lists, different species of birds are all grouped together in no particular order. The basis for classification here is place and time. All those I met also spent time keeping an eye on their 'patch'. They keep track of the birds over the year. On 1 January the RSPB encour-ages a bird-counting day where people go out and record what they can see in their area. On Insh Marshes, there was a regular monthly counting day, one of which I participated in. It was cold and clear with little wind so a good day to see as well as hear. There was a touch of snow on the ground and the marshes spar-kled in the soft winter light. We toured the reserve making some rough estimates on the numbers of different birds that we saw at fixed counting points. To some extent, the existence of lists is a way of organising perception; people will be more likely to see birds that one is searching for to add to a list (Law and Lynch: 1990). However, the lists themselves are a product of the experi-ences of the birder; they are 'embedded in practice' (Bowker and Leigh Star: 1999). There are an infinite variety of potential lists that could be created, as new situations arise; birders therefore will improvise, making up their own rules (Bowker and Leigh Star: 1999).

The specific birding system of classification can also be seen in a discussion between John and one of the Insh Marsh volunteers, Bo, during a birding outing. They had a debate about what kind of bird book is best, a general one or one that is organised by area. One view is that a general book means you might be open to see the unexpected, but an area book helps you know to what to look for and also makes it easier to identify birds. The organisation of field guides, like the lists, may have a role in structuring the activity (Law and Lynch: 1990), but this example shows how birders use them according to their own needs.

Another innovation in the scientific system of classification is the introduction of new classifications such as the LBJ or Little Brown Jobbie. This class of bird refers to those birds that are so difficult to identify because they are so similar, often small and brown, especially without the aid of binoculars. But this does not mean that these birds are unappreciated. Identifying a bird as such can often mean that more time is spent in finding out what it really is. For me as an amateur, LBJ took on its own meaning. So often was I unable to identify the bird, even if close-up, that I remained content with the label LBJ and then just enjoyed watching the bird.

A classification system created by birders themselves out of a practical need contributes to the hierarchy of seeing. Depending on which list one is working on, the sighting of certain birds will be given more priority. When people are working on their life list, it is the rare and the unusual that is noted. Whereas if the focus is their own patch, they will notice and count the more common species. The same bird could either be noticed or not noticed depending on the context. Ailsa, a local from Kingussie who had recently graduated from the University of Aberdeen with a zoology degree, remarked on this when we saw a coot on a pond. She said that maybe in London, where coots are a common sight in the parks, you wouldn't notice one, but here in Scotland they are unusual. However, if the local London birder is doing a list for their patch, then the coot will be noticed and counted. The following extract from my field notes during the Insh Marshes Christmas outing illustrates how a particular bird will be seen amongst hundreds of others.

Birding was a combination of a quick glance with a tick and spending longer watching birds like the whooper swans. The goal seemed to be to see something unusual. We spent some time in one field where Chris searched and searched for a pink-legged goose amongst the grey-legged ones. I couldn't tell the difference. He didn't seem to notice the cold at all and kept going further into the field to get a better look at the pink-legged one that he had finally spotted whilst the rest of us were freezing and wanted to go to the pub.

Without discounting other types of lists, the life list underlies all the others. It is within the structure of the life list that seeing a rare bird takes on specific significance. Strathspey attracts many birders because of the chance of seeing species that are specific to the area: capercaillie, crossbills, dotterel, ptarmigan, snow bunting and osprey. Andrew, who would describe himself as 'mildly obsessive' about birding, made sure that he came to see me in Scotland. He had already been on a birding holiday around the west coast of Scotland the year before and seen a number of rare species but not the dotterel, which nests on top of Carn Ban Mor above Glenfeshie. His pilgrimage to find this bird involved a five-mile walk up to 900 metres. Andrew does not do a lot of hill-walking normally but he forged ahead, despite the strong headwind that we had to struggle against on our way up. From my field notes:

We climbed over the last steep rise and I started getting my mind in gear for dotterel hunting; this is where they were supposed to be. Then I looked up and right in front of me, about ten feet away – was a dotterel! It seemed oblivious to us, maybe because we were downwind. Andrew was over the moon. Catching the first glimpse is an important moment – it's unexpected – the initial surprise and delight. He rated this even higher than the osprey moment because this was the bird he had come to see.

This birding experience ranks very highly in the hierarchy of seeing for a number of reasons. Andrew saw a rare bird, rare not in the sense of its being endangered but because it can only be found in a few sites. The sighting also involved effort; he made a considerable investment in time and energy in order to see the bird. In addition, he not only saw the bird but it was immediately in front of him so he did not even need his binoculars. And he found the bird himself; it was his own discovery. Andrew said that it is these moments that 'stand out', ones that 'remind you of why you go birding'.

Naming and identifying

Making a list requires naming the bird. It isn't enough for people to just see the bird, they have to identify it and say what it is. The process of naming can tell us much about how humans relate to the species in question. Hearne (1982) refers to the process of naming as 'Adam's task'. Naming has two aspects; it can demonstrate interest and respect, as illustrated by the work of the early naturalists (Morris: 1996), or it can show one's power to command and possess. 'Naming to possess' has been an integral part of the history of science. Though scientific inquiry has been a vehicle for opening people up to the world around them, it has also been motivated by the desire to control, dominate and rationalise (Merchant: 1980, Plumwood: 2002). Francis Bacon, one of the leading proponents of the 'subjugation of nature' perspective, says about naming: 'the first acts which man performed in Paradise consisted of the two summary parts of knowledge; the view of the creatures and the imposition of names' (quoted in Hollander: 1995: 42). By classifying and ordering, naming and identifying, scientists have brought the natural world into the human orbit, ready to be used and exploited for human ends. This has culminated today in companies searching out different life forms to patent, an extreme form of 'naming to possess' (Shiva: 2001).

The aspects of naming can be distinguished in the birding world in the contrast between birder and 'twitcher'. Tom and John at Insh Marshes were concerned that I realised the difference between a birder and a twitcher, though they were quick to stress that all birders could be twitchers at times. Therefore, it is important to see this in terms of particular practices rather than types of people. They define twitcher as someone who is only interested in ticks and who ignores birds that they have already seen. People will go to great lengths to get a tick. Tom and John didn't like it when people said 'just a crow' or 'just a robin'. Just as many of the Victorian collectors sought out the rare and exotic, so do the twitchers. Once they have seen them they can add them to their list and claim ownership; they do not name and let go. Birding takes on the modern-day form of collecting: consumption. Thomas (1983) recognises this tendency in the new natural history fashion. There is an element of wanting to possess or consume: a natural history version of keeping up with the Joneses.

> Much of this activity was distinctly acquisitive in character. Ladies vied with each other to emulate the great collections of shells, plants and insects amassed by aristocrats like the Duchess of Beaufort and the Duchess of Portland (p. 283).

Similar to those who tick off places they have been or continually add a new consumer item to their house, twitchers tick off birds. They may not physically collect the bird but they do so symbolically and this can be just as powerful.

Photography also enables possession. Ross had recently taken up photography as an activity related to his birding. It was no longer enough to see a bird, he also wanted to get a good photograph of one. This required him to get much closer to the bird, which is an added challenge to the whole activity. This desire is reminiscent of deer-stalking, discussed in the next chapter. Instead of a deer-antler trophy, the successful bird stalker displays a photograph over the mantelpiece. The expression 'to capture something on film' is relevant here. Interestingly, John shot birds before he started watching them. His view was that watching rather than shooting was a sign of evolution; people had moved beyond their hunting ancestors. However, photography is compatible with non-twitcher practices, as it is in the case of Ross. Though he liked having the photos, the act of taking the photos required greater effort and afforded a better sighting, thus contributing to a fuller appreciation of the bird.

Most of the birders I met do not exhibit the possessive characteristics of a twitcher that are potentially contained within the activity. Tom and John got excited about birds even if they had seen them many times before. Whilst working on the reserve, John would stop to look at the whooper swans even though they were around us all the time. John looks at his patch every day and talks about getting to know the birds as individuals. Therefore, identifying a bird by naming it can mean something much different to wanting to possess it; it can show that by making the effort to identify and name the bird, the birder is showing respect and appreciation. Michael Fiennes (2002) realises this as part of his quest to follow the snow geese.

'Learning the names is a method of noticing. The ducks were transformed – fleshed out, coloured in – when I matched them to names: bufflehead, wigeon, gadwell' (2002: 95).

By giving a bird a species name, you are opening yourself up to the world, as Fiennes' example shows. You are actually noticing features of a specific bird species – it is not just a bird. According to Cocker (2001), birding is particularly suited to Britain. The 200–225 species that breed in this country are just enough species to give variety. There aren't enough mammals and trying to identify the 20,000 species of insect in Britain would be too much of a challenge. Naming birds is therefore possible and meaningful for anyone. Naming a bird in the sense of noticing requires much more than an observation of the structure of the bird. We have seen that the birder uses the senses in a sophisticated manner.

Sight may give the birder some of the structural characteristics but perceiving GISS seems to go beyond basic structure, to a sense of the whole bird in movement. Also, the key part played by bird calls defies classification. The role of observation in natural history is based solely on the visual.

Another key difference between birding and twitching practices is that once the bird is named, the birder goes on to watch the bird. This is done out of sheer enjoyment, unrelated to the bird list. This appreciation of birds was recognised early on. Thomas (1983) quotes G. M. Trevelyan: 'To preserve the bird life of the country is required in the spiritual interests of the human race, more particularly of the English section of it, who find such joy in seeing and hearing birds' (quoted p. 302).

In the case of Andrew's viewing of the osprey and the dotterel, it was not just a case of 'tick and go'. He spent at least a half an hour observing the birds. With the osprey, he enjoyed watching how it fed its young. Because he had such a close view of the dotterel, he could notice the details of the bird itself such as the colouring and the way it moved on the ground. I witnessed many more examples of the joy of observing birds on my day out with Pete and his group.

Birding as an apprenticeship

Birding can be an activity between the individual and the birds. However, there is an important social aspect involved in becoming a birder. We have already seen how a society infused with consumerism and the desire to dominate and possess can affect the way that birding is practised. Another key factor in the making of a birder is apprenticeship. The first experiences of birding may be unstructured (Cocker: 2001), but once tuned-in, the activity becomes increasingly complex and requires the acquisition of many competencies. This requires a kind of apprenticeship with other more experienced birders. Birding is a 'situated activity' where learners participate in communities of practitioners (Lave and Wenger: 1991). My experience in the field was indeed an apprenticeship. I had been vaguely interested in birds, but unless they were very obvious or remarkable in some way, I did not see them.

Once I started volunteering at Insh Marshes and going out with John and the trainee warden Ross, it is was if a new world had opened up to me, one that I soon realised had much more to it then I would ever have imagined, having lived a life of limited radio 'frequencies'. Birders are very proud of the skills that they learn. The day I spent with Pete and his birding group from Speyside Wildlife on a trip to the north-west coast of Scotland illustrates the process of undertaking a birding apprenticeship, and shows how the sensual, mental and social work together. My findings from this day demonstrate how all parts of birding come together to construct a birding sense of place. As mentioned above, this process is guided, an education of the senses.

People went out of the house with their bins already around their neck. We had only driven a short distance up the road when the guide stopped because he thought it might be a good place to see a crested tit, one that is local to this area and therefore of interest to the clients. Our search began with a scan of the area using the bins. This is a specific way of looking that means moving our binocular-assisted vision slowly and systematically over an area. It took about fifteen minutes of scanning before someone first heard and then spotted a crested tit. You could just make it out at the top of the tree. Alan and Beth discussed whether such a view counted. Most people felt that it could count as a tick but they wanted to see it again with a better view. This stop provided the occasion to discuss binoculars. One of them lent me his to compare with mine. They showed things up so closely and clearly. Through this incident I began to integrate a number of lessons. I was beginning to learn patience. I was developing a desire to be able to recognise birdcalls. And, I was starting to think that I needed to have a better pair of binoculars.

We got back in the minibuses and the guides organised an inter-bus bird quiz. The group was keen to show off their knowledge and got very involved. The questions were very detailed and included questions that could only be answered by those who have a high level of knowledge, like naming birds with 'square white rumps'. I had no idea that there was so much to learn. I was very frustrated at not being able to answer any questions so the answers helped increase my own knowledge as well as making me want to learn more.

Our first major stop was in a lay-by off the Inverness–Ullapool road surrounded by high, rocky crags. Pete knew that there was an eagle's eerie. We did the usual scanning and focussing-in when a nest was spotted. Unfortunately, no one was home. The stop did provide the opportunity for what I was told was a typical birder encounter. A couple with their young daughter pulled up by us. The man tried to get information out of Pete but wouldn't come right out and say that he was interested. Pete says that there are certain phrases that are used such as 'what have you got?' 'What's about?' Pete resented telling this guy anything because of his casual manner, pretending that he already knew what was there. Pete said that you had to be careful because of the danger of egg collectors. In any case, when we pulled out, the man followed us and managed to pull up in the next lay-by that we'd chosen. I had not realised the need for secrecy before and this would affect my future encounters with other birders.

When we got to the lay-by near the coast and Gruinard Island we proceeded to start searching for our prime target of the day: a sea eagle. The clients may not have been classic twitchers, but Pete was very concerned that his group would be able to tick this bird off. They had had three bad days due to horrible weather, which made things miserable for both them and the birds. This day was glorious and Pete was hoping it would be a good one for birding. We got started with our scanning. We must have been there for at least an hour. People didn't look the whole time for sea eagles but used the telescope to get a really close-up view of some other species that were reasonably fixed points. The telescope, even more than the bins, provides incredible detail. The procedure is to scan, find something and then, where possible, to focus in with the telescope that we would all share. It requires incredible patience. People were on constant alert. But even the keenest got bored after a while and we decided to move on. Someone said as much for the view as anything else. The general view was not in the forefront of everyone's mind – I had pointed out a fantastic view of the mountain An-Teallach and no one seemed that interested – but they still commented on how birding gave them chances to see nice views. Again, this was a real lesson in patience. In addition, I got to know about the telescope and the advantages it afforded.

The next spot provided a good choice, but not for sea eagles. We had managed to give our shadow the slip by this time. Here we spotted a pair of surf scoters. This provoked great interest because they are an American species that one doesn't expect to find here. Such species that do not regularly breed in Britain are especially sought-after. Andy told me how he makes a special effort to go to the Isles of Scilly every year. Birders come from all over Britain to see the many species of migratory birds that may only be in Britain for one day. Therefore, the group was concerned to let others around Britain know of this sighting. Andy sent the information about the scoter to Birdline. People who subscribe to this service get messages on their pagers, which tell them of the latest unusual sightings around the country. This can prompt people to set off immediately in hopes of adding the bird to their list, even if it requires travelling long distances. This is obviously important information for an apprentice birder like me. It also initiated me into the hierarchy of seeing. This sighting ranked highly because we saw something that was unexpected in this context as well as being able to observe the birds close-up for a considerable length of time. Though we didn't see any sea eagles people still enjoyed the good views of mergansers and divers. People were very good about explaining things and helping me to spot and identify birds.

The next stop was a farm near the bay. We spent quite a lot

of time just looking at some very ordinary birds – wheatears, pipits et cetera – in just one garden of a house. So, despite coming to look for a few key birds, some of the group got very involved in just watching the famous LBJs. My apprenticeship continued as people pointed out how the plumage had changed from winter to summer, as I enjoyed an excellent view of a wheatear. I began to realise how people could learn to appreciate this LBJ.

We still had the goal of seeing the sea eagle and Pete was keeping an eye out. He had the telescope trained on Gruinard Island because he expected them to come from that direction. We had been in this spot for some time, looking at the various species of divers, when, suddenly, all the gulls who had been sitting on the water just took off. Immediately people's minds turned to what had disturbed them. Gary looked up and saw it – it came towards us quite slowly so we could fully appreciate it. It flew right over us and then disappeared over a rise behind us. People were estatic. The sea eagle could be ticked off. I could now understand the satisfaction of seeing a rare bird. It was especially rewarding because we had spent so much time searching for it. A desire to seek out other firsts was growing inside me. I had enjoyed watching the other birds, but this stood out – the contrast with the usual.

In the minibus on the way home we talked about what it meant to be a birder. The people came from a variety of backgrounds and had different stories about how they started out. However, what they most talked about was what they liked about the activity itself. Pleasure in the birds themselves was not explicitly mentioned but that this played a part was obvious from their enthusiastic and appreciative comments throughout the day.

Some mentioned the feeling of accomplishment as they added to their list. However, as with the Munroists, there is more to it than the tick. Beth said that it was good to have a hobby. It gave a focus for visits, a way of deciding where to go and what to do. She and her husband have visited over fifty countries as a result of their interest in searching out rare birds. She says that she gets satisfaction out of seeing the rare bird, but it is the way it gets her to explore new places in a different way that is more important. Andy likes the skill aspect of birding. He gets intense satisfaction out of becoming a better birder – learning to recognise birds quicker, learning to recognise calls. He said he had enormous respect for Pete, the group leader who has developed his skills to a very high level. On the day out it was obvious that people looked for the chance to display their skill.

These two comments highlight the importance of the social aspect of birding. Exploring new places and developing skills are done with other people – the 'community of practitioners.' This is further illustrated by the way Pete ended the birding day. After dinner, the group gathered together in the sitting room to go back over their day, summarising what they had seen and discussing what the highlights were for each of them. This moment of sharing is very important, according to Pete. They all felt that this day was the best they'd had so far and asked me what I thought about it. I could only say that I too had really enjoyed it and wanted to go birding again. Maybe I was even becoming a birder!

A birding sense of place

I have shown how birders use their senses and minds in a social context to bring forth a world. They learn, perhaps initially on their own, but primarily through apprenticeship in a community of practitioners how to be in a place in a particular way that is known as birding. Though it means opening oneself to the world, it also leads to the closing down of perception, and, in some cases, becomes just another form of domination and consumption. This is because by noticing birds, other features of the world go unnoticed. The pivotal role binoculars play illustrates this point. The birder focuses in so closely on the bird, that nothing else has room to fit in the lens.

The birding sense of place has many similarities with moun-taineering. They both take up the affordances of the natural envi-ronment and use their skill to develop their relationship with that environment. Both have an aesthetic appreciation of a part of non-human nature and experience immense enjoyment from their interaction whether it be with a rock face, a view or a bird. They also make a contrast between the activity of birding and everyday life. However, birding is something that can still be done in the urban environment, with a garden bird list. Nevertheless, the visits to places like the Cairngorms are particularly valued, partially because they offer the opportunity to see different kinds of birds, but also because of the beautiful surroundings. Andrew's purpose for climbing to the top of Carn Ban Mor was to see the dotterel, but he also spent considerable time contemplating the extensive views over the Cairngorms and down to Loch Einich. Similarly, mountaineers also value their experiences of bird spot-ting. John, the mountaineer, often takes binoculars with him on a non-climbing day and is able to recognise a range of birds. Therefore, both senses of place can be considered to be forms of a general environmentalist sense of place. The consequence of their passions is a desire to protect that environment so that they can continue to enjoy their hobbies.

However, the birding sense of place can also form the basis of a more generalised approach to other species. Whereas moun-taineers stress the importance of having places where they can 'recreate' themselves, many birders have a tendency to see birds and other species as having intrinsic value, worthy of conserving. In other words, it is important that birds exist, even if humans are not there to see them. Though mountaineers are often involved in campaigns to promote their interests, such as the freedom to roam, it is a concern for the preservation of other species, normally referred to as conservation in the UK, that has been a more important stimulus for birders, as well as moun-taineers with a concern for wildlife, to participate in the growing ranks of an environmental movement. Birding and other wildlife interests have evolved into a general conservation sense of place whose presence is felt in the Cairngorms region as in the rest of the world.

Birding, the love of nature and conservation

Birding has created an intense passion and an appreciation of the natural world that is manifested in the way conservation organisations and businesses have increased in membership and in political and economic influence. Conservation is a distinct way of relating to the environment and is one strand of the broad environment movement. It has a long history and current organisations are part of this tradition (Pepper: 1996, Morris: 1996). Morris (1996) argues that some of the first conservationists were naturalists. Darwin showed that humans were also part of these life-processes and in fact had emerged out of them. Humans were just one species, linked by a web of life. A number of scientists were thus becoming critical of the traditional anthropocentric worldview of nature as something to be exploited and dominated. Instead, it was something to be studied and understood as well as loved and respected. Naturalists did not develop their views in a vacuum but as a result of both new ideas in science, for example from Darwin, their own experiences and by observing what was going on around them. And it was the work of these naturalists, both professional and amateur, that contributed to the first conservation legislation.

It was from those who studied birds for recreation or curiosity that the pressure for conservation would arise; and it was the naturalists who pushed through a series of Acts, which from 1869 onwards, gave an increasing degree of statutory protection to wild birds. This was the culmination of several hundred years of mounting interest in the natural world (Thomas: 1983: 280–81).

Various organisational forms have emerged in Badenoch and

Strathspey as a result of people's knowledge and love of nature. I came across organised conservation in several forms, from small informal groups to large organisations with international influence, such as the RSPB. The individual's experience of birding both influences and is influenced by this social environment. In other words, one moves from the existence of people who go birding, to a public conservation approach, to land use. Within this wider context, many tensions are revealed that are not so apparent during the moment when the birder is engaged in the activity itself. Though birders and others interested in protecting various species of flora and fauna agree on the intrinsic value of non-human species, there is disagreement about how to go about the protection of those species as well as which species are priorities. Learning to perceive and appreciate something like a bird, also involves a closing down of perceptions such that other aspects of the environment are not seen. This forms the basis for potential conflict with other approaches to land use that are examined later in the book.

RSPB member

Everyone I met through birding was a member of the RSPB. They are often people who don't join traditional political organisations but they join the RSPB because they want to protect birds. Many members are from urban areas and have little understanding of rural land management issues and the perceived conflict between protecting birds and other land uses.

I came across much hostility to the RSPB during the course of my research. The reasons for this are very complex and tied up with politics and image. According to Smout (1992), the focus on a particular species that is protected in human-free zones, is a legacy of an English approach to conservation. Whether there is such an approach may be open to question, but the RSPB is very much an English organisation in terms of membership. Though it has many properties in Scotland, only 82,000 of its over 1 million members are in Scotland, with few of these in the Highlands itself (https://ww2.rspb.org.uk/our-work/rspb-news/news/details. aspx?id=tcm:9-228008). The vast majority of wardens and volunteers are of English origin, the only exception from my own limited observations being Ross at Insh Marshes. As seen in the popularity of the SNP, nationalist sentiments are strong in Scotland, so that the 'Englishness' of the RSPB could be a factor. However, I found that there were many specific local attitudes that show that the view of English = bad, RSPB = English, therefore RSPB = bad is too simplistic.

The RSPB aims to protect birds through strategically buying up key properties that are significant for certain species that they have targeted for protection. In my fieldwork area, the RSPB manages two reserves. One is the very high-profile Abernethy reserve, site of the reintroduction of the osprey. It covers hundreds of acres from native pine forests, the home of capercaillie and blackcock, to the tops of the hills near Cairn Gorm. The other is the much smaller Insh Marshes, which is very important for its flood plain habitat, attracting a number of species including the whooper swan.

Tom, the warden at Insh Marshes, was not satisfied with an exclusive focus on birds. When I first met him he was very excited about a visit from some specialists who were coming to examine the aspen trees on the reserve because they are one of the few places where a particular species of fly can breed. One of the jobs the volunteers undertook was building a rabbit fence to protect these trees. Tom saw himself as a deviant within the RSPB, saying 'the members do not pay for him to be spending his time protecting insects'. He later left the RSPB to work for a butterfly conservation organisation.

Tom felt that the RSPB reserve at Abernethy focussed 'too much on a few high-profile' bird species. Their publicity material supports this claim. In the 1999 Abernethy Newsletter, despite acknowledging the importance of other species on the reserve, the only ones given detailed reports are the osprey, black grouse and capercaillie. The Osprey Centre, a 'national promotion site' (Management Rationale, Aims and Policies) has become a major tourist attraction, and the introduction of video viewing of the capercaillie has been very successful. The nearest village to the reserve, Boat of Garten, calls itself the 'Osprey Village'. Whether or not it is true that the reserve mangers neglect other species, the outward impression is that they are prioritising only a few. There is of course debate about whether they spend too much time on these species. As stated in 'RSPB in Scotland': 'resources are limited, making it essential that we prioritise our work'.

Local conservation groups

Tom's broadening of perception led him to form a local naturalist group. He was concerned to make links between different specialists working in conservation of other species apart from birds, as well as including the many interested amateurs. He was well aware that many of these people were English incomers who had recently moved to the area, but he thought that by forming a group and taking field trips, he could include a wider variety of people. He also wanted to extend his own interest in birds to other species and by bringing together lichen, moss, plant, mushroom and butterfly and moth specialists he hoped for some 'cross-pollination'. Instead of just birders or botanists or lichenologists, he hoped to create a broader front of people who all shared a conviction in the importance of enhancing biodiversity. The first outing was an example of opening of perceptions. From my field notes:

> *I thought I was going birding but I was given a magnifying glass and most of the day was spent looking at mushrooms, lichen and moss. Looking through the magnifying glass made all the difference. Les, a lichen expert, said that it is a different world and he is right.*

There was so much to see – the little bumps were so intricate and detailed. One lichen had little bumps that looked like mushrooms through the glass.

Many people on the field trip shared Tom's concerns and wanted to extend their knowledge beyond their own area of interest. Viv, a botanist and local ranger for the Highland Council, said she enjoyed learning about species that are not really her speciality. As a ranger, she wanted to expand her knowledge of all the flora and fauna in the area. Tessa, also a ranger, had a breadth of knowledge that she had accumulated as part of her role in taking children on environmental field trips. However, some of the others only focussed on 'their' species. Tom went off on his own to pursue his newly discovered interest in butterflies; the mushroom specialists, a retired couple, looked at mushrooms; and the lichen specialist at lichen. The use of the magnifying glass opened up a whole new world, but even more than with birds it closed off many others. We were all in the same place, yet there were many different senses of place within one square yard.

This was only the first trip of the group and Tom hoped that future trips would see more opportunities for sharing. Despite their differences, they all had a common interest in maintaining habitats for the various species that they care about. The forest that we visited for our field trip had recently come under threat from developers. A campaign to save a forest, home to birds, plants, lichen, moss and mushrooms, could therefore unite everyone in the common aim of conservation. Threats from developers were the impetus for the formation of the Badenoch and Strathspey Conservation Group. This group takes public stands on a variety of general conservation issues, including the need to take down deer fences to protect capercaillie, opposition to planning applications on a rare butterfly breeding site, campaigns to stop housing developments in forests where the capercaillie breed, and general promotion of native tree regeneration. From a collection of individuals with a knowledge and love of various species, they have created a conservation interest group in Badenoch and Strathspey (https://www.bscg.org.uk/).

Wildlife tourism

Another sign of the increased interest in observing wild creatures is the success of wildlife holidays. In the Badenoch and Strathspey area, there are many such operations, including Speyside Wildlife and Heatherlea Birding. My contact with Speyside Wildlife was mostly through the owner, Sally, who arranged for me to go out with Pete and his group. Sally formed the company together with her partner, a keen English birder. They were able to sell property in the south and use the money to set themselves up in business in Strathspey. The business has been very successful. The clients stay in a steading out in Glenfeshie that has been converted into comfortable accommodation. The success of the business depends on whether or not the clients see what they have come to see – the species that are specifically Scottish such as crossbills, sea eagles, dotterels and corncrakes. Therefore, the interest of the business is to maintain the natural habitats in which these species are found. Sally has a strong professional interest in conservation. Though these types of businesses are relatively new, the impact of their success is beginning to be felt within the business community. Sally was Vice-chair of the Cairngorms Chamber of Commerce and also became a member of the new National Park Board in 2003. This only happened because of the way an interest in birds and other wildlife has become a valued pastime for so many people.

*

Birding is a situated activity. Though the birds themselves are affordances provided by the physical environment, a person learns to be a birder as part of a social process. The various ways of seeing, the role of binoculars, the hierarchy of seeing, the birding list, the act of naming and the acquisition of skill are all part of a social environment. This then creates a particular sense of place in which the bird is the central feature of all perception. By becoming tuned-in to birds, one has learned to perceive in new ways and, as a result, to care about the objects of this new awareness (Milton: 2002). However, because of the intensity of the experience, which is both intellectual and emotional, there is a potential tendency for people to see and value only birds, to the exclusion of all else. This process is not confined to birding but can equally be applied to interest in other species, whether butterflies, lichen, mushrooms or moss, and may have consequences for decisions about land use. However, there are a number of areas of overlapping concern and in these cases, when there appears to be a threat to a habitat, people come together to form groups or join larger organisations, which then increase their power in the public arena. In this sense there is a general conservation sense of place. The general increase in interest in wildlife has also led to greater economic power as conservation organisations become landowners and wildlife businesses become key members of local business associations.

However, as there is disagreement amongst those that might come under the broad heading of conservationist, there is even more potential for disagreement with those whose experience of the land is as a place to work. The next chapter is based on those who work on the land, showing how a very different context – work rather than leisure – can lead to a very different sense of place.

CHAPTER FOUR

Sense of Place
and Livelihood

Activities: Producing, Cultivating, Nurturing, Looking, Feeding, Counting, Stalking, Beating, Driving, Shooting, Culling, Mending, Managing, Spotting, Organising, Transforming, Entertaining

> I was out with a gamekeeper on Kinveachy – watching him work and chatting. We stood on a vantage point, looking around. He waved his hand, pointing out particular hills and burns and said: 'This is my garden.'

The gamekeeper's comment epitomises the livelihood approach to land that will be examined in this chapter. The 'garden' stands in contrast to 'wilderness' or 'wild land'. Whereas mountaineering and conservation senses of place both value land that has minimal signs of human impact, those who work on the land – farmers and sporting estate workers – assign a value to land that has been tended and cultivated, transformed from wilderness into a garden that produces something for human use. 'Farmers assume a right to enter the world, tame it and reshape it, farm it' (Brody: 2001: p. 10). This sense of place is developed out of a day-to-day engagement with the land that has the express purpose of transforming nature into something that can be exploited to provide a livelihood for human beings.

My detailed ethnographic research with land workers shows how a livelihood-based sense of place is constructed in practice.

As with mountaineers and conservationists, the farmers', game-keepers' and stalkers' activities give rise to distinct perceptions and ways of relating to the land: their sense of place. However, it is the overarching purpose of transforming the land into a garden that provides the backdrop for people's activities. As a result, the sense of place is linked to land-use goals that will often be in conflict with other land uses.

The people and places: hefted to the land

My experience of life on a sporting estate started on the morning I arrived for my first stint as a grouse-beater. Thanks to Frank, the sporting estate manager who took me on as a beater for the grouse shoots in order to help me with my research, I was able to get to know a world that was not easy to access. We were told to meet at the car park at Slochd, just off the A9 north of Carr-bridge. It was all new to me, yet the sight of all the estate workers in their Kinveachy black and white tweeds, the Land Rovers, the dogs, the guns seemed very familiar – it was just how I imagined it would be. I was immediately taken in by the pageantry of it all. This was to be the first of many experiences with the estate workers, people who went out of their way to make me feel welcome, giving me many opportunities to participate in the day-to-day running of the estate.

At the time of research, Kinveachy sporting estate was run by a team of people who had a large degree of autonomy from the owner and his factor, neither of whom lived on the Strathspey part of the Seafield Estate. Frank was the overall manager and under him were the head keeper, John, who looked after the grouse, and the head stalker, Alastair, who was in charge of organising the deer-stalking and culling operations. Alan and Ian were the other keepers and David and Peter worked with Alastair. However, there was a large degree of overlap. Everyone was involved in the grouse drives and the keepers would sometimes assist the stalkers if they had extra guests to take out. They were a close team and I felt very privileged to be able to spend so much time with them.

My research on farming also depended on people letting me be involved in their daily activities. The farm of Mary and Jimmy consisted of their own land and land leased from Kinveachy. Gordon had his own beef farm, which he has now sold, and Douglas, a good friend of Gordon, was the sole employee of a beef farm nearby for twenty years. His father was a farm manager on a sporting estate near Kincraig near Glenfeshie. There is a certain intermingling of the two groups. I was introduced to the farmers Mary and Jimmy by John from Kinveachy. Their farm backs on to a grouse moor and there are friendly exchanges when their animals sometimes stray into grouse and stag territory.

In Badenoch and Strathspey as a whole there was a tendency for farmers and estate workers to see themselves as part of the same social group. Douglas differentiates 'land-workers' from 'villagers'. These groups may not always mix due to where they live, often far from villages, and also due to work requirements. Many sporting estates have farm managers who know other local farmers. Some farmers let keepers onto their land to shoot rabbits and other 'vermin' since the keepers are usually not allowed to keep their 'kill' at the estates they work on.

Often farmers, unlike many others, can trace their roots in the area back several generations. Mary inherited the farm from her father who originally came to this farm from another a few miles away. Gordon lived and worked on the farm he grew up on. Even in retirement he lives on a part of that land, having kept a large plot for his house and his wife's horses. The keepers and stalkers cannot normally claim such a lineage but their link with the land comes from the long hours spent working in all conditions over a period of many years, as well as from the fact that they live where they work, in tied cottages provided by the estate. All the Kinveachy Estate workers came from outside or 'outwith' the area. However, they saw themselves as carrying on a tradition that had been in place on this estate for over a hundred years. In addition, they have been trained by those who worked the land before them, ensuring a continuation of knowledge and practices. The expression I often heard, both from these workers themselves and others referring to them, is that they are 'hefted to the land'. This term is also used to refer to deer that are attached to certain parts of the hills. To say someone is 'hefted to the land' implies long-term commitment and extensive knowledge that carries with it the 'right to belong'.

Such a relationship can be characterised as 'historical ecological' (Balee: 1998, Crumley: 1994). These land-workers have a history of intervention on the land. They can visibly trace the effects of that intervention and know that their current work will contribute to the future of that landscape. Farmers and estate workers are aware of how their lives and the land are bound together, each having an impact on the other. It is this interaction that has created the present landscape. It is not a question of achieving some kind of stable equilibrium but of constant intervention to deal with new problems as they arise, all within the context of achieving a specific end or purpose. For John, Alastair and the others on the sporting estate, this means maintaining a healthy population of deer and grouse. For Mary and Jimmy, Gordon and Douglas on their farms, it is to raise good quality cattle and sheep. According to the historical ecological perspective: 'Individual and group interests may drive specific initiatives that create environmental impacts; these in turn, are part of processes leading to ongoing problems, options and pressures that rebound on individual and group interests.' (Henderson: 1998).

Other land-users such as mountaineers will also have an impact on the land, which will in turn have an impact on their future activity, for example path erosion. However, it is the land-workers who have continual contact with the land and explicitly aim to transform the land. It is in this way that land-workers can be described as hefted to the land as part of an historical ecology.

There is at present a great fear that this 'hefted history' is coming to an end. Both farming and the sporting estates are undergoing considerable upheaval. In order to understand the sense of place of farmers and estate workers, and the challenges and issues they are now facing, it is necessary to examine the 'historical ecology' of the area. In other words, the current relationship with the land and the kind of activities farmers and sporting estate workers undertake, are the direct result of how humans and nature have interacted previously. The way humans have intervened to transform the land, the land management practices, have created the conditions in which they are now working. However, these practices must also be seen not just as technical, natural history or ecological questions, but as products of particular social, economic and political contexts (Balee: 1998).

Farms and the sporting estate:
history of land and people

As in other parts of Scotland, agriculture was the mainstay of the economy up until the nineteenth century. Prior to the seventeenth century, farms were largely subsistence farms, based on arable crops, cattle and goats. During the eighteenth century, demand for cattle increased, stimulated by the need to feed the British armies, and the Highlands was increasingly drawn into the wider market (McCarthy: 1998). Farming was assisted by the introduction of the turnip in the eighteenth century, which meant cattle could be kept through the winter. Up until the early eighteenth century this economic activity was part of a set of social and political relations in which families belonged to a clan, headed by a clan chief, relatively independent of any national state structure. However, with the increased commercialisation of farming and the decline of the clan system after the defeat at Culloden in 1746, the Highlands were more firmly brought into the market and state structures dominated by the rising capitalist class based both in England and in the Lowlands of Scotland. The clan chiefs were incorporated into this hierarchical system, taking on a role of private landowner. Commercial pressures, the Industrial Revolution and the related agricultural changes transformed the nature of farming, and therefore every other aspect of life in the Highlands (MacAskill: 1999).

The biggest change came with the surge in demand for sheep to supply wool to the new industry. The turning over of the land to sheep and the subsequent 'clearing' of the land of people is now notorious, with debate still raging about the extent to which the Clearances were simply a by-product of economic development or the imposition of an imported system of profit-driven landlordism (Prebble: 1969, Hunter: 1996, McCarthy: 1998, MacAskill: 1999, Wigan: 1998, Bayer: 2004). In Badenoch and Strathspey, the impact of the Clearances was not as marked as in other parts of the Highlands, though in Badenoch returning army officers in the early 1800s cleared the land and put it to sheep, much like in other parts of Scotland (Glen: 2002). In Strathspey, on the other hand, sheep were never introduced on a mass scale. Cattle farming may have become less widespread, but it was still the main type of farming. The reason for this lack of interest in sheep may have been due to the fact that forestry was still a more financially attractive option for the landowners. Grant of Rothiemurchus 'did not approve of sheep farms' (Glen: 2002: 57) and concentrated more on developing his timber operations. It was certainly at this time that the area became an important producer of timber with many areas of hillside given over to new imported trees in addition to the native species (Glen: 2002). Though sheep did not replace cattle in other parts of Strathspey, they were still an important addition to the farmers' livestock that has consequences today.

The introduction of commercial shooting on the estates in the late 1800s had serious repercussions for farming in the area. As the hillsides were increasingly transformed into grouse moors and deer preserves, farming was confined to a narrow strip of the strath. The origins of killing animals as a form of recreation lie with the ruling class (Shoard: 1997). The sport goes back at least to Norman times. William the Conqueror was a keen hunter and whole areas of the country were cordoned off and called 'Deer Forests' (despite often including no actual forest) and were the special preserve of the King and his entourage of knights and nobles (Shoard: 1997). Heavy punishments were given, including hanging and transportation, to anyone who dared poach a deer or even a rabbit. In Scotland, sport shooting began to reach the Highlands in the early nineteenth century, made possible by the pattern of private landownership where large tracts of land were owned by the ruling elites of both England and Scotland (McCarthy: 1998). Queen Victoria added impetus to the sport when she and her hunting consort began their tradition of taking up residence in Balmoral, in Deeside, for the 'season', a practice still maintained enthusiastically by the current Royals (Richards: 2004). The grouse season begins on the Glorious Twelfth (of August) and extends into December. The stalking season overlaps with this, beginning in July and finishing in October. Hind shooting can go on until February. Balmoral became the model for the Highland sporting estate which then proliferated all over the Highlands, having an impact on both the landscape and the economy (Richards: 2004).

In Strathspey, in the 1830s and 1840s prior to Queen Victoria's influence, what became the Seafield Estate had already started making changes that would severely alter farming practices (Glen: 2002). Lord Seafield made the transition to sporting estate by clearing the forest of cattle and sheep thought to be in competition with deer for food. Therefore, farmers faced restrictions on where they could graze their stock. As both deer-stalking and grouse-shooting increased in financial significance in the next decades, both the forests and the open hillside were increasingly off-limits to graziers. The practice of grazing animals on upland lands in the summer – on sheilings – came to an end.

The impact of these changes can be seen today. Farms are still there, but only about 250, all of 100 hectares or less. These have been consolidated between fewer owners and, like most upland farms in Britain, are heavily dependent on subsidies. It is still an important sector, employing seven per cent of the local population, whilst the Scottish average is three per cent (interview with a Farming and Wildlife Advisory Group, or FWAG, representative). Many of the farms are scattered between Carrbridge and Grantown, along the Spey and Dulnain rivers. Farmers still raise cattle and sheep but the grazing land is even more restricted to the strath. Mary used both her family's farm and pastures leased from Kinveachy. This meant that she had to drive from one to another. One tract was adjacent to the grouse moor of Kinveachy and there was frequent good-natured banter about whether her livestock were causing any problems for John's grouse. The smaller amount of land available for farming means that less is given over to crops: Mary Grant, now in her nineties, remembered that on the farm where she grew up they had many more fields of oats and neeps (swedes) as fodder for the livestock. Now farmers tend to buy in feed from elsewhere. Ruins of former sheilings can be seen adjacent to the Burma Road in the Dulnain valley on Kinveachy and Mary's sheep graze amongst ruined farm buildings.

Frustration at this decline is widespread amongst farming people. Seamus Grant, the son of a railway worker who lived near farmers on Rothiemurchus Estate and who, at the time of research, was a lecturer in Gaelic Studies, singled out the decline of agriculture as a major problem for the wellbeing of Scotland. The glens, once inhabited and used by people are now empty. Robbie Burns, one of the earliest Munroists, would often stay with a family living in a remote glen on his explorations (Allan: 1995). No walker would be able to do this today. The decline of farming has also meant the decline of Gaelic culture. Seamus emphasised the concept of 'duthchas' in Gaelic that means 'derived from the land' and refers to one aspect of people's identity. Seamus believed that with the loss of the connection to the land people have lost part of themselves. This is because people's identity is seen as tied up with a sense of purpose – a reason for being on the land.

Fear of losing one's purpose for being on the land was a major theme of a National Union of Scottish Farmers conference held in Aviemore in March 2000. This theme continues today with the uncertainty of post-Brexit agricultural policy. The President stressed that farmers 'should not have to defend getting support'. They have 'environmental, social and economic reasons for being there.' Many farmers expressed anger that they had to have environmental reasons for being on the land. A dairy farmer from Argyll insisted that they are economically viable but that government policies have increased costs and supermarkets do not pay fair prices. 'I sell milk for seventeen and a half pence a pint to a co-operative by arrangement; this is then sold to be processed. But the supermarkets double that price'. He thought that people in Glasgow 'don't give a f*** about buying Scottish' and that this lack of identity with Scottish farmers is causing them problems. This farmer's opinion was that people in the cities do not see a link between the food they buy and the people producing the food.

Farming has come further under pressure after foot-and-mouth disease. Gordon sold the family farm. Many others wonder why they should continue. Mary and Jimmy did not want to give up farming, but they do not want their son to go into farming: 'There is no future'. Their son did in the end take over the farm on Jimmy's death but he had first found a trade as a joiner. With the inclusion of the area in the Cairngorms National Park and the development of the area as a commuter belt for fast-growing Inverness, many farmers will be tempted to sell their land at a premium for housing developments. The farmer Douglas worked for had already built a number of holiday homes on his land, which brought in more money, and took more of the farmers' attention, than looking after the cattle.

Despite all the problems, for many of these people farming forms part of their identity and they wouldn't know what to do if they didn't farm. Even Gordon has been back farming, helping out Mary and Jimmy during a difficult time. Mary and Jimmy were bewildered by how their occupation was now considered to be economically unviable. They were aware that they are dependent on subsidies but they do not see these as handouts, they're simply the only way they can make a living in what is an unfair system. They worked hard – Mary and Jimmy rarely had a holiday and regularly worked twelve-hour days, longer in the lambing season, and, they produced something. They could actually see the physical outcome of their labour. They shared the confusion of many other workers who have witnessed the disappearance of their jobs, as the primary and secondary industries become an increasingly small share of the economy. Douglas, for example, berates the fact that so much food is imported. If food was produced and consumed locally then there wouldn't be any talk of 'over supply', he reasons.

Survival of farming, according to several speakers at the Scottish Farmers conference, including the president and the Rural Affairs Minister Ross Finnie, depends on diversification, which is now being encouraged by government initiatives as a way of preparing for the removal of subsidies and to halt the decline of farm incomes. Some farmers, like Alistair MacLennan, have done this very successfully, taking full advantage of money available for this purpose. His farm was a showcase of the environmentally-friendly farm. He had a bed-and-breakfast business and a holiday home on his land and talked of how he could take advantage of the newly opened long-distance walkers' route, the Speyside Way, to expand his income from tourism. He was doing a Masters in Environmental Studies and he sat on the new National Park Board. He had visited France to study how farmers there have promoted farm tourism. In many ways, his purpose remained the same – making a living out of the land. However, the focus had changed somewhat. Instead of having a physical output, he was providing a service: looking after the land and enabling other people to enjoy it. Farmers like Mary and Jimmy find such changes a threat to the very core of what farming is about. Jimmy said, 'I don't want to be a hobby farmer'. To Jimmy, what Alistair is doing with his farm is not really farming. The farm is more of an object of consumption, a spectacle for the tourist, than a place of production so therefore it is not 'authentic' farming but 'hobby' farming (Boyle: 2003, Shepherd: 1995). The skills that Mary and Jimmy had in abundance, raising and looking after animals, are not the same ones needed for running what is much more a service industry business than a productive farm. The Farming and Wildlife Advisory Group (FWAG) was set up to help such farms take advantage of the many environmental initiatives, but Mary found it difficult to get on with the university-educated 'expert', 'half her age', who came to advise her. She said that she, and farmers like her, will have difficulties making the kind of changes the government requires.

Economic and political realities clearly structure the relationship farmers have with the land. The decline in production-based industries and the increase in the service sector in Britain and in other Western economies has transformed their labour into something that has use value but no exchange value and is therefore superfluous to the economic system. A number of farmers from the Scottish Farmers conference echoed the concerns of Mary and Jimmy, namely that they are a dying breed. However, farming will not disappear without a fight as can be seen by the determination of Mary and Jimmy to continue farming in the traditional way as well as by Alistair's efforts to adapt to these new realities. The sense of place of farmers is constructed within this ecological, economic, political and social history. Their current practices and the choices they make now about how to respond to their situation will determine the future of this land.

The sporting estate, one of the key factors in the decline of farming, ironically shares many common problems. Owning a shooting estate in Scotland is a sign of status: a place to invite friends and family for a shooting holiday. Though it started as the preserve of the aristocracy, the sporting estate soon became popular for the new capitalist class. It is difficult to assess the exact impact of shooting in Scotland. According to the website of the Scottish gamekeepers, 4.4 million hectares of Scotland's 7.8 million are 'influenced by shooting'. The number of jobs supported depends on whether the employment is direct or indirect. Again, using the same source, '11,000 full-time jobs are sustained'. At the time of research, 2,171 was given as the number of full-time jobs that depend directly on shooting. (British Association of Shooting and Conservation: 2000, www.scottishgamekeepers. co.uk).

Keepers are responsible for managing the grouse moors and organising the shoots for the guests. They also co-ordinate the work of a team of beaters, who are grouped into military-like formations in order to drive the grouse to the 'guns' (guests). The stalkers manage the deer population, carrying out culls (killing the least healthy deer to reduce numbers and preserve a quality herd), and ensuring that the deer have food through the winter months. Then, during the season, they entertain paying guests, talking them deer-stalking and providing them with a traditional Scottish experience in the shooting lodges.

Shooting on a sporting estate is a form of recreation that symbolises belonging to the elite. According to John and Alastair, food was not the objective of the shoot. They exported most of their venison. What matters is the size of the 'bag' of grouse (the term for the number of grouse killed) or the quality of the antlers. A twelve- or fourteen-pointer is the most sought-after trophy for the mantelpiece. One of the grouse-beaters (the seasonal workers who drive the grouse towards the guests), derided the paying guests on Kinveachy because they never came near to matching the skill of the Royal shooting party, known to kill almost 600 grouse in a day. The animal or bird is thus seen as a symbol of one's skill.

Recently, the nature of the sporting estate has changed. Estate owners usually earned their wealth outside and the estate was a form of conspicuous consumption. Now, for many, there is some

View from Glenmore campsite to Northern Corries of Cairngorms

Craig and the author at Harkai's

Home

Anne planning her route

First outing with Strathspey Mountain Club, at Strawberry Cottage

John's weekend

Northern Corries in winter

Cuillin Ridge in Skye, with Ed and Douglas

Author on Glenmore Lodge course

Top of Cairngorm plateau in winter

Ed and Douglas climbing
Photo by Dorothy Carse

Ross on Insh Marshes

The TGO coast-to-coast team

Stuart in the secret howff

River Spey meandering through Insh Marshes

Insh Marshes with Tom, Kate and John

Nature study in woods near Grantown

pressure to make the estate pay, or at least reduce the losses. Shooting has become more commercial. Whole companies, such as Holland and Holland, exist in order to market shooting holidays in Scotland. The guests come mostly from abroad. There are many reasons why the rich of the world choose Scotland. The main prey is grouse and red deer stags. Some people come to shoot roe deer or hares but they tend to be less well off, often working-class people from Germany, Holland or Italy, because this type of shooting does not have the same status. In these countries, with a larger rural population and fewer restrictions from landowners, there has been more of a tradition of shooting small animals for the pot. Hares are an expensive delicacy in Italy and a trip to Scotland with a rented refrigerated van can make a tidy profit. Despite shooting's popularity, the costs of organising the shoots are quite high and many estates are still losing money. However, the owners are reluctant to abandon this tradition, as it is still an important part of elite culture. As a result, many people's livelihoods and the whole pattern of land use in the Highlands is linked to the continued existence of these estates.

In Badenoch and Strathspey, at the time of research, the sporting estate was an important feature of the landscape. According to David, the Holland and Holland representative in this part of the Highlands, Kinveachy and Glenfeshie had an international reputation for good shooting and were promoted by his company. However, there is a sense that this is under threat. One indication of this is that Holland and Holland's bookings are on the decline. There are also signs that landowners are themselves changing. A Dutch owner on a neighbouring estate to Kinveachy has banned commercial shooting altogether because she is against shooting animals. Hector MacClean, taking over the family estate in Angus, introduced the idea of wildlife safaris rather than shooting holidays. He is acutely aware of the antagonism from society in general concerning shooting animals as sport. And Glenfeshie is now being managed for conservation by its Danish owner. David, from Holland and Holland, thinks that

the image of shooting is too exclusive and this gives it a bad reputation. Sporting estates are also under pressure from the Deer
Commission and conservation organisations such as Scottish
Natural Heritage, to reduce deer numbers. This stems largely
from the widely accepted view that Scotland needs to encourage
native tree regeneration and that deer are a major obstacle to
this (SNH: 1994, Cramb: 1998). Landowners are offered financial incentives to reduce deer numbers on their estates. As the
tradition of the shooting estate becomes less important, owners
will consider where their economic advantage lies and this is now
often in obtaining grants for trees rather than offering commercial shooting holidays.

Like farmers, gamekeepers and stalkers construct their sense
of place within a landscape that has a complex history. Though
the methods they use to carry out their work have changed over
the years, for example using all-terrain vehicles such as Argocats
and Land Rovers, rather than ponies, to transport the deer, the
activities they are engaged in and their purpose have remained
largely the same for the past 100 years. This purpose is bound-up
with a cultural tradition that emerged partly as a result of a very
specific combination of economic and historical circumstances
in Scotland. Though the land provides certain affordances that
create the possibility for grouse- and deer-shooting, the continued presence of the sporting estate in the Highlands is due to
cultural traditions rather than what the land is 'naturally' suited
for or what is economically viable.

Common purpose: the land as a productive garden

The historic ecology of the area has united farmers and the
sporting estates against what they see as a common threat –
the end to a certain way of life that shares a common purpose,
which is to transform the land so that it will yield a product for
human consumption. For farmers, it is raising animals to be

consumed as food; for the keepers and stalkers it is managing the land in such a way as to produce animals that can be consumed as part of people's recreational activities. Even though they work in quite distinct economic sectors, (agricultural and the tourist industry), both farmers and estate workers go about their work and engage in activities in ways that create a very similar relationship with the land, which can be contrasted with that of others who live in the area or who come as visitors. Though many of the activities are similar to those of the mountaineers and conservationists – walking over the land, observing and managing the flora and fauna, appreciating the views and having epics – there are some crucial differences. It is not enough just to consider what people do on the land, what activities people are engaged in, but one must also take into account why they are there.

Farmers and estate workers move through the land, notice particular features and construct a sense of place in a way that reflects this different purpose, which can be characterised by using the metaphor of the garden, that is to say, their purpose is to make the earth bear fruit. By stressing the importance of production over consumption, they give particular value to their work. They legitimise their purpose by defining what is an acceptable activity in a rural environment. The increase in recreation activities in the countryside and the emphasis on what Williams (1973) calls the aesthetic as opposed to the practical side of our view of the countryside has brought the contrast from the realm of the abstract and is now manifested clearly on the ground. Jimmy highlighted this point with his comment about not wanting to be a hobby farmer. He didn't want to be a provider of holiday homes and guest houses and the farm experience to urban dwellers. McCarthy (1995) in his study of the Wise Use Movement in the western United States found a similar reaction. The fight of the working-class resource producers to maintain productive, extractive activities as a fundamental part of rural land use was directed against attempts to turn them into service providers for urbanites.

The stalkers and keepers on the sporting estates also see themselves primarily as producers rather than service providers. According to an interview with a long-term employee, the stalkers at Mar Lodge on the southern side of the Cairngorms bitterly resented being asked to change from stalkers to 'wildlife rangers' when the estate was taken over by the National Trust for Scotland. The Scottish representative of the British Association of Shooting and Conservation calls it 'consumptive recreation'. Scotland is the only country in the world where red deer are so numerous. The guests do not have to go on big wilderness treks to get their trophy. The deer are on open ground so that they can be stalked with minimum effort. All of this, together with the romantic image of the Highlands, makes Scotland a much sought-after destination. It is the stalker's job to ensure that the guest gets his or her trophy of antlers. So, in many ways their role could be compared to that of a mountain guide or a birding tour leader. However, they see it differently and this is illustrated in the nature of their work and in their attitude towards their shooting guests. My research shows how estate workers have chosen to define their work as part of the productive sector rather than the service sector. They do this by generally playing down the aspect of their work that involves looking after the guests. Instead, they stress their land management role, tending the garden, where they manage the land to 'produce' a healthy population of deer and grouse.

The conflict between the consumption aims of the guests and the productive purposes of the stalkers and keepers emerged in a number of ways in the course of my research. The season only lasts from July to the end of December at the latest, with occasional winter shoots for hares or forest deer, but there is nevertheless a tendency to see guests as an inconvenience. One estate worker was concerned that management made them spend too much time taking people out shooting, leaving them not enough time to do their work. Grouse and deer may be technically wild animals but on the sporting estate there is significant human intervention, in many ways similar to the raising of livestock. The keepers needed to maintain fences to keep rabbits out of the grouse areas, do the heather burning to create new shoots for the young grouse chicks, and give anti-worm tablets to the grouse. The stalkers may help with this work but theirs consisted primarily of undertaking the deer cull. They did this as part of government policy, administered by the Deer Commission, to reduce deer numbers, but also because they needed to keep numbers at an optimal level for the carrying capacity of the land.

A day on the estate spent deer-stalking with Peter and some American guests is indicative of the conflict between those who work the land and those who consume its product. Stuart is a CEO from an American steel company. He had been shooting all his life, everything from bears to deer with bow and arrow. He invited two other top executives to come on a Scottish shooting holiday. They came in couples, the men shooting whilst the women shopped in the tourist shops of Grantown or Inverness. In addition, the shooting holiday was a form of corporate bonding amongst the executives. On a worldwide level, these wealthy businessmen often belong to the 'Safari Club', an exclusive group of the most prestigious hunters, who travel around the world to get trophies. This is the basis of the conflict between production and consumption. Peter and the other stalkers managed the deer population carefully. They had to ensure that the gene pool was maintained and that the healthiest stags needed to be kept for breeding purposes. The size of the antler was thought to be one of the signs of good breeding potential. Therefore, they did not allow guests to shoot a twelve-pointer or a 'royal'. The guests, on the other hand, were looking for a big trophy, so the bigger the antler the better. As we drove around in the Land Rover looking for a potential target for Stuart, he badgered Peter in a half-joking manner, asking why he couldn't shoot a twelve-pointer, offering him more and more money. Peter was not going to give in and later told me that he had been quite angry that this sort of thing happened regularly; the guests just didn't understand what they are trying to do on the estate. The situation got even more tense when Alan, normally a keeper looking after the grouse, took one of the other steel executives on what was for Alan his first stalk with a guest. They had to drive up the hill a fair distance to spot a suitable deer. Alan thought he had one but they had to trek for some time before they could get close enough to shoot. But when Alan got the stag in his sights, he realised that it was a twelve-pointer and couldn't be shot. Alan had to tell the guest and by the time he joined us towards the end of the day, they still had not managed to get a stag. The guest was angry and the stalkers were annoyed by his lack of understanding.

This example shows how the interests of production take priority over the interests of providing a service to the guests. It was as if the guests were privileged in being allowed to help them in their normal work of culling the deer population. Alistair's goal was for the guests to shoot the least healthy deer. He instituted a special award called the Donald Award. This award was named after a particularly ugly deer who had been a 'pet' of Frank and who was shot accidentally by Alastair when he was new to the estate. This went to the guest who shot a deer that the stalkers were most keen to cull. This was a strategy to encourage the guests to see themselves as part of the production process rather than as being consumers of a service.

The keepers and loaders exhibited similar attitudes to those guests coming to shoot grouse. They found a group of French champagne executives exasperating. In each butt there is a loader, someone who loads the gun and passes it to the guest. However, in this case, the loader had to do more. One loader said, 'We have to hold their guns for them!' The 'bag' was especially low this time – thirty-eight birds for 3,000 shots. Ian compared this with the Royal family who, according to Ian, get four birds for every five shots. One beater commented that the guests must be 'Animal Liberationists' because they gave the birds so many 'chances to get away'. The guests themselves didn't mind – they were enjoying themselves, with crates of champagne opened for lunch. But the keepers felt that all the work they had put in over the year, to ensure that there were plenty of birds for guests to shoot, had not been taken full advantage of. Later in the year, they told me that the poor shooting of the guests had caused problems for the health of the population. Normally, the guests shoot a lot of the older and weaker birds, and this had not happened sufficiently this year because the guests had been such bad shots.

The attitude towards the shooting guests is in many ways similar to the keepers' views towards recreation in the hills in general. 'Real' shooting to them is 'walked-up' shooting where you go out on the hill with a gun and shoot grouse or rabbits for the pot or shoot vermin. One loader told me: 'I couldn't imagine going out on the hill without a gun'. Alan said he couldn't see the point of going into the hills 'just for fun'. They thought it a strange idea and laughed when Isobel, one of the beaters and a member of the Strathspey Mountain Club, told them of her hill-walking plans for the weekend. Mary had a similar attitude, laughing at me when I asked her if she had ever been up walking in the Cairngorms. Their walking was more legitimate, since it had a purpose. Alan and David had done a survival course at the outdoor centre, Glenmore Lodge. They bragged to me that they had out-walked the instructor, indicating that this showed who the real outdoor people were.

The work of farmers and estate workers can also be contrasted with the goals of the conservation sense of place. Instead of managing wildlife as an end in itself – for biodiversity (Milton: 2000), there needs to be a productive purpose – the land needs to be changed in some way. They see their activities as an integral part of the land, not as something that is alien. It is this basic disagreement about what the natural environment is for that is at the root of conflicts between different land users. Walkers, climbers and conservationists aim to have minimum impact on the land. The walker's motto is 'take nothing but photos and leave nothing but footprints'. The conservationists aim is to recreate areas of wild land, free of human intervention in natural processes

(Milton: 2000). By contrast, farmers and estate workers aim to have an impact and exploit the land for human use. They want to move about the land and see signs that they have been there – the proof that they have fulfilled their purpose. To succeed in one's purpose, it is important that one can see the result of one's efforts.

Making a mark on the land

The Zafimaniry (Bloch: 1995) in Madagascar in their admiration of the 'clarity of the view' showed similarities with mountaineers. But this is not all they noticed. They also scanned the view for signs of human habitation. Bloch quotes one woman who seemed to be appreciating the aesthetic beauty of the forest. When probed about why she appreciated it, she surprised Bloch by saying 'because you can cut it down' (p. 65). He concludes: 'The Zafiminary's concern with the environment is not with how not to damage it but with how to succeed in making a mark on it.' (p. 65).

Farmers and estate workers look upon the land in a similar way. 'Making a mark' can take a number of forms. One of the most crucial indications of making a successful mark for both farmers and estate workers is the number and health of their animals. The lambing season is the critical period. Lambs are usually born when it is still cold in Scotland. Mary would be up all night in very bad conditions, providing shelter for the new lambs. She said if one dies it is 'like a pet dying'. Douglas does everything in his power to ensure the survival of all the calves and admits to getting 'upset' if one dies.

The grouse, despite being wild birds, have a similar amount of attention given to them. There had been serious problems with worms in recent years and the keepers spent considerable time in the winter going out and finding grouse in order to feed them their medicine. They counted the birds every spring both before and after the new chicks had been born to check on numbers. John kept records of all these counts and could trace the success of his own management. Four years had been selected and he looked at the pairs, the chicks and the bag. He was convinced, and the statistics certainly support him, that his intervention in the land has been a major contributing factor in the increase in grouse numbers, which would later provide a sizeable bag in the autumn shooting season.

Once the grouse season is over, the keepers move on to the work of ensuring the success of next year's shoot. A key part of this is creating conditions conducive to the survival of the new generation of grouse. These activities are instrumental in creating the landscape that is the grouse moor (Richards: 2004). One of the most important activities is heather burning. Keepers devote many days at the end of the season in October and November to this work. It is necessary because it clears patches on which new heather shoots will sprout in the spring, important food for the young grouse. It is vital that the patches are just the right shape and size. If they are too small, then there are not enough new shoots, but if they are too wide, the young grouse will not be able to escape back into the cover of the longer heather if a bird of prey should threaten. I joined John, his young son, Alan and Ian for a day of heather-burning. We spent the day setting fire to patches of heather and then using large, flat beaters, like giant fly swatters; we would control the course of the fire until it created a vague rectangle up the side of the hill. It was incredibly hard work but exciting with flames blazing around us. Alan admitted that he really likes doing the heather burning: 'how often do you get to set big fires legally?' It all had to be done just right. John was scathing about other estates where they do not have the skill and let the fires get out of control. He was very pleased with our efforts, training up Ian and Alan, as well as giving his young son a chance to get involved.

The significance of what we'd done became more apparent as we drove away after the end of a full day of burning. We parked the Land Rover on a knoll and looked back at the hillside where we had been working. John was clearly extremely pleased with the mark we had made. 'It's beautiful, look what you have been part of'. His appreciation of the view was based, as for the Zafimaniry, on the fact that we had made our mark. I found myself picking out the patches that I had been instrumental in determining the shape of. And for months after, any time I drove up the A9 and saw that hillside, I would show anyone who was with me what I had done. I could understand why John said heather burning is a part of the job he takes most satisfaction in. His aesthetic appreciation was firmly rooted in the sense of a job being skilfully executed.

This meaning of being in the hills can be contrasted with that of many who walk or climb. Instead of the focus being on your subjective response to the environment and how what you have done might have changed you, the stress in the case of farmers and keepers is on producing and creating, with the land forming the material that you are working with. Those that work the land, as in Peiolta's study of the Ukraine (2000) emphasise the importance of human labour and its contribution to the land.

> The historical/ideological foundation for the land–labour conjunction is animated and enlivened by the real, practical, physical engagement of body and soil on the household plot for forty hours each week, fifty-two weeks a year – an engagement that produces food and a future (p. 173).

This does not mean that there is not any aesthetic appreciation or subjective response. The beauty lies in its usefulness and to what extent the work has been done with skill – very similar to Aristotle's virtue ethics in that making your mark is a moral activity. Everything in the world is designed with a purpose; virtuous action is that which fulfils that purpose with excellence. We had done a job that fulfilled an identified purpose and we had done it with excellence. Therefore, the act had meaning.

Knowing the land

Ellen and Harris (2000) describe a distinction between knowledge that comes from books and knowledge that comes from real-life experiences. They argue that knowledge has become a body of thought held in institutions. They cite many cases from non-Western societies, where local people struggle to maintain the validity of their own knowledge practices in the face of powerful outside interests, usually from Western-dominated organisations. Similarly, Hobart (1993) distinguishes between 'world-ordering knowledge', or scientific knowledge and localised, context-specific knowledge. Scientific knowledge is seen as a body of knowledge that is constituted prior to practice, applicable everywhere. On the other hand, local knowledge is 'a practical-situated activity, constituted by a past, but changing, history of practices' (Hobart: 1993: 17). Such debates surrounding what constitutes knowledge are also significant in the context of my research. Farmers and estate workers believe their definition of knowledge is at odds with the dominant one held by society. They feel that their knowledge is not respected and, in some cases, are told that their practices are harming the land. They deeply resent what they see as being the prevalent attitude: that the knowledge of university-educated 'experts', who 'come in' to give them advice on how to manage their land and the animals, is more valued than their own, practically-based knowledge.

According to the estate workers, the RSPB Abernethy reserve, adjacent to Kinveachy, was an example of a managed estate that had a reputation for being run by university-educated conservationists, largely from outwith the area. (This has been changing and people like Ross, the son of the Alvie farm manager mentioned in the previous chapter, was employed by Abernethy for many years). They receive considerable publicity for their work on fostering the osprey population in Scotland; I encountered many examples of resentment of the attention and respect given to the knowledge of these official conservationists. One of the first things Mary pointed out to me was an osprey nest on her land. She took pride in informing me that no one knew about this nest – but she did, unlike the one on the RSPB reserve. She pointed out various birds to me in the course of the day, stressing that she and other farmers know more about the wildlife on the land than the conservationists. Alistair also felt irritated by the fact that conservationists seem to dismiss his knowledge. He said he knows exactly what has happened to the bird life on his farm over the past ten years and asked why they do not consult him rather than doing their own survey. His knowledge, as is Mary's is thus based in a 'history of practices' (Hobart: 1993).

Similar attitudes were expressed on the sporting estate. When I showed John an article in the local paper about how to burn heather correctly, written by one of the land managers on the RSPB reserve, he agreed with what was written but was annoyed that the RSPB person had been asked to write it. He said: 'they hardly ever do heather burning so why was he asked to write the article rather than me?' This just reinforced his view that there are certain people whose knowledge is more respected because it comes with a university degree. For John, on the other hand, this knowledge was less valuable because it did not emerge out of practical use.

The difference between the scientific knowledge of the RSPB and the considerable store of practical knowledge held by the farmers and estate workers is illustrated in the contrasting experience of capercaillie, a native Scottish bird that is on the endangered list. The RSPB wardens put in much effort to ensure that conditions are conducive to their breeding. To see a 'caper' is considered very rare and the RSPB offer a viewing of capercaillie similar to that offered for the osprey. They set up a special video link so that people can observe from afar. Therefore, when I actually saw several capercaillie whilst deer-beating in the forest of Kinveachy I was taken by surprise. They assured me that they saw them quite often. They appreciated the fact that they saw them but it was a fairly common occurrence. This sighting of wildlife is contrasted with the incredible effort that birders go to in order to see different species. For Mary and the stalkers and keepers at Kinveachy, seeing animals occurred as a matter of course and their knowledge came from this day-to-day experience. As one of the stalkers told me: 'I see a lot of birds every day, it's one of the reasons I like the job, but I don't deliberately set out to see them. It just happens.'

Those working in conservation, however, could equally feel aggrieved that their knowledge is not respected by many land workers. People like Gus Jones, of the Badenoch and Strathspey Conservation Group, have spent years researching the capercaillie and the wardens of Abernethy have a vast knowledge of the osprey. Farmers and estate workers may resent these people because they represent expert knowledge, but Tom of Insh Marshes thinks that the problem is more complicated. It is not so much where the knowledge comes from but 'what the knowledge is used for'. Because conservationists and land-workers have different purposes, they also clash over what counts as knowledge.

The place of animals on the land is another source of dispute. When the RSPB bought the Abernethy estate, they threw the sheep off the land, arguing that sheep made tree regeneration impossible. Farmers and shepherds argue the contrary, that grazing is compatible with forest regeneration. They base their claim on years of experience. There may well be other ideological reasons why this knowledge has been constructed in such a way as to cast grazing animals as the enemy. I have already noted how landowners cleared the forest of grazing animals to make way for deer. In other parts of the world, shepherds have been equally demonised, often as part of the process of turning an area into a National Park. In Baviskar's (2000) study of conflict in the setting up of the Great Himalayan National Park, powerful conservation experts from the West used their power-knowledge to impose restrictions on grazing.

Stalkers make similar arguments. Alastair agreed that the red deer cause problems for tree generation but felt that the amount they cull every year was sufficient. To cull more would, in his view, have had serious repercussions for their livelihood. In 2004, with encouragement from conservation agencies, the Deer Commission undertook a massive out-of-season cull of deer on the Glenfeshie Estate. This provoked a protest demonstration on the estate from stalkers and keepers. A key concern is what counts as legitimate knowledge: the estate workers believe that their years of experience on the land have given them the knowledge to ensure the regeneration of trees and the maintenance of a large deer population. They argue that the conservationist agenda is based on book knowledge, mobilised by political forces that want to see the end of stalking.

Farmers and estate workers acquire and use knowledge of the land in a distinctive way. Within the recreation sense of place, maps are a crucial way of knowing where to go and identifying features of the land. Farmers and estate workers do not use maps. At first, I found this very disconcerting. When grouse-beating, we would start at one point and then just move in a more or less straight line to a line of butts where the shooters were waiting. It was a struggle to keep up as we plunged through thick heather, into ravines and back up the other side. There were no paths. The grouse would fly out in front of us towards the butts. We stopped what I hoped was a safe distance from the butts, given the reputation of the shooters as poor shots! Once we had done one drive, we were then moved to another part of the moor, often in the back of a Land Rover, and we would get out and repeat the procedure. In the evening, after I had recovered from my exertions in the jacuzzi of the Hilton hotel, I would get out my map and try and figure out where we had been. I could never do it. Alan, a long-standing local mountain guide, was doing his first ever grouse-beating on Glenfeshie. He expressed the same concern that I had: 'Where are we? I'm not used to being out without my map!'

So, how do they find their way? The grouse drives were established patterns, routes taken that would sweep the grouse towards the butts. However, the heather-covered landscape looked so similar all over the estate that I did not know what landmarks they could be using. Burns were crossed between hills but they all looked very similar. The keepers knew the land so well that they could organise the beaters into lines according to fitness. The fittest ones would be given the point in the line that would require the greatest descent and ascent. The skill that must be involved came to the fore one day when visibility was nil. Alastair was in charge of the drive and we moved through the hills for several miles without seeing anything, yet we arrived exactly where we were meant to. Alastair laughed when I asked him if he ever needed a map. Being on the land, day in and day out, gives them this intimate knowledge, something quite alien to the mountaineer who, even if they visit the area regularly, will never obtain the same level of knowledge – they are still outsiders. According to Gell (1985), the 'experienced native' bases way-finding on images reinforced by habit and familiarity. When travelling with his Inuit companion for several weeks in order to reach a distant settlement, Brody (2001) asked him how he had managed to find his way over the seemingly featureless terrain. He assumed that the man had been there recently. It turned out that he had not been there since the 1930s when he was a boy! He explained that once was enough. It seems as if being on the land, in a certain type of terrain, trains the senses such that one is much more able to remember and use features for navigating that many people would either not notice or not remember. David, one of the stalkers on Kinveachy, said he got 'a better feel for the whole estate' through the stalking. Instead of just looking at your feet or just in front of you at the next steep hill to go up, you use the binoculars to scan for deer. You then locate the deer in relation to particular places – Vince's knoll, the rabbit knoll, the Dell, Eil burn. These were places that are not on any printed map. Once a deer is shot, then you have to say where it was shot for the records, so this practice necessitated the giving of names to any key features.

Gradually I built up a reasonable knowledge of where things were on the estate and I could point out features and remember if I had been somewhere before. My knowledge built up through the months I spent out with the keepers and stalkers. A crucial part of building up a picture, however, concerns the events that took place. Finding one's way more resembles storytelling than map reading (Ingold: 2000). Native maps are not so much representations as condensed histories. In other words, because things happened in particular places, the name of the place would be referred to and my overall picture of the estate was built up through these stories. I remembered clearly Eil burn because that was where I saw my first stag being shot and where Alastair and I went with the Argocat to pick it up. The stalkers and keepers would similarly relate place to stories such that you could create a map out of these tales.

The contrast between knowledge held prior to experience and knowledge arising out of experience is relevant here. Though mountaineers develop their skill through practice, they use maps as a way of bringing prior knowledge with them to the experience. The estate workers, on the other hand, have no knowledge until they gain it through their work. However, the way farmers and estate workers learn about the land is not completely different from that of mountaineers in other respects. Both are looking for affordances. However, because their purposes are different, they notice different features or they see the same features in different ways. When walking, the wind is an enemy. The best place to have it is at your back. When organising a grouse shoot, a wind is an asset. The drive is organised so that the grouse fly into the wind that prevents the grouse flying too fast over the butts. Slower flying birds are easier to shoot. Alan, the mountain guide, pointed out flat, grassy spots that would make an overnight camp as we were grouse-beating. Mary would have judged the same patch of grass for its grazing potential whilst the keepers wouldn't have noticed it at all, except maybe as a place to park the Land Rover. A walker might choose to stop for lunch at a flat and scenic spot along the Speyside Way, but the farmer Alistair would look at this piece of ground as an ideal location to build his bunkhouse.

In all cases, the people are acquiring knowledge through their activities, building up a store of information that could be useful, contributing to their overall knowledge of the land and improving their skill in relating to the land. But with those who work on the land, this is always done, not for aesthetic beauty or pleasure, but for the contribution this knowledge will make to its productive potential. Their knowledge has the characteristics of what Ellen (2000) calls 'indigenous' knowledge. This is often devalued in the face of institutionally produced knowledge, which is used to implement agendas of powerful agencies, both government and private (Ellen: 2000, Baskar: 2000). This lack of recognition of their knowledge contributes significantly to feelings of marginalisation, expressed by farmers such as Mary, and helps to fuel the conflicts that are discussed in later chapters.

Animals

One of the main ways to distinguish the livelihood approach to land from others is how people relate to animals. One key difference I noted is the way land-workers can raise livestock to be killed, yet still care for these same animals. This relationship with animals can be incomprehensible to those not raised in this environment. For example, one birder I met criticised the RSPB reserves in Strathspey for killing rabbits. He said it was a contradiction for an organisation to kill animals when it is supposed to be protecting them.

Mary had 900 sheep and 60 cattle. She had a name for every cow and could distinguish many of the sheep as well. As I joined her in her daily round to check on her animals, she greeted every cow by name and remembered any problem they might have had from the day before. One of the tasks we had was to find a lamb she had seen the day before who looked like it had pneumonia. We eventually found it and gave it an injection. She preferred not to think about what would happen to her animals when they go off to slaughter; the focus was on caring for them now. As Douglas says: 'I don't get sentimental when they go off to be slaughtered but when they're in my company they are my calves'. Like Mary, he knows his animals as individuals and says many are 'characters'. He also prefers not to think about them after they leave his care. It is a characteristic of modern farming. Killing is no longer done in the same place as the animals have been raised.

> Specialists emerged to cart animals to the slaughterhouse and thus separate the farmer from complicity in killing. Husbandry was a wholesome, caring, nurturing industry to be insulated from the stain of death and slaughter (Franklin: 1999: 41).

Keepers and stalkers, however, do the killing as well as the raising of animals and they still have the ability to separate out the two tasks. I found it disconcerting the first time I saw a stag being shot. As it lay on the ground, Alastair commented with satisfaction on its health and David from Holland and Holland admired the quality of his first stag; a stag they had been admiring alive only moments before. I found that it was remarkably easy to attain a calm disinterest. When asked to reach in and pull out the intestines after Alastair had slit open the belly, I did it with an objective detachment. Later in the larder I helped weigh the stag and cut it up for storage, making sure that the penis and backs of the ankles got put into the right bucket for export to Asia, without batting an eyelid. To me at that moment, the living animal was just an object.

Stuart, the mountaineer, was taken aback when grouse-beating by what he thought was Ian's callousness as he wrung the neck of a hare that had been injured by one of the dogs. However, there is no contradiction if one keeps in mind that they are operating according to their purpose, with the moral 'boundaries drawn in different ways, depending on how it suits'. (Ellen: 2000: 27).

Keepers and stalkers have a job to do and lines are drawn according to whatever aspect of that job they are engaged in at any given moment. They do not consider shooting animals as cruel. At Kinveachy, the stalkers went to considerable lengths to ensure that stags are shot 'clean'. If a guest did not kill the stag outright, then the stalker took over and finished off the job. When one of the steel executives only injured the stag, we approached it, now on its knees. The animal was dispatched in silence. David said they wanted to kill the stag without it knowing what is coming; this situation was not how they wanted it to be.

Their anti-cruelty sentiments came through even more strongly in the 'driven' deer shoots. This involves walking through the forest in a line, driving any deer towards towers where the guns would be waiting. Afterwards, David told me how distasteful he found it. He said this was because it is difficult to shoot a moving deer so the guns often just injured the deer and the stalkers would have to find the deer in the forest. He said once he followed a trail of blood for two hours before finding the deer. 'The deer shouldn't have to suffer like that', he told me.

The fact that animals can be cared for yet killed can be partially explained by the way they fit into different categories. Leach (1964), outlines the different categories that the British adopt for their animals including: wild animals, foxes, game, farm animals, pets and vermin. On Kinveachy Estate, the same species of animal could fit into a number of different categories all at the same time, depending on the context. When David was off work he often watched the deer for no reason except that he liked watching them. Or he will admire birds of prey, usually seen as enemies of the keepers because they prey on the grouse. Frank, the sporting estate manager, had his pet stag Donald, who would frequently come to visit him at his house. When Alastair accidentally killed Donald, he seriously feared for his job. He managed to save the situation by writing a poem, 'Ode to Donald', and presenting the poem and a box with Donald's antlers to Frank for his birthday. John's son was very proud to show me his pet rabbits – Topsy and Cottontail, whilst at the same time having a pet ferret that killed rabbits regularly. They also had a pet pheasant, again odd to me for people on an estate where they raised pheasants for game. And juxtaposed in the yard were the corpses of dead rabbits that had been recently shot. The boy did not seem to find this at all disturbing.

Animals are classified according to their use value rather than their structural characteristics. Or rather, individual animals are classified according to their role at any one time as defined in the purpose of the work. Even pets are kept mainly for their contribution to the tasks being carried out. People become very close to their dogs, in particular. This closeness comes from the fact that human and animal work together on a day-to-day basis and the humans develop enormous respect for the skill of the animal. Billy was brought over from Northern Ireland regularly to help train the dogs. Many people I met later in the research who had no direct connection to the shooting estate had heard of him and the magic he could work with dogs. He himself had over twenty bird dogs whose purpose in life was to flush out game. Billy's dogs were pointers which means that when they sensed game, they would point with their muzzles. He said they stopped him from marrying until recently (he was in his sixties at the time) because he preferred the company of his dogs to humans. He spent hours training them and this time spent meant that he got to know all their characteristics. I spent an afternoon with Billy as he was training three of his dogs. We went out on an expanse of low scrub just next to the A9 and Billy put the dogs through their paces. He showed me what to look for, such as how each one moves and whether or not they are cautious or rush into things. Even the way each one points is distinctive.

Animals may also be classified as vermin. These animals undermine the very basis of the work being done on the land. According to Knight (2000), this is an anthropomorphic, utilitarian term that arises when wild animals somehow threaten or undermine the resources that humans are trying to use for their own purposes. Rabbits are one of the main problems, and achieve the category of pest. A large part of the keeper's time is spent shooting rabbits and building rabbit fences to keep them away from the grouse-breeding areas. Shooting vermin is one of the main objectives of walking in the hills with a gun. It is your purpose for being out. A rabbit can go from being a family pet to vermin in the space of a few hundred metres, depending on the point at which the rabbit becomes a threat to the work of the keeper.

Mountain hares are a prime example of how different groups, depending on their purpose and values, have very different definitions of vermin. I came across this when John invited a group of Dutch shooters from a farming community in eastern Holland where they worked as bricklayers and plasterers but helped out farmers in their communities with their shooting skills. Grouse numbers at Kinveachy had been suffering because of a virus and it was believed that mountain hares facilitated the spread of the virus. Therefore, it was deemed necessary to cull the hares in order to protect the grouse. The hares were not killed out of cruelty. In fact, the Dutch farmers were called in because they were excellent shots so there would be no slow deaths. I went along on the shoot and found it very difficult at the beginning given that, as a hill-walker, my own experiences and view of hares was so very different. To me, hares were something I loved to see when out walking – always a special treat – such beautiful creatures. We were out on the moor most of the day, focussing on one large area. It was carefully organised to make sure none of us was shot by accident. Dogs would fetch the dead hares and the bodies began to accumulate. After a while, I became immune to the killing. It was just something that was happening, a part of the work of the gamekeepers. In the end there were scores of corpses piled up. John estimated that 112 hares were shot that day. Whether or not this actually helped the grouse population is hard to say. As always, there is conflict over what counts as knowledge. One of the Dutch farmers told me that he thought gamekeepers and farmers were the real conservationists, the ones who, despite shooting them, cared about the animals. What they do is wildlife management. He thought conservationists came from outside and didn't know what they were talking about.

What gets classed as vermin therefore depends very much on where you are coming from in terms of land management. For hill-walkers and many others, hares are wonderful creatures that should be protected. Grouse moor managers see it differently. Similar is true of birds of prey: though many admire them, estate workers bitterly resent their presence and have been accused of killing them. This had been a major source of conflict with the neighbouring RSPB-owned Abernethy. Ian was convinced that their pro-birds of prey policies are responsible for killing young grouse on his patch.

On Kinveachy itself I saw no indication that the keepers did anything more than complain about birds of prey. However, there is considerable recent evidence from grouse moors in the UK as a whole that estate workers do kill birds of prey, in particular the hen harrier which is meant to be legally protected. A study undertaken on the Buccleuch Estate in Langholm with the support of the Game Conservancy Trust and the RSPB in the 1990s found clear evidence that the presence of hen harriers, who feed on small mammals and birds, including red grouse chicks, affected the number of grouse available for shooting in the autumn (Avery: 2014). It also showed that if there is no intervention to eliminate hen harriers, the number of pairs increases dramatically. How to deal with these facts is a problem and various campaigns have been set up calling for a ban on grouse-shooting in Scotland with bitter resentment from those who work on grouse moors. This is a key example of the conflict between a livelihood and a conservation sense of place.

Hill-walkers may enjoy the sight of the different forms of wildlife from stags to grouse to mountain hares, as do the keepers and stalkers. But for the latter, this enjoyment takes place firmly in the context of the land's purpose. Animals are part of the historical ecology of place. The sporting estate workers are aware of their own role in managing this ecology and have a greater knowledge of the history of that land. Creating the conditions for life, as well as taking life, are aspects of the same managed ecology. Those who work on conservation reserves are also involved in this human-managed ecology. Hill-walkers may look forwards to spotting deer on the hill but deer are considered to be a major problem for reforestation in Scotland and so could be classified as vermin. Conservation organisations such as Abernethy undertake a regular deer cull. There have been instances of deer being killed en masse with helicopters brought in on some estates, such as Glenfeshie. Tom at Insh Marshes employed local farmers to shoot rabbits. Ian was building a rabbit fence on his patch at the same time as John and Ross were building one at Insh Marshes. In this respect conservationists who work on the land, unlike those who go birding as a hobby, have much in common with the keepers and stalkers on the sporting estates. However, it is their different purposes that distinguish them. Keepers and stalkers are raising animals to be killed and conservation managers have different objectives, thus creating different values.

*

The sense of place that emerges out of a livelihood-based relationship to the land has been shown to be distinctive in many respects from those of mountaineering and conservation. Whereas the latter's aim is to keep impact to a minimum, the land workers' reason for being on the land is to transform it into a garden, to make a mark, as the means to achieving their purpose of production. The term 'wild land' is used as an ideal to be pursued by both recreation and conservation organisations. For example, the Scottish Wild Land Group was formed 'in order to raise public awareness of the main threats posed to the wild character of Scotland's natural heritage' (SWLG: 2002). Wild land is defined by the National Trust for Scotland as being 'relatively remote and inaccessible, not noticeably affected by contemporary human activity' (NTS: 2002). Though recognising that all land has been changed to some extent by humans, the goal is to let the flora and fauna on the land take its own course, as far as possible, without human intervention (Milton: 2000). Such a view is echoed in the work of some anthropologists and others writing in the field of human–environment relations. Seeing the earth as a human garden is thought to be the foundation for the anthropocentric (human-centred) values and practices that are in turn thought to be the source of current environmental ills (White: 1967, Brody: 2001). In contrast, the land-workers whose everyday work is a constant struggle to manage and guide nature to particular ends, would argue, like historical ecologists, that the mutual influences of people and non-human nature are an inevitable part of the ecology of the planet. And, rather than damaging the environment, they are actually enhancing it. What they do could be called 'resource management'; which, according to Balee (1998) is 'the human manipulation of inorganic and organic components of the environment that brings about a net environmental diversity greater than that of the so-called pristine conditions with no human presence' (p. 19).

The farmers and sporting estate workers would be able to identify with the historical ecology approach in that they would question whether it is human intervention as such at the root of environmental ills. Balee (1998) argues that humans have always intervened in their environment, transforming it to suit their needs. Therefore, to set up an ideal of untouched, pristine nature is futile. The Scottish Highlands have been worked over for centuries. To rid the land of grouse and deer, as is sometimes recommended, in order to achieve some kind of imagined wilderness, is strongly opposed by the stalkers and keepers I encountered in my research. Balee (1998) also argues that to assume that humans are either biologically pre-disposed to destructive or harmonious relations with the environment is ill-founded. Human beings have done both. This contention would be supported by estate workers and farmers who feel that by adopting the correct land management practices, they enhance the quality of the environment through their work. They take issue with the conservation ideal of wild land existing separately from humans. Instead, the land-workers' view is that the life of the land is part of a carefully balanced process of human interaction and intervention. They do not believe that they are guilty of damaging the environment. Rather, they would argue that they have contributed to biodiversity and the health of the land.

However, farmers and sporting estate workers are in many ways seen as clinging to outmoded practices and a culture that is at odds with current economic, social, political and ecological realities. According to Moran (2000) in his study of the Amazon, individuals operate in a history of past resource use and the customs relating to that environment may or may not reflect current conditions. According to those coming from a recreation and conservation approach, this is indeed the case for farmers, keepers and stalkers. Though it is hard to see much damage done by farmers in Strathspey, industrial farming techniques and over-grazing by sheep have been held up as examples of where concern for production and profit has caused environmental problems. With climate change and the post-Brexit withdrawal of subsidies now on the political agenda, the activities of farmers will be carefully scrutinised.

Sporting estates are under attack for maintaining high deer numbers because of the damage they do to trees. In addition, the whole way of life of estate workers and the shooting estate is rooted in a tradition based on a very unequal class society, raising questions about the desirability of maintaining a form of land use which is mainly for the benefit of a tiny minority of wealthy people. This was illustrated for me by the way estate workers were actually excluded from the products of their garden. They put in long days for relatively low pay and were not allowed to shoot themselves or have the meat from the grouse and deer (not that they complained about this to me). And they had to put up with clients who looked down on them and treated them purely as a means to an end – getting their trophy. Towards the end of the grouse season, John was allowed to organise a staff shoot, or keepers' day. This was because the guns had been so poor, and not enough grouse had been shot, so the staff were going to have a go. It was a great day, despite the poor weather. Keepers and stalkers were invited from neighbouring estates to make it a fun social occasion. There was a buzz of excitement as people congregated in the morning. However, in the end not that many grouse were shot. I was told by some that this was because the staff, despite being good shots generally, had very little, if any, experience of shooting driven grouse. I am not even sure they were able to keep the grouse they shot. So, the attachment of keepers and stalkers to the sporting estate as a way of life is bound-up with the fact that they do not own the land nor do they benefit from the fruits of their labour, though they themselves expressed no serious dissatisfaction with their situation. In a society where land reform and social justice are high on the political agenda, the sporting estate is seen as an obstacle, a symbol of a wealthy elite holding on to their privileges at the expense of the majority, perhaps even at the expense of their own employees.

However, this chapter has shown how farmers, keepers and stalkers have a particular sense of place; one in which they are hefted to the land. They have a dedication to, and knowledge of, the land that is invaluable. This needs to be remembered when policy decisions are made about the future of farming and the sporting estate.

CHAPTER FIVE

Disputes

In the preceding three chapters I have shown how different senses of place emerge out of the activities people are engaged in as well as historical and cultural contexts. These differences often lead to conflict over land use. Now we examine in more detail how these conflicts have unfolded in the Cairngorms.

Hill-walking, climbing, birding, mending fences, grouse-beating, stalking, herding cows, skiing – just a few of the activities I was involved in. These different experiences changed my perceptions and made me more confused. This is because the different senses of place that emerged out of being physically engaged with these activities led to views that are in many ways contradictory. For example, it was hard to go out hill-walking with a major hill objective in mind and at the same time do serious birdwatching. Depending on which activity I was doing I would notice different things. When I saw a hare or deer on the hillside, was it something to be shot as vermin or a thing of beauty? Even when activities that people are doing are very similar, the purposes may vary and therefore cause different species to be valued.

Different senses of place can therefore lead to disagreement and conflict. The individual learns the activity through doing it with other people. This apprenticeship involves both an opening out as the individual's perceptions are tuned in to previously unnoticed affordances in the environment, and a closing off of other perceptions as the individual is disciplined to give attention only to that which is relevant to the chosen activity. In addition, the activities take place within a historical ecological context, influencing the meaning and interpretation given to them.

The result of these processes is a tendency for people to have a particular approach to land use, which can be marked off from others. In other words, the experiences people have within a specific physical and social environment create both a sense of place and a sense of who they are in relation to others. This then allows for the possibility of establishing boundaries between groups (Barth: 2000). According to Lund (nd):

> It is thus knowledge gained through moving through different spatial and temporal environments, that determines how people place nature and themselves in it. It is evident that they not only place themselves in nature but also situate others in relation to it, which establishes the boundaries between the groups (p. 9).

Just as the individual becomes part of the group, so the group is part of a wider social, economic and political context, structuring how the groups relate to each other. These groups may, in certain circumstances, become more than loose identities and form into interest groups that have the potential to come into conflict with each other. In this way, relations with the land provide the basis for which wider social and political identities are formed (Bender: 1993). However, these identities are fluid, 'contingent on the circumstances and relative positions of significant others' (Cohen: 2000: 3). This chapter examines which circumstances contribute to the formation of these clearly delineated groups with self-identified, opposing interests, by considering two disputes in order to illustrate, on a micro level, this process of moving from a sense of place to being part of an interest group. These micro conflicts then provide the grounding for examining in Chapter Six a much larger conflict between two polarised sides – local livelihood versus outside conservation and recreation interests. The two disputes concern the use of the river by anglers and paddlers and the conflict between conservationists and land workers over deer numbers.

'The Spey ain't big enough for the both of us': conflict between anglers and paddlers

They were all waiting for the moment when the fish would catch. This moment was described by Chris – the consultant physician – as 'electric'. Lionel, the head ghillie from Kinveachy, said it was 'magical' and told stories of casting his line and the fish leaping out of the water – 'an amazing experience that makes it all worthwhile'. You have to let the fish run, and then slowly draw it in. It is at this point that they form a relationship with the fish and the adrenaline surges. They don't seem to mind the fact that they have to wait a long time for that moment. Chris says he enjoys just being in the river, in such a beautiful spot, seeing the bird life, totally immersed in the activity.

I first thought that paddling on white water just meant sitting tight. But on the Findhorn we got a real taste of the sport. All the practice of manoeuvring the canoe had to be in earnest. I kept worrying about what was around the corner. Shaun, the Glenmore Lodge instructor, just kept saying 'it gets better'. The first 'better' rapid involved a manoeuvre around various boulders and then a sharp left, through a narrow gorge. I just managed to avoid a wall, my paddle just touching it, as it seemed to come straight at me. It was exhilarating and then I felt the relief as I broke out into the eddy. I thought the worst was over but I was wrong. The next 'better' rapid looked OK from the top – a few shallow boulders, slowish waters, then as I got closer, the speed picked up and the boulders grew in size. I was heading for a narrow gap between two of them – worrying about the waterfall further ahead. I missed the gap and ended up on top of one of the boulders, teetered and capsized. Next thing I knew, I emerged from the water to see that I had gone upside

down right over the waterfall! I decided to have another go, took my
boat out of the water and dragged it back up to the top of the rapids.
I sat in the kayak feeling terrified but determined. I headed off, came
close to that left boulder again but just glanced off it. I was now in
the pool below and heading on course for the water chute. I knew I
would make it and was able to just relax and enjoy the ride.

From the above accounts, it is difficult to see that the two activities are taking place on the same river. One is mostly quiet and sedate, a scene of peace and tranquillity, with the only interruption being the occasional appearance of a fish. The other is one of rushing rapids, intense effort and speed, with moments of calm and relaxation the exception. In fact, each activity values different parts of the river. Rapids are sought out by the paddlers – the whole river defined as a grade 1, 2, 3 or more by the difficulty of the rapids, whereas the fishers look for quiet pools where the fish will lurk. These activities should take place in separate locations. However, paddlers cannot go from one set of rapids to another; theirs is a journey that encompasses all parts of the river. In addition, pools or eddies are needed for rest. It is here that the conflict lies. The ghillies and their fishing guests argue that the paddlers scare off the fish. The paddlers argue that the fishers are rude and hostile, sometimes throwing things at them.

An even greater issue is the raft trips that are organised for groups by the outdoor centres. I was sitting quietly on the bank with my fellow apprentice paddlers and our instructors from Glenmore Lodge, getting ready to 'put in' (launch our canoes). We were watching some fishers on the Spey, when four minibuses pulled up. They unloaded their excited teenagers right behind a woman fishing. The anticipation of the adventure they were about to have made them extremely noisy and contrasted sharply with the calm of a few minutes earlier. Eventually the woman moved and I could just imagine what she would be reporting back to the ghillie, further fuelling the already hostile relations between the two groups.

Because the paddlers and anglers are both in the same space, the individuals involved are more likely to see themselves as part of a group, in contrast to another group. And because their respective sports not only engage with the river differently but have contrasting ways of behaving whilst on and around the river, this leads to the perception that they are fundamentally incompatible. Particular incidents reinforce this group identity in which individuals see themselves as one group whose interests are in conflict with those of another group. However, these interactions have shaped and been shaped by the wider context. As isolated disputes become part of a generalised debate on use of the rivers, both groups mobilise wider political and social discourses that have an impact on encounters between paddlers and anglers. One of the main issues affecting the disputes between anglers and paddlers is the debate about land ownership and who has the right to actually be on the river. What might have been just two different senses of place now become public conflicts between interest groups.

Genealogy of dispute

One aspect of the dispute concerns the facts. The anglers believe that, objectively, paddlers are disturbing the fish. Paddlers argue that these facts are 'wrong'. Disagreement over facts takes on such significance because of the wider context in which the dispute is unfolding. The salmon population in many Scottish rivers has reached a critically low level. The reasons behind this were the topic of conversation over lunch on the day I was out with the ghillies and their tenants. They could not reach agreement as to the main cause but contenders include: seal numbers, fishing trawlers in the North Sea and fish farms. The problem was only too obvious to this group of tenants. Ten of them had been there almost a week and had only managed to catch three salmon. The ghillies were very sensitive, understandably, to the disappointed mood of the tenants. Would they continue to come back if they had no success this year? One man said he had caught nothing for five years but kept coming back. Others, however, may not be so committed. One man said that Alaska is becoming a popular destination because they would be guaranteed a good catch.

It is within this context, then, that we must understand the antagonism to paddlers. As with other conflicts over wildlife (Knight: 2001), it is the people at the margins, those whose position is precarious, who are most hostile to the presence of 'predators'. Ghillies may not threaten to shoot paddlers as predators but the situation is similar. If the fish were plentiful, then a canoeist doing turns in a pool wouldn't be seen as such a problem, but in a situation where the tenants may not have caught a fish all week, then that canoeist may be disturbing the one fish waiting to be caught.

Disputes between paddlers and anglers have their roots in the wider historical context. The key issue is illustrated by the following comment from Lionel:

> The agreement is supposed to be that paddlers have navigational rights one way – downstream – and that they need to get permission for doing these turns from the ghillie because they involve more than just going one way. But he (the canoeist) acted like he had a God-given right to be there. The river can be for both but it is the paddlers that must ask permission from the ghillies.

This illustrates the fundamental divide: the ghillies believe that they and their tenants have a greater right to be there because they are the ones who are part of the estate, the legal landowner. The ghillies, like the stalkers and gamekeepers, have a livelihood sense of place. They see themselves as belonging to the land because of the fact that they are managing and looking after their garden. Lionel lives on the riverbank on his 'beat'. The tenants are on the river as paying guests of the landowner. The paddlers are only there under sufferance. As a result of this legal and social position, the ghillies and their guests have adopted certain discourses in order to legitimise their being on the river (Mels: 1999). It is the group identity of a 'producing, income-generating local', together with the ideology of the sanctity of private property that justifies fishing. On the other hand, the paddlers have mobilised their own discourses. As I heard from many paddlers – similar to mountaineers – 'how can anyone "own" a river?' There is a very real and immediate dispute, but to understand the basis of the day-to-day antagonism, it is necessary to examine the contrasting perspectives on land ownership as expressed within the institutional and historical framework in Scotland (Mels: 1999).

Owning the river

In 2003, three years after my time on the Spey, new access legislation was passed by the Scottish Parliament. This granted access rights to paddlers for inland rivers and lakes. Similar to access rights for non-motorised transport on land, there are qualifications to this and paddlers are encouraged to work in harmony with other river users. The access code also establishes responsibilities for landowners, such as providing places of access for paddlers (https://www.outdooraccess-scotland.scot/practical-guide-all/watersports/canoeing-rafting-rowing-sailing). However, there are still conflicts between paddlers and anglers (http://canoescotland.org/news/spey-access-update) and though paddlers now have the law on their side to an extent, they still do not own the land and therefore these new rights of access will not have the same legitimacy as ownership in the eyes of the ghillies and other estate workers.

The newly established Land Commission, a product of the 2016 Land Reform Act, has produced a number of papers on land ownership. It is difficult to know exactly who owns what because of the lack of a complete and transparent land registry. However, the Land Commission report into concentration of land ownership (2019) confirms the basic idea that, particularly in rural Scotland, a small number of large landowners own the majority of land. From the report:

> From the seventeenth century, into the late 1800s, there was an increasing concentration of landownership into fewer and fewer private estates (Callander, 1987; LRRG, 2014). Although the majority of public land was acquired during the first half of the twentieth century and there was a growth in the number of owner-occupied farms in some lowland areas, particularly during the 1920s and 1930s, private ownership of large properties continues to dominate (LRRG, 2014; Thomson et al., 2016). In the last 40 years, the proportion of public landownership as compared to private landownership has remained broadly similar (Wightman, 2013). Research by Hindle et al. (2014) has continued to explore the pattern of landownership, with their findings resonating closely with the estimation made by Wightman (2013) that 1,252 owners hold 67 per cent of privately-owned rural land. Hindle et al. estimated the size and characteristics of the 'estate' sector, using available databases and other information, reaching the conclusion that 1,125 owners hold 4.1 million hectares (seventy per cent of Scotland's rural land).

The focus on rural land is understandable considering that it makes up 97.4 per cent of the total land in Scotland. Also, most of this rural land is privately owned: 83.1 per cent. The remaining rural land is divided between the public sector (12.1 per cent), heritage sector, such as the RSPB and National Trust (2.5 per cent), and the community sector (2.2 per cent) (Wightman: 2015).

In the Highlands, which is predominantly rural, research by Wightman in 1999 found 'fully half of the private land – over 3.6 million acres – is owned by fewer than 100 landowners and three-quarters of it owned by around 300' (1999: 30). Furthermore, much of this land has been bought by the rich in order to pursue certain leisure interests associated with their social class: shooting and fishing. This is the legacy of the economic and social transformations outlined in the last chapter. 'This country has become a haven for the rich because it has been emptied of people' (Short- 1991: 75).

The Seafield Estate, within which lies Kinveachy, is typical of the Highland estate. The current Lord Seafield, Ian Derek Francis Studley, the thirteenth to hold the title, owns the land and has power over it. For the ghillies and their tenants, this ownership is not something they question. However, it is not just this 'jural' (the legal) aspect of the land (Abramson: 2000) that underlies the passion that the ghillies and tenants feel about their right to be there. Instead, it is what Abramson calls 'mythic' land, which refers more to the symbolic aspect of land, where people associate it with particular meanings and values. In the case of the Scottish Highlands, landowners present themselves as part of Highland tradition. It is a form of what Hobsbawm (1983) calls 'invented tradition' which 'seeks to inculcate certain values and norms of behaviour by repetition, which automatically implies continuity with the past' (p. 1). This was seen in the last chapter with Queen Victoria's popularisation of the sporting estate. Short (1991) calls this the making of the 'Highland myth'. Ghillies, as do the stalkers and keepers, see themselves as keepers of this tradition.

The ghillies' claim to belong on the land is the result of both their activities on the land and the cultural context. Their everyday work looking after the land and managing it for a productive purpose is embedded in tradition. In their view, despite the access laws, paddlers do not have the right to be on the river to the same extent as they do for several reasons. Firstly, from the jural perspective, the paddlers do not own the land and therefore do not have the same legitimacy as those who have been expressly been put there by the legal owner. Secondly, the ghillies are involved in a traditional activity that has mythic significance for the Highlands and Scottish identity, whereas the paddlers are not. In other words, the ghillies have the legitimacy of history behind them. However, the use of the word mythic could be misleading. It is not just that these land workers see their being there as having symbolic importance. As discussed in the previous chapter, they believe that their traditional activities bring material benefits to the land. The stalker Alastair criticised walkers and mountain bikers for wanting to have access but put 'nothing back', whilst he and the other estate workers maintained the tracks and paths. Similarly, Lionel argued that he lives and works on the river; it is his 'responsibility'. The paddlers come for a one-off trip, showing no long-term commitment and giving nothing back to the river.

Freedom to roam

The canoeing instructors, Shaun and Claire, say that the conflict with anglers is a regular feature of a canoeing trip. They make a point of moving to the other side of the river and asking the ghillie the best way to move past. But sometimes, the river is so narrow that there is no choice but to ask the fishers to take their lines in. This provokes much hostility. One instructor had rocks thrown at him in the past. Another said both groups are using the river and should be able to get along, but the problem is that landowners think that the sport they do should have 'first option'. The instructors are willing to give in to the ghillies up to a point. One said 'if they give a good reason why I can't go down a stretch of river, like salmon spawning, then I won't go down. But if they are just being bloody-minded, then I'll insist on passing'. An instructor from an outdoor centre told me of all the access problems he had on the rivers, saying the ghillies have 'Victorian values'.

The resentment felt by paddlers is the basis for the public debates over river access at a public level. In other words, the personal history of particular instructors is linked to wider struggles (Holland and Lave: 2001). Though canoeing organisations in Scotland have been successful in getting access enshrined in law, in other parts of Britain this is not the case. Under current law in England and Wales, public access to rivers is restricted, and only 2 per cent of all rivers have public access rights. The River Access Campaign in England and Wales has stepped up its efforts because of the access rights given over land in 2000. Campaigners argue that there is a right to roam but not a right to paddle (http://www.riveraccessforall.co.uk/). 'There are 300 Welsh rivers and only six have some kind of access agreement. We want to paddle these rivers just the way ramblers can walk in the countryside' (BBC Countryside Files: 16 January 2005).

At the public level, the dispute between fishing and canoeing is represented as being a conflict between different attitudes towards land ownership and access. This has a long history in Scotland, often related directly back to the Clearances (Chenevix-Trench and Philip: 2001). Whereas landowners mobilise the myth of tradition and their role as guardians of the land, those campaigning for wider access state that 'the land belongs to the people'. This can be seen in many of the arguments for land reform in Scotland. This approach gathered momentum under the devolved parliament with Land Reform Acts passed first in 2003 and then more comprehensively in 2016.

> Culturally, land and its ownership and use have shaped the outlook of the people of Scotland. Contemporary debates about land ownership are a clear expression of a deep-seated feeling, unaffected by two centuries of urbanisation, for the land. Whether expressed as national pride in landscape and wildlife or anger at abuses to land, the concerns are real and widely expressed in poems, books, music and plays' (Wightman: 1999: 1).

The fight against anglers can be interpreted as part of the general struggle to reclaim the land in the name of the people. In the views of paddlers, though the fishers are paying clients in the same way people pay Glenmore Lodge instructors, the difference lies in the fact that salmon fishing is an upper-class sport, fostered and protected by the landowners. According to Robbie Nichol in an article supporting the paddlers' position, the fact that access has to be negotiated with landowners 'masks an extraordinary absence of the natural heritage which each one of us is born with' (1999: 13). In this way, paddlers can also use the discourse of tradition to legitimate their claims.

Though there is an element of imagination (McCrone: 1992, Macdonald: 1997) in the way tradition is used, the different claims are based on material and class differences. One instructor legitimised his claim to his right to be on the river by stressing how, in terms of history, kayaking is very old. He mentions the Inuit and Rob Roy. This could be seen as romanticising kayaking and could therefore be part of the 'landscape of the mind' (McCrone: 1992: 16), but at the same time, there have been very real conflicts over land ownership between Highlanders and the new landowners who imposed new regulations on the use of land by ordinary people. The Spey itself was the object of a court case in which Clive Freshwater, one of the first canoeing instructors in the area, took landowners all the way to the House of Lords in order to establish that historically there had been a right to navigate the Spey. Such historic rights have also been used by the Scottish Rights of Way Society to establish routes that had been used historically by local people to travel from one place to another.

The two groups therefore mobilise different mythic views or stories of land in their conflict over access to the river. These views can be seen in the actual encounters on the river, but only become fully articulated at the public level as part of a general debate. Until recently, the landowners' view of land has been predominant. However, with the changes that have taken place in the economy and politically, those who argue for the freedom to roam have gained a power base and are now in a position to challenge the dominant ideology. Power relations determine which myths become part of the national identity (Daniels: 1993) and because there is currently a power struggle, both myths co-exist as part of Scottish identity.

The conflict is further complicated by the social origins of the people making the claims to tradition and rights. Both sides make claims to these rights on the basis of 'belonging'. Landowners and their employees stress that many of those using the river or the hills for recreation are 'outsiders' and therefore don't belong. This is reinforced by the fact that the land workers both live and work on the land, unlike the paddlers and mountaineers, who come as visitors, 'consuming' the river, and then leaving. The paddlers, on the other hand, and land reform campaigners, point to the fact that landowners originally took the land from the local people and that it is the descendants of these Clearance victims who are coming back from the urban areas to enjoy what should be their land. Moreover, they can also use the number of foreign and absentee landowners to strengthen their case.

However, the issue is further complicated by the increasing number of instructors who work on the river in the same way as ghillies. Instructors, both in the river and on the hills, argue that they have as much right to make a living out of the land as the ghillies. What delegitimises their claim in the eyes of the ghillies and other estate workers, is that outdoor instructors are not working for the landowner. They are using the river but not contributing to its upkeep. In addition, outdoor instructors are largely incomers, new to the area and therefore do not belong in the same way as the ghillies do. The guests of the ghillies may be visitors just like the paddlers, but they are invited guests of the legitimate owner of the land. The fact that these guests are wealthy and part of the same class as the landowners reinforces their legitimacy. As discussed in Chapter Four, the sporting estate was originally a place for the owner and his friends to enjoy shooting and fishing. It is only relatively recently that estates opened their doors to wealthy paying guests.

A similar analysis can be made with reference to disputes between hill-walkers and keepers and stalkers who also occupy the same space, but on opposite sides of the ownership divide. A number of walkers commented on problems they had on certain estates in the area. These individual incidents form part of the general conflict at a national level over access legislation. The arguments are very similar to the ones made by ghillies and paddlers. Hill-walkers demand the right to roam; estate workers insist that the hills are a place of work, such that deer-stalking and grouse-shooting take precedence over leisure activities. At a national level, a hill phone system has been established in the stalking season so that walkers can phone to find out what areas to avoid. However, many walkers resent that their activities have to take second place to the activities sponsored by the landowners. Kevin, a regular visitor to the area from Fife, recounted an incident in which he was out in the remote hills on a backpacking trip with his children. They had been swimming in a stream when 'two posh English women' came up to them and told them: 'you are disturbing our fish which we have paid for'. Kevin's children told them to 'go back to their own country' and then wrote the incident up in the events book in the mountain bothy where they stayed that night. Kevin's story illustrates how issues of who belongs are used in both sides of the debate, furthering the construction of distinct interest groups.

The dispute between paddlers and ghillies and their fishing tenants, as with hill-walkers and stalkers, has its origins in their different senses of place, arising out of different activities. The fact that they are using the same space in different ways may cause one activity to interfere with the other. However, this problem need not necessarily take the form of an ongoing dispute over land use. Skiers and mountaineers also inhabit the same space on Cairn Gorm and in the Aonach Mor ski area near Fort William. Mountaineers walk through the area on the way to climbs. There is potential for a dispute because walking on the runs can ruin the snow grooming. Similarly, walkers complain that mountain bikes ruin some paths. However, though ski operators may reprimand walkers, and walkers may shout at mountain bikers, there is no dispute on the level seen with paddlers and anglers. There is no sense of one group having more of a right to be there than others.

However, with the paddlers and ghillies, as with hill-walkers and stalkers, the two senses of place clash because of differing perceptions of land ownership and tradition. It is a dispute about who has the right to be on the river or on the hill.

The paddlers from Glenmore Lodge generally accepted the rules of the ghillies, and asked for permission. This led to a smooth passage down the river. The rafting group from the outdoor centre did not do this, and have potentially fuelled future conflict. The fact that private land ownership is being challenged by the pad-dlers and hill-walkers, who advocate a 'freedom to roam and to paddle' and mobilise a discourse of 'land to the people', has caused what was a disagreement between two activities to become a more generalised conflict that is increasingly manifested in the wider public arena. Hill-walkers campaigned for years for access legis-lation and now paddlers have done the same (BBC: Countryside Files: 16 January 2005). The results of their efforts in Scotland (not in England and Wales) has been the inclusion of 'inland water' into the general access legislation that came into effect in March 2005. This issue of who has the right to be on the land, in other words who belongs, wrapped up with struggles over tradition, will become a crucial feature of the conflict to be examined in the next chapter.

Deer versus trees: who belongs?

In the same way that the activities of fishing and canoeing give rise to tensions between individuals and groups with contrasting ideas about the land, arguments about deer numbers and native tree regeneration highlight antagonisms between individuals and groups that can be understood in terms of the contrasting priori-ties created by conservation and livelihood senses of place.

Walking for the first time with Alan and George of the Strathspey Mountain Club, we were ascending a hill in Glen Affric and Alan stopped to point out the fence that was running parallel to us up the hillside. He said that this marked the boundary between land owned by a conservation body and a sporting estate. He said it represented two types of land management. The sporting estate owner had put the fences up to stop deer getting into any new tree areas, without having to reduce deer numbers. The conservation body didn't believe in fences; they just reduced the deer numbers. This was the first of many conversations over the next months concerning what to do about deer.

As I have shown in previous chapters, it is possible to distinguish between conservation and livelihood senses of place. This difference in perception and attitudes towards the land lies behind the conflict over red deer. It is not only a question of different groups having different representations of deer (Lorimer: 2004). Rather, it is how people live their relationship with the environment that is most significant. It is this lived practice that can, in certain circumstances, give rise to distinct representations and discourses. Therefore, though the source of the dispute lies in these different senses of place, the dispute itself, occurring at a public level, has created distinct ways of seeing and talking about nature that have become associated with identifiable interest groups. These discourses are then, in turn, taken up by individuals and used to argue for a specific perspective. Individuals who have come to identify themselves as conservationists have publicly clashed with other individuals who have also developed a public identity in opposition. In this section, we discuss how the public conflict reinforces identity as a particular interest group and also how this disagreement begins to take the form of an outsider-versus-local conflict.

The dispute over red deer emerged in both my face-to-face fieldwork encounters and in public debates and documents. During the weekend in Glen Affric, George and Alan talked extensively about the problem of deer. Their interest was prompted by the fact that conservation organisations are trying to encourage native tree regeneration in the area. This is accomplished by dramatically reducing deer numbers; overgrazing is thought to be the cause of deforestation. Sporting estate mangers do not want to reduce the numbers to the same extent and therefore prefer to put up fences rather than kill so many deer. George said that Scotland had once been covered with trees and that the current state of Glen Affric was not natural. He said that 'conifer plantations are also not natural and that native tree regeneration would not mean rows and rows of trees but that the trees would be more randomly dispersed with open spaces between the trees'.

George is assigning a particular value to native trees by calling them natural. This view accords with the wild land ethic in which land has intrinsic value. Roy, a member of the Badenoch and Strathspey Conservation Group and the John Muir Trust, regularly voiced this opinion at meetings. He attacked those who use an argument based upon 'preserving for the next generation'. He says that 'we need to care for the land for its own sake'. These arguments are part of an eco-centric environmental discourse, which blames environmental destruction on human intervention and domination (Pepper: 1996, Peterson: 2001, Hay: 2002). A key part of creating wild land is to restore the land to its pre-human state as much as is possible.

> What gives the distinction between human and non-human processes a greater importance for conservationists is the fact that 'naturalness', in the sense of freedom from human interference, is seen as a quality worth conserving in itself (Milton: 2001: 240–41).

George and Roy's views contrast with the land ethos of the livelihood sense of place. At a meeting with the local landowner Jamie Williamson, Roy asked him why he did not just set aside one patch of land and just let it be, not do anything to it. This was an alien concept to the landowner who, like the workers in the previous chapter, conceives of the land as a garden, there to be cultivated and used to produce something. He could not understand why he would possibly want not to make productive use of his land. For him and other land workers, the land has extrinsic value, based on its output. Speaking at an educational conference designed to teach 'townies' about the countryside, he said:

> For most of our population, our countryside is seen as a place for recreation, relaxation and dumping litter. Or somewhere to be preserved like an artefact in a museum. Or even restored to some romantic past. Relatively few seem to appreciate the link between making our living in primary production and the landscape we have today (Maxwell: 2000).

The foundation for the conflict between deer and trees lies in these contrasting views of the land's purpose. For the conservation sense of place, trees represent what the land would have been without human interference and therefore they need to be restored as a point of principle. For those working on the sporting estates, deer have been put there by humans for a purpose and now also belong, enhancing the land as a place of production. The land workers in this case have the unknowing support of many walkers and climbers who enjoy seeing deer. This corresponds to their own unique sense of place in which they notice and appreciate what enhances their own personal experience on the land.

Land workers versus conservationists in Glenfeshie

Glenfeshie, under the ownership of the Dane Povlsen, has become a conservation show case but previously it was a top sporting estate. The change did not come without a fight. In the spring of 2004 stalkers and gamekeepers came from around Scotland to Glenfeshie in order to protest against what they saw as a 'barbaric cull of deer', including pregnant hinds. They presented their case as an animal welfare issue, but their reasons for protesting are much broader and have their origins in an ongoing battle with both local and national conservationists who want to dramatically reduce the number of deer in Glenfeshie, targeted because it contains remnants of the native Scots Pine. Many groups would like to expand the pockets of trees to cover a much larger part of the glen. However, Glenfeshie is also home to many deer, which often stray into the glen from neighbouring estates. Government money is available for taking measures to encourage regeneration. Until the recent extensive cull, the preferred option had been to put up deer fences to protect the areas where regeneration was to be encouraged. This option, however, has always met with hostility from many conservationists who argue that the fences are a menace to the capercaillie, another native species that is endangered.

This conflict takes place largely between those with a conservation sense of place and those who work on the land. Those who come to the Highlands for recreation have mixed views depending on how influenced they are by conservation discourses. The conflict over what to do about deer numbers and whether to take down fences is played out in the public arena, as well as in informal private conversations. It encapsulates many important debates: what counts as knowledge; the relationship between facts and values; debates around what is defined as natural; and the relationship between social and cultural factors in the construction and mobilisation of these definitions.

Knowledge: battle over facts

In Chapter Four, I showed how stalkers, keepers and farmers resent the accusations made by some conservationists, that their practices cause harm to the environment. In this case, they oppose the proposition that the deer are a problem. They agree that some culling is necessary but that fences are adequate to deal with the problem of deer eating the young shoots. They do not believe that the fences do any harm to capercaillie. Moreover, they argue that taking down fences has caused a number of problems. In a letter to the local paper the landowner Jamie Williamson writes:

> Climate change, a reduction in sheep numbers and the removal or lack of maintenance of deer fences has resulted in red deer expanding their range and increasing their reproductive potential. In Glenfeshie, damage of farm groups and deer competing with winter feed for cattle is also an issue. The problem has been created by the Forestry Commission and Scottish Natural Heritage removing or failing to maintain deer fencing. As a result deer have moved onto farmland (*Strathspey and Badenoch Herald*: 15 April 2004).

On the other hand, conservationists, many of whom have extensive knowledge of the capercaillie, are adamant that these fences are a major cause of deaths for both capercaillie and blackcock and that they therefore have to be removed and the deer culled instead. The BSCG published the findings of what they call 'a leading authority on capercaillie in Scotland'.

> There are two main reasons for the decline of capercaillie. First, the bird is rearing fewer young than in the 1970s. Second, the adult birds' main single cause of death is flying into forest fences. The scientific evidence shows that, with no deaths from fences, the decline could be reversed (Moss: 2000).

This difference in interpretation of the facts is illustrated by the visit of the BSCG and the local John Muir Trust group to Mar Lodge Estate on the southern side of the Cairngorms. This estate is unusual in that it is a former traditional sporting estate that has been taken over by the National Trust for Scotland and is being managed for conservation objectives, including native tree regeneration. However, for various pragmatic reasons, according to the head ranger, they have continued with guest stalking rather than just culling all the deer themselves. He admits that they could cull more deer if they just went and shot them without the guests, but that for both financial and political reasons, such as maintaining the support of the original staff, they have carried on with the traditional practices. Because they have not managed to lower deer numbers significantly, deer fences have had to remain in order to protect the new trees. This was going to be an issue for debate on our walk around the estate; we had with us the now late Dick Balharry, a well-respected conservationist and one of the most vocal opponents of deer fencing, and Gus Jones of the BSCG who has been monitoring the situation with capercaillie for many years. Both have been passionate about the importance of preserving native species. Gus has studied everything from butterflies to ants and led a major campaign to stop building on land that was home to several species of rare butterflies. Dick was a former gamekeeper who left his job after an incident with the head keeper. Dick had a reputation for rescuing injured birds such as crows when he was supposed to shoot them as pests. One day, his favourite 'pet' crow escaped and flew through a window into the house where the head keeper was having tea with the vicar. Chaos ensued and Dick was sacked. Since then he metamorphosed into a conservationist (though he refused to label himself) and devoted his life to what he calls 'restoring the land'. Both Gus and Dick are convinced that deer fences are not the way to protect the trees because of the threat they represent to capercaillie. On our walk around the estate we soon crossed our first deer fence. Gus was aghast. He would not accept the explanations put forwards by the ranger and just said: 'How many capercaillie have to die before the fences come down?' For Gus and Dick, there is no room for compromise. The capercaillie are an endangered species, they are native to Scotland and therefore they must be preserved at all costs. Dick argued with the ranger's interpretation of the facts. He said that research done by checking 'hits' on the fence is an underestimate of the number of casualties – many will not show up. The rest of the group supported Dick and Gus, another example of how a particular discourse becomes established and disciplines the way the group perceives the land. This became apparent when I dropped back from the group with Robert. He is a retired vet and though very informed on conservation issues is not employed in that capacity. He admitted that he disagreed with the majority and thought that deer fences were the only way or it would take too long to regenerate. He said: 'It's not ideal but there are so many problems with taking them down. Of course, I wouldn't say this in front of Dick Balharry!' Robert's views are not necessarily incompatible with having a conservation sense of place. For example, Justin Dillon, Chair of London Wildlife Trust writes: 'As protectors of biodiversity we should ask if there is a scientific reason why "non-native" means bad' (*LWT Journal*: Spring: 2004). However, in this case, his comment mirrors that of the estate workers themselves rather than the conservation group he belongs to. In this sense he is something of an anomaly.

I let the others continue on their walk to sneak off back to the Lodge and found one of the employees who had worked on the estate before the National Trust took ownership. My conversation with Malcolm (name changed), who had worked on the estate for over thirty years, presented a very different view of the facts. He talked as authoritatively as did Gus and Dick about why deer fences had to remain. He said that the only way they could get deer numbers down is to make a big effort and have no guests at all. It would still be a huge operation as deer numbers are high due to mild winters. Also, they are in places that are difficult to get to. He says that: 'The deer are just too resilient'.

Both sides are convinced of their facts. The problem is exacerbated by the different social positions of the two groups and the sources of their knowledge. As in disputes in other parts of the world (see for example Bashivar: 2000 and Walley: 2004), locals like Malcolm resent being told by perceived outside experts, such as Gus and Dick, that practices they have traditionally pursued are damaging the environment. Conversely, the conservationists who have devoted years to studying and learning about certain species do not understand how these local land workers can be so unwilling to listen to the them (Lund: 2003). As one member of the conversation group, who happens to be an English incomer, said during the visit: 'people like Dick and Gus are needed to educate people that just don't understand'.

Land workers expect this kind of comment from incomers. As we've already discussed, the knowledge they have, based on over thirty years of experience in the case of Malcolm on Mar Lodge, is thought not to be valued by those who work professionally in the field of conservation. Such resentment can be seen in the following quote from the letters page of the local paper, known as the *Strathy*, concerning whether or not sheep and deer overgraze. This is just one example of the many exchanges between these two protagonists. Gus Jones had written to the paper, outlining the arguments of various studies that had found overgrazing to be a problem for tree regeneration. The following letter was written in response by a shepherd who has been living and working in Glenfeshie for decades, arguing that it is the mismanagement of conservationists, not sheep, that has led to the environment being 'ruined'.

> When I first noticed the name of Mr. Gus Jones, he was writing about trees in the *Strathy*. In fact, he was writing about the lack of them in what he called treeless Badenoch and Strathspey. I immediately thought what a ridiculous statement from an obviously ignorant incomer/would-be conservationist.
>
> The truth, whether Mr. Jones and his ilk like it or not, is that the greatest disaster for all bird life, wildlife and hill life has been the arrival and misunderstanding of conservationists.
>
> *D. W. Ross, Leault Farm, Kincraig*
> *16 December 2004*
> Badenoch and Strathspey Herald

The debate over the facts is entangled with who presents which facts. Roy, Gus and Dick, coming from a naturalist or conservation approach, use scientific discourses as a way of presenting the facts, what Ellen (2000) calls expert knowledge.

This knowledge gets defined as such because of the way it is presented, citing studies and research, but also because of who says it. Despite being long-term residents, Gus and Roy's origins in England are a sufficient reason for some to categorise their knowledge as that of 'outside experts'. Once this has been done, this knowledge can be dismissed. Local knowledge is also categorised by conservationists. Local knowledge cannot be objective because it is bound up with particular groups' vested interests – in this case, the maintenance of a specific occupation and way of life. Therefore, this knowledge cannot be trusted. Letters to the Editor, because they are public and are motivated by opposition to something, play an important role in creating entrenched positions and defining interest groups. By linking the differences in opinion to particular social positions – local or incomer – the letters create a framework for the debate. These issues will be discussed in more detail in the next chapter.

Native and natural: what belongs?

'Nature conservationists, by definition, conserve what is natural; without an understanding of what is natural and what is not, they would have no basis for taking decisions about what issues to become involved in' (Milton: 2001: 240).

A key feature of the conflict over facts is the question of what is natural. One of the main ways of defining what is natural in this context is to include all species that are deemed native (Milton: 2001). Such reasoning involves a value judgement. To say a species is native is to say 'we should encourage its growth'; to say a species is alien, means 'it must be eradicated'. This is a form of boundary maintenance. Native species contribute to the purity and therefore health of the land, whereas alien species 'pollute' (Milton: 2001). The argument for native tree regeneration is based on this belief – that native means natural and that natural is good. The debate also involves questioning the role of human intervention: to what extent can humans change their environment without affecting its ability to support human life? Sheep and deer have been introduced by humans, so they are in some respects both domestic animals. Domesticated animals have a different status to wild animals (Lien: 2004) and therefore there is disagreement about their effect on the natural ecology of the land. Some, like the shepherd from Glenfeshie or the landowner Jamie Williamson, argue that these animals have contributed to the wellbeing of the land and people. Gus and Dick, coming from a conservation sense of place, see this intervention as destructive, making it difficult for what is natural to flourish. Each side also holds different criteria for evaluating the presence of these animals. As shown in the last chapter, the livelihood sense of place stresses the importance of the land in providing for human needs.

When out walking with Alan, we discussed the landscape around us. We could see nothing but grouse moors and bare hills. I was explaining to him how John on Kinveachy saw these moors as beautiful, especially when he could see evidence of heather burning. Alan could not understand this. His perception is different. He says: 'When many visitors come to the Scottish Highlands and look at the vast expanse of treeless hills, they see wilderness. When I look, I see desolation.'

Alan's views are echoed in the literature from conservation organisations. Frazer Darling, one of the first naturalists to write about the Highlands is often quoted:

> We are apt to view with pleasure a rugged Highland landscape and think we are here away from the works of the mind and the hand of man, that here is wild nature. But more often than not we are looking at a man-made desert (*Natural History in the Highlands and Islands*: 1947, quoted in Cramb: 1998: 1)

The transformation of the Scottish Highlands into a 'wet desert' (Cramb: 1998) was a slow process over the centuries, largely due to agricultural practices. However, by the eighteenth century, the degradation of the land had been slowed and a certain balance had been achieved. According to Lister-Kaye (1994), this was due to the expansion in cattle grazing – cattle are considered to contribute to the quality of the soil as well as to tree regeneration. However, by the nineteenth century, with changes in political and economic structures sheep were introduced, spelling disaster for tree regeneration. Up to this period, poaching pressures and lack of economic value kept deer numbers low. This changed dramatically as landowners moved from sheep to sporting estates. The new estates embarked on a major campaign to rid the land of any predators of deer and grouse. The result was a major transformation of the wildlife in the Highlands. From only six deer 'forests' (a forest of deer, not of trees) before the nineteenth century, by 1912 over 3.6 million acres were dedicated deer forests. The number of red deer was estimated to be around 360,000–400,000 in 2013 (www.parliament.scot/ResearchBriefingsAndFactsheets/S4/SB_13-74.pdf) and the total of all deer to be 750,000 in 2018. This is a considerable increase from the figure of 150,000 for 1959. In the Cairngorm and Speyside Deer Management Group area, numbers have gone from 8,232 (Williamson: 2004) to 4,103 in 2010 (www.speyside-deermanagement.com/deer-planning). However, estimates are sketchy. In addition, according to Williamson (2004), comparisons cannot be made with previous years because the counting method changed in 2000. The problem with the deer, according to conservationists, is not so much that they are not native to Scotland but that they have been introduced in unnatural numbers, whereas other native species, such as the Scots Pine and the capercaillie, are severely under threat. The aim is to restore the balance. According to many from a livelihood sense of place, like Williamson, the conservationist view is romantic, one of a timeless, transcendental landscape (Hirsch and O'Hanlon: 1995). In Scotland, many writers refer to an idealised past which must be 'restored' or 'revived'. Lister-Kaye (1994), writing on behalf of Scottish Natural Heritage, looks to the past as a model for the future:

A fast-forward history of land use in the Highlands should be accompanied by a pibroch lament. Ten thousand years ago man arrived to find a pristine wilderness of rich climax vegetation: Scots Pine, sessile oak and downy birch, willow, hazel and alder, rowan and gean, with a patchwork of heather clearings and slopes, mountain grasslands and sphagnum-rich bogs. Open forest and blanket bog covered the whole of the hinterland from sea-level to upwards of two thousand feet with arctic-Alpine scrub rising to stony, moss and tundra-lichen summits. There were altogether some five million acres of upland through which moose, reindeer, red deer and roe deer, wild ox, brown bear, wolves, lynx, beaver and wild boar roamed, each according to its ecological niche, side by side with the familiar wildlife we know today (p. 8).

Such an attempt to restore and revive was made on Creag Meagaidh National Nature Reserve between 1986–1996 under the leadership of Dick Balharry. He talked about his work at a public meeting I attended, arguing that the criterion for any land management policy must be the 'health of the land'. In his view, the choice between deer or trees is not a matter of aesthetics or personal preference for one kind of activity or another. Instead, land policies must be based on an objective assessment of what is good for the land – and good is defined as what is historically natural. Dick was keen to provide me with a copy of the publication that documented his work on Creag Meagaidh. He hopes that the policies implemented there will be adopted more widely across the Highlands. The goals are set out in the summary:

When it was acquired by the Nature Conservancy Council, now Scottish Natural Heritage, the land in the old forests of Aberarder and Moy had been grazed for centuries by deer, sheep, goats and cattle. These uses of the land had created a wet moorland in which trees were scarce, the situation prevailing in much of the Highlands. When the land was acquired by the NCC, the aim became to restore the ecological health of the land. This was to be achieved by reducing grazing pressure to enable native trees to grow tall, where previously they had been checked by browsing, and to enable the plant life of the corries to flourish (Ramsey: 1996: 7).

One of the main ways in which conservationists present their case is by mobilising discourses of native and national identity where the nation is seen as synonymous with particular native species (Short: 1991, Bender: 1993). The Glenmore Forest Visitor Centre run by the Forestry Commission has a major display devoted to the importance of restoring the native forests. I came across the following quote on one of the posters:

> The change of name of the Nature Conservancy Council to Scottish Natural Heritage is significant. Instead of conserving nature, their task is to secure the conservation and enhancement of Scotland's unique and precious natural heritage – the wildlife, habitats and landscapes through the long partnership between people and nature.

In this way nature is given even more of a timeless, transcendental quality as it is linked to what is timeless about the nation.

Land workers reject the conservation view that the land has inherently natural or native characteristics. They accept that the red deer have been introduced and see nothing wrong with this. The existence of the red deer provides them with a livelihood. From the conservation perspective, nature is not just a social construction, but is a set of real laws and processes that cannot be ignored. The livelihood approach on the other hand, sees human intervention as of value in itself. The historical practice of locals is not irrelevant, as the conservationists would argue (Mels: 1999), but is what the land actually is – not some idealised vision of what it should be. Conservationists are seen as outsiders who bring in an idealised, unhistorical vision of the natural landscape (Hobart: 1993, Walley: 2004).

Land workers, like many anthropologists, are very aware that their arguments and interpretation of the facts are based on their own subjective opinions and interests. Alastair had been a stalker at Craeg Meagaidh before the takeover by the Nature Conservancy Council. He says that the council had a 'particular agenda' that he 'can understand'. However, he says: 'They need to recognise that this is not my point of view. My job is under threat. There are many agendas'. And, like the shepherd Donnie Ross, Alastair is aware that the battle is about more than a species; it is about a way of life. The deer are defended, not because of some scientific definition of natural or native, but because the deer have meaning in relation to the group's goals (Entriken, quoted in Proctor: 1995: 275). And, the goals have to do with maintaining livelihood and a way of life that is also identified with the nation, though a different nation and a different heritage from conservation and recreation perspectives.

Conservationists argue that there cannot be many perspectives – that the facts speak for themselves. Theirs is a scientific approach to knowledge; science can be used to discover the facts and then policies will flow automatically from those facts. Anthropologists have queried conservationists' and other scientists' belief in the existence of objective facts (Berglund: 1998). The argument is that society constructs facts and by deconstructing these we can see how so-called facts emerge from different perspectives and values, like the way a sense of place shapes people's views on land use. However, many critiques of social constructionism or deconstructionism have come to the defence of the conservation argument. Soule, a conservation biologist, is vicious in his attack: 'Deconstruction is an ideological tool used as part of the assault on nature' (1995: p. 137). He is supported by social scientists (Soper: 1995, Hayle: 1995, Peterson: 2002) who argue that if there are no facts to be discovered about eco-systems, and humans' relations to them, then the implication is that it does not matter what we do. By denying that anything is natural, then everything becomes arbitrary (Soper: 1995).

> If this is true, and there is no real nature – no nature not consti-
> tuted by human interpretation or intervention – then we are left
> with no grounds on which to evaluate one environment as better
> or worse or to resist some forms of intervention and support
> others (Peterson: 2002: 64).

Dick Balharry and others would strongly support this view. The consequences of refusing to accept that trees are important for the health of the land, are not just theoretical but could have devastating effects. With climate change looming as a major threat to us all, it is important that we are aware of how land management has an impact on this. Trees have a vital role to play by acting as a carbon sink in the UK, removing about 10 million tons of carbon from the atmosphere every year (http://www.cityoftrees.org.uk/why-trees-climate-change). There is a similar argument about grouse moors. Much research has shown that management of land for driven grouse creates problems for the land, increasing greenhouse gas emissions and flood risk (Avery: 2015). However, as with the trees-versus-deer debate, land managers on grouse moors would dispute the fact and stress their key role in wildlife management and conservation.

The problem then is what to do when both sides believe they have the facts and they lead to different practical conclusions on land use. Whether these facts are really facts is not necessarily the central issue in these conflicts. When confronted with two versions of the facts the debate then centres around whose count. It is not that people are making them up or socially constructing facts about a non-existent natural world, but rather that they are selecting observations of the world that fit with their values and interests – for example, what they want Glenfeshie to be used for. Worster (1995) explains the problem:

> If nature is nothing but a bewildering panorama of changes,
> many of them induced by human beings, going back to ancient
> hunters setting fire to the bush, and if our attitudes towards nature

are themselves demonstrably in a state of constant flux, so that yesterday we hated wolves, now we love them, then what should conservation mean? (pp. 67–68).

A similar dilemma arises with the question of what Glenfeshie should look like. We have already discussed how a livelihood-based sense of place sees beauty in a landscape where a mark has been made. In the case of the deer debate, estate workers do not see deer fences as an aesthetic problem – they have a purpose to fulfil in the work of the estate. They also do not see trees as any more aesthetically pleasing than deer. By contrast, the mountaineering and conservation senses of place are more likely to appreciate the qualities of wild land. However, in the case of deer or trees, the divisions are complicated by the fact that hill-walkers have a variety of views depending on the group they belong to. Those from outside the area tend to have a view of Scotland as empty wilderness and see the appeal in this emptiness. The hills that are the most valued are those that are bare. John, the mountaineer from London, could not understand why there was such a dispute about reforestation. He identifies forests with the conifer plantations – but these are to him aesthetically displeasing. He wants the feeling of space. A friend from the Strathspey Mountain Club agrees. After a John Muir Trust meeting at which Glenfeshie had been discussed, she confessed to me that she had not dared say anything at the meeting, but that she thinks that the 'openness of the glen, with just a few stands of scattered trees is attractive'. This corresponds to what many environmental psychologists have found where humans are said to prefer open savannahs to forests, perhaps the result of our ancestors' very real fear of the dangers of the forest (Cave: 1998).

In addition, for many people, a highlight of walking in the Highlands is seeing the red deer. It is deer, not trees, that are associated with the Scottish hills. As a stalker told me: 'Deer are now part of the Scottish hills. They are a source of income from shooting and most visitors like seeing deer on the hills.'

His view was confirmed to me in the many times the people I was walking with stopped to watch the deer – pointing them out excitedly. One woman, recently moved to the area, described to me one of her most memorable walking experiences.

I saw a reddish-brown spot on the hillside that turned out to be a herd of deer – over 200 of them. Then they moved, running en masse down the hillside. It was one of the high points of my life. I have never seen anything like it.

Tree-supporters also try to mobilise the aesthetic discourse. They point to the ugliness of the deer fences. It would enhance the beauty of the landscape if the fences were taken down and the deer culled instead. Some local walkers, such as Alan and George, concur and constantly pointed out fences to me in a negative way, attempting to educate me. However, walkers and climbers from outside the area are not so familiar with the various arguments. Dick believes that their kind of attitude is the result of ignorance. He says, 'People do not really see. When they walk through Glenfeshie, they are not aware that it is like walking through an old people's home with ninety-nine-year-old humans. This is not healthy.' Health can be related to both beauty and heritage. In a Forestry Commission publication on native tree species, I found the following comment: 'Our native tree species – trees natural to this country – have been linked with Scottish culture and society throughout history. They are pleasing to the eye. They seem to belong (1998: 2).'

*

The positions adopted in both disputes discussed in this chapter come about through the blending of a complex mixture of factors that make up their senses of place. It is impossible to separate out the activity one is involved in, and the appreciation it gives of certain aspects of the land, from the perceptions of what are the facts and what should be done. This chapter has also shown that the sense of place based on activity is infused with views on wider cultural issues such as debates about knowledge, aesthetics, rights, tradition and heritage.

One's sense of place underlies positions on the deer-versus-trees and the paddlers-versus-anglers debate. However, a particular sense of place does not necessarily lead to the individual becoming part of an identifiable group in contrast to another. For this to happen, there need to be circumstances in which the groups come into contact with each other as groups, accompanied by specific discourses and supported by institutional frameworks. Different positions don't exist in the abstract as contested natures (Macnaghten and Urry: 1998, Proctor: 1995), they emerge out of situations in which choices have to be made. As disagreements move from individual encounters to the public arena, relations between groups become more codified and structured, with discourses and institutions playing a much more dominant role and clearly defined positions of interest groups emerging.

As we move further into the public arena, the issues themselves are transformed. As shown in the letter exchange between Gus Jones and the shepherd Donnie Ross, the discussion incorporates a different set of issues concerning who belongs and who should be making decisions about the land. As I have shown in previous chapters, these wider contexts are also there, but they are not so prevalent in the everyday activities of the various individuals I have described. However, in certain circumstances, as outlined in this chapter, they become increasingly important. My findings are supported by an interview with Roy Dennis, a leading conservationist, who was also married to a crofter.

I think what you're picking up as well is that a lot of it is nothing to do with nature conservation; it's to do with power. In the recent debate about beaver in Scotland, if you were able to really check it through you would find that a lot of people who are against it or for it know very little about beaver. Some of the views as to why they want it or don't want it are not based on the ecology of the animal, they're thinking if SNH want it then I don't. If this group don't want it, then I'm for it. So I think that any of these discussions, whether in Strathspey or the rest of the world are based on these relationships and power and who thinks they should be in charge. It's very wrong to think it's only to do with conservation.

The dispute between anglers and paddlers and the debate about deer and trees are both infused with power relations. There may be real differences of interest, arising out of their sense of place and the activities they value, but power struggles obscure and complicate the situation. We have seen in the two conflicts studied in this chapter that the groups differed not just in terms of their sense of place but in their social position. Paddlers resented the power of the landowners and ghillies were defensive of their precarious economic position vis-à-vis the recreation industry. Land workers are also worried about their future in an age that is turning against the sporting estate as the conservation organisations grow in influence. Conservationists are frustrated by the power of the traditional landowners who resist their efforts to restore the natural heritage. Permeating all the debates is the question of who should have power to decide, often portrayed as a choice between the local community and outside interests. Commenting on who will make the decisions in the new Cairngorm National Park, the local MP Fergus Ewing writes:

Will it be the board members with the strong local input which they encompass? Or will it be the powerful special interest groups and outside quangos who seem to exert an ever growing and unconstrained power and influence on rural life? (*Strathspey and Badenoch Herald*: 21 August 2003)

CHAPTER SIX

Conflict and Power

Senses of place in conflict

The local people can never be trusted to run a National Park. Anyone who would build a railway up a mountain can't care very much about the environment. They're just greedy. (Conservationist living in the area)

We don't want all those conservationists parachuting in from down south and telling us what we can and can't do. They don't realise that we have to make a living. (Employee of ski shop)

The locals don't value what they have. They never go out in the hills to see what's there. (Hill-walker visiting the area)

The conservationists just want us to gaze at the land from the outside, as something pristine and pure. They don't want us to get active enjoyment from it. (Cairngorm Partnership Recreation Forum member)

An international spotlight was focussed on the Cairngorms in 1994 when the Cairngorm Chairlift Company (CCC) put forwards a proposal to upgrade the skiing facilities by building a funicular railway. Not only was the chairlift considered to be out of date, it could not operate in the typical high winds. Unable to get skiers up to the main slopes on many days, the old chairlift meant much business was lost. It was also argued that the funicular would serve as a summer visitor attraction, more appealing to tourists, including the disabled, than the old chairlift. People could take the funicular up to the top, and then walk up to Cairn Gorm or over to Ben Macdhui – both 4,000 feet peaks. This is where the problem lay. By attracting more summer visitors, it would cause severe damage to the fragile plateau environment that lies between the top of the funicular and Ben Macdhui, others argued. They did not want the area to be made any more accessible than it already was. During the next six years, a conflict ensued between supporters and opponents of the plan.

The legacy of the funicular debate is still felt strongly today, both in ongoing arguments about the success of the mountain railway and in the new National Park where 'all the old tensions between conservation, development and recreation are still evident' (Magnusson: 2001: xvii). The mountain railway became the centre of local attention again when it was declared out of action for the ski seasons of 2018–2020. Its future is still therefore in doubt and many of the old arguments are resurfacing.

This conflict mirrors many other conflicts around the world. According to Lambert (2001), disagreements over land use were evident as far back as the late eighteenth century when visitors first began to come to the Cairngorms. The funicular debate and then the discussions surrounding the creation of Scotland's second National Park mean that 'the Cairngorms now represent the most public and bitter manifestation of these conflicts in the UK' (Lambert: 2001: 1).

The previous chapter has shown how conflicts ensue when groups with different senses of place find themselves involved with the same land. Groups that co-exist in most circumstances find themselves at odds with each other when situations arise where a choice must be made about how that common space is to be used. The conflict over the building of the funicular brings together all of these players on an international stage, also drawing in other individuals, institutions and structures. Small-scale, informal disagreements over other issues, such as deer numbers, metamorphose into formal positions, which are then exaggerated and solidified into interest groups. The battle lines are drawn between two distinct sides: 'local' development interests against 'outside' conservation and recreation. This chapter builds on the analysis developed in the previous chapters in order to understand the genealogy of this conflict.

Anti-funicular and pro-funicular

The construction of the funicular or mountain railway had just begun when I arrived in the area in late summer 1999. Though it had been approved and was going ahead, it was still a source of controversy. I encountered anti-funicular views on day one of my fieldwork. The source of opposition was two walkers from the Dundee Mountaineering Club. I walked with them down from Cairn Gorm, through the beginnings of the work on the funicular. They gave me a range of reasons why the funicular should not be built, arguments that were echoed by many others who engage in the activities of hill-walking and climbing. I showed in Chapter Two how the mountaineering sense of place involves perceptions of land as the location of adventurous activities and as a means of escaping from normal life in urban areas. This perception has led to a particular position on the funicular for many moun-taineers; Richard typifies this. He is a walker and climber from Sheffield who often visits the Scottish Highlands. In 1994, he had just returned to Aviemore, after a multi-day backpack trip in the Cairngorms, when he heard the announcement that the Chairlift Company, supported by their landowner Highland and Islands Enterprise, was proposing to replace the chairlift with a funic-ular railway. He said he was so angry that when he got home he immediately joined the John Muir Trust, a conservation organi-sation that he thought would campaign against the funicular, and wrote countless letters of protest. Mike Dales, the Conservation and Access Officer for the Mountaineering Council of Scotland, at the time of research (now Mountaineering Scotland) said in an interview that skiing is 'inappropriate' for the Scottish Highlands and that the funicular would just 'prolong it'. Another visitor referred to it as representing the 'Disneyfication' of the Scottish hills. A frequently stated view is that a mountain railway does not fit in with what they expect to see – it doesn't belong – in the same way as conservationists see certain species as not belonging. A mountain railway does not fit with a sense of place that is attuned to views, and the appreciation of adventure unfettered by human technology.

Conservationists have similar but different arguments arising out of their sense of place. One expert on the dotterel was worried that the plateau, as a major breeding ground, would be made more accessible to tourists, increasing the chance of disturbances. Other scientists in the area told me of their concern for rare moss and lichen, supposedly protected by various directives. They want the Cairngorm plateau to be free from human disturbance, not made more open to that disturbance.

I also came across pro-funicular views on my first day. These were expressed typically by the shop assistant in the gift shop of the ski area. I heard these views repeated by many others whose livelihood depends on the tourist industry. There are an estimated 1.87 million visitors to the Cairngorm National Park every year (cairngorms.co.uk/caring-future/local-economy/tourism/). Tourism makes up 30 per cent of the economy and provides 43 per cent of the employment. For the Highlands as a whole, tourism is considered the most important industry (www.strathspey-herald.co.uk/news/highland-council-welcomes-tourism-tax-consultation-plans). The sense of place of those who have some direct engagement with the land, through activities such as farming and working on a sporting estate, represent a significant number, but not all, of the possible outlooks of those who make a living in the area. I also met many other people who are characterised not so much by how they interact with the land as by the fact that they are not engaged in activities that cause them to come into direct contact with any aspect of the hill environment. They therefore have a sense of place that is defined by an awareness of the 'low ground', the area in the villages and the immediate surroundings.

The divide between those who experience the high ground and those whose lives are led in the low ground came sharply into focus when I took a job in a local restaurant. I was still staying 'up' at the Glenmore Campsite with its Cairngorms view, and drove 'down' the ski road to the restaurant in Aviemore.

Several local teenagers were employed part-time at the restaurant. Apart from the fact that they were both fun to work with and very helpful to me in my new role, they also proved an excellent source of information. They knew about my research and were keen to help out by patiently answering my questions (when we were not rushed off our feet working, of course!) They did not ski or go walking so had never spent any time up at the ski area and had never been on top of the Cairngorm plateau. This contrasts so much with my own pre-fieldwork experience of the area. I had come to Glenmore Lodge for several years to take courses and then rented houses in remote places with friends. If I stayed at Glenmore Lodge I would not even need to come down to Aviemore to shop. Most of the time was spent at the Lodge and on the hills. I knew the Cairngorm plateau better than I did Aviemore.

One weekend, they were very excited about the Harley Davidson festival but knew nothing about the Glenmore Lodge open day that was also taking place, offering free taster sessions for local kids. Fourteen-year-old Craig, son of a taxi driver and a childminder, said his parents work long hours and he works every weekend so there is no time. Going into the hills is something tourists do, not him. When the snow fell for the first time, one local customer said that she finds it 'inconvenient but at least it will bring in the tourists'. I heard similar views expressed in the course of my daily errands around town. The hairdresser told me that for her, the hills are just something 'in the background' that she would miss if they weren't there but isn't usually aware of.

These local residents see the surrounding natural environment as something that provides them with an income. According to one local councillor, the Cairngorms are 'an economic asset'. However, though this sense of place is based on perceiving the land as a source of livelihood, it is different from that of farmers and estate workers. The general perspective may be the same, but, as mentioned in Chapter Four, people from the farms and estates tend to not mix with villagers and therefore were not involved to the same extent with the debates surrounding the funicular. Mary the farmer, for example, was not against development on the mountain but did not even know that it was a funicular that was being proposed. The sense of place is also different because many of those working in the tourist industry have no direct knowledge or contact with the land. They know the hills are there and that they are the reason for tourists, and therefore themselves, living in the area, but it is the tourists' domain, not theirs. Even many of those who worked in the ski area have not ventured further. I met one local lad working in the restaurant at mid-station. He saw from my clothes and ice axes that I had been out in the hills and he asked me about it; he said he'd never been and wondered what it was like. He has never had anyone to go with.

Support for the funicular, therefore, was most often expressed by those working in and around the tourist industry. The area had been going into decline since the demise of the Aviemore Centre. It was this that many locals, such as Mary Walker and her grandson Craig, brought to my attention as the major issue. In the 1960s, Aviemore had been a boom town, with visitors coming all year round, both for the skiing and for general entertainment, for example stag weekends and hen parties. The Centre had many attractions such as a major ice rink and a cinema. People remember those days with fondness. Not only was business good, but there was a lot for locals to do. At the time of research, the Centre was derelict and its future unknown. Some plan would come close to being adopted then it would fall through. Waiting to see what would happen was something of a local joke. The redevelopment of the Centre was considered crucial for the future of Aviemore, which hoped to return to a Golden Age, and the funicular was supposedly the key. The head of the local Tourist Board said it is 'vital' for the future of Aviemore and a waiter in a popular restaurant said he is 'in favour of anything that would attract people to the area'. A shop assistant in an outdoor shop said he did not understand all the arguments but that at least it meant change – something needed to happen to counter the demise of the Aviemore Centre. Other arguments stressed the extra income generated directly and indirectly from the increase in tourist business as reasons to support the funicular. Owners of attractions such as Waltzing Waters in Newtonmore (closed in 2011), described on its website as: 'The world's most elaborate water, light and music production', thought that the funicular would attract more coach parties, who might then add their attraction to the list of things to see. Locals were also hoping more jobs would be created.

It is not my aim to evaluate the success of the mountain railway as such – I am more concerned with what the debate tells us about conflicts over land use. In any case, at the time of writing the jury is still out as to whether it did have the desired effect on the economy and local livelihoods. It has been dogged by difficulties, culminating in the most recent owners, Natural Retreats, going into receivership after a history of bad management. However, reviews did show that though the mountain railway did not increase skiing visitors, it did attract significantly more summer visitors – from an average of 36,750 visitors in the years 1997 -2000 to an average of 165,000 after the railway was built (Review+of+Cairngorm+Funicular+Railway+-+Audit+Scotland+Report+-+Main+Report+-+October+2009.pdf).

Those who were pro-funicular expressed their resentment of those who campaigned against the funicular in terms of outsiders versus locals. Seamus Grant, the Gaelic scholar from Rothiemurchus, saw the conflict as being typical of the 'Southern oppression of the Highlands', not wanting the region to develop but to remain as a kind of backwater for their own enjoyment and benefit. Meanwhile, those against the funicular explained the conflict in terms of the same dichotomy; the locals 'can't be trusted' to look after their environment.

Therefore, the conflict arose because different senses of place value different aspects of the land and have different views on how the land should be used. It would appear that the positions were so entrenched and represented such real differences in opinion, that the conflict could only be resolved by having a winner and a loser. Walkers have an interest in maintaining the sense of wildness in the Cairngorms. Conservationists have an interest in preserving the habitat of the dotterel. Those in the local tourist industry have an interest in developing the area to attract tourists. It seems to follow logically from this that they will hold distinct positions on issues such as the funicular, the National Park or development of land for housing. However, by looking at conflicts as a complex process of interactions between individuals and groups, within institutional, discursive and structural contexts (Mels: 1999) my data will reveal that conflicts between locals and conservation and recreation senses of place are by no means inevitable. Conflicts are often about more than a choice between two options. There is no inevitability about one sense of place leading to particular material interests or any particular interpretation of what may serve those material interests. Like-minded people with shared experiences form into interest groups and come into conflict with each other because of specific circumstances that involve relations of power at a number of levels (Wolf: 1999).

Making of interest groups

It was taken for granted amongst many in the mountaineering community that climbers would be against the funicular. Rosie, an instructor at Glenmore Lodge, spent the majority of her time either working, climbing or socialising with the other instructors. When she asked me to find some 'guinea pigs' to practice for her Mountain Instructor Award assessment, I invited Anne and George from the Strathspey Mountain Club to assist. The subject of the funicular came up and when Rosie expressed her opposition, she was shocked to hear that they were in favour. She told me later that she had never heard this before, especially from people she sees as fellow mountaineers. One's identity as a mountaineer comes from associating with others, learning through apprenticeships. And it is not only the skills that one learns, but the attitudes that go with it. The pressure to conform is not the result of coercive power (Lukes: 1986), but is much more insidious as the individual comes to internalise the value system of the group. The activities of mountaineering and birding share many similarities with ritual. The process of becoming initiated into the activity involves a major shift in perceptions and worldview. The emotional power of the experience changes the person such that, depending on the intensity of their response to the activity, a bond to the group is formed. In groups as dispersed as walkers/climbers and conservationists, national organisations (for example the Ramblers Association and Mountaineering Scotland), together with magazines and websites, help to create a 'community of interests'. Because of their position as representatives and spokespeople for this community, they play a formative role in group identity and worldview. In the case of the funicular, climbers and hill-walkers are presented with an unashamedly anti-funicular position. Under its former name, the Mountaineering Council of Scotland, it published 'Proposed Cairn Gorm Funicular Update' in 1999. Its position is unambiguous:

The Mountaineering Council of Scotland will continue to:

- Oppose the funicular option
- Press for a sensible alternative
- Inform our members of the latest developments in the case

- Highlight the disastrous consequences of pursuing the funicular option

Magazines have taken a similarly bold approach. For example, a major national magazine for walkers published an article called 'The Runaway Train'. The opening paragraph reads:

> The Cairngorms – the highest, wildest, the most untouched mountain range in Britain. Seven hundred and fifty square miles of subarctic slopes, deep corries and rare, fragile, natural history. And a spanking new train, ferrying 100,000 tourists a year to a large building 3,600 feet up the mountain for a bite to eat, a quick potter around the souvenir shop and a gawp at the view. Welcome to the future – it's pretty ugly (Schofield: 2000).

The Angry Corrie (1999) referred to the funicular as 'the carbuncle on Cairn Gorm' and 'a white elephant'.

Such writers act as opinion leaders, presenting particular perspectives that become accepted by others in the group. It is not a case of the 'hypodermic syringe' where readers are 'injected' with a view they automatically accept; rather the readership already shares many of the same values and sensibilities. The author is seen as an authority on the subject and writes about the funicular in such a way that the reader comes to associate his or her sense of place with being anti-funicular. A local bed-and-breakfast owner might pick up the same article and remain unconvinced, no matter what facts may be presented. Both the Scottish and British Mountaineering published strongly negative comments. The comment made about 'Disneyfication of the Cairngorms' was from a mountaineering magazine. Being part of a group means that certain views are encouraged and reinforced.

Birders and others with a conservation sense of place developed their anti-funicular views through a similar process. They are surrounded by a similar community, brought together through membership of organisations such as the World Wildlife Fund (WWF) and the RSPB, and by various media forms (the RSPB's *Bird* magazine, nature programmes on TV) that shape and influence their views. In addition, as with the mountaineers, they are unlikely to come into contact with people who have opposing views. Both the mountaineering and conservation communities can be very insular, especially during their time in the mountain regions. Those attending Glenmore Lodge courses have little contact with local people. At the time of research, only one of the instructors was originally from the area and though many of the others had lived here longer, they tended to mix with others like themselves, and who have the same interests, as in the case of Rosie. Those who come on birding holidays stay in especially designed accommodation in order to maximise their time talking and learning about birds. There were no local instructors working for Speyside Wildlife when I was there in 2000. At a Scottish Natural Heritage conference in Pitlochry, a conservationist presented the research he was doing in the Kincraig area of Strathspey. Even other conservationists from Strathspey at the conference said they didn't know about his project and he admitted that he did not have any contact with people in the local area. It is not as if people are deliberately kept away from or are not interested in other views. Rather it is the nature of the activity and the context within which it operates that closes the group off from alternative perspectives.

As a result of the processes described above, aspects of one's sense of place that have been only vaguely articulated form into more precise discourses. Certain vocabularies, views and opinions become solidified within the group context. In the case of mountaineers and birders, discourses include the importance of wilderness or wild land, biodiversity, freedom to roam and the intrinsic value of nature. It is through these discourses that the group comes to define the world. In the case of the funicular, many people who identify themselves as hill-walkers or climbers, birders or conservationists, through contact with 'authoritative' magazines, documents, websites and individuals, adopted an anti-funicular view.

It is not random that certain discourses are more accepted than others (Wolf: 1999, Foucault: 1986). Magazine editors will call upon those they see as experts to write on certain topics. These people tend to have full-time positions that give them the opportunity to research and write. Mike Dales, the Access and Conservation Officer for Mountaineering Scotland at the time of research, devoted considerable time to researching the problems with the funicular. He worked closely with Bill Wright of the Cairngorms Campaign, which was set up and funded by organisations such as Mountaineering Scotland and the WWF as part of a strategy to influence debates on the funicular and the National Park. Bill wrote articulate and well-researched articles, including a regular column for the popular *Climber* magazine. It was through such writing that the anti-funicular position became hegemonic within the mountaineering community. The situation was similar for those in the broad environmental movement. The WWF and the RSPB have millions of members and their official anti-funicular position could not help but have an effect on the views of their members. The power of group identity and ideas have contributed to the way the conflict evolved.

However, we need to also examine the process by which certain ideas and organisations reach a position from where they can then influence others. This requires us to take a step back from individuals in order to examine the workings of structural and institutional power (Wolf: 1999). Many of those who favoured the funicular commented on the power of the 'unelected institutions' that 'interfere' with local issues. One of the main targets is the RSPB. As it is a large landowner in Scotland, with 125,858 acres under its control (Wightman 2015), it can determine what happens within its territories. As discussed in previous chapters, the RSPB owns Abernethy Reserve and has made itself unpopular with many locals. I was repeatedly told that they 'discourage' locals from walking on their property and others expressed outrage that all the sheep were expelled when the RSPB took over, thereby affecting local livelihood. In addition, being such a large organisation gives them the ability to lobby politicians and influence policy (Chenevix-Trench, H. and Philip, L.: 2001). The RSPB represents over a million people but decisions are largely in the hands of full-time employees and local reserve wardens. The RSPB's emergence as a major player illustrates how the balance of power is shifting away from traditional institutions (Rose: 1999). This has ramifications for local politics. The financial and political power of these organisations means that they are able to participate as equals alongside private landowners, politicians and local business associations and therefore have to be included in any consultations.

Mountaineering Scotland, together with the British Mountaineering Council south of the border, may not have the same financial and political power, but together with the Ramblers Association (RA), they represent a very large section of society. The RA has around 123,000 members in Britain and Mountaineering Scotland is supported by around 140 affiliated clubs. As a result, they are able to employ full-time staff to research and make representations to government on issues such as access, the National Park and wind farm or hydroelectric developments. One of the main points they stress is the importance of recreation to local economies. With ever-increasing participation in outdoor recreation, organisations that set themselves up to speak on behalf of these people will continue to gain influence in the corridors of government.

Parts of the state had also been instrumental in supporting an anti-funicular position. Scottish National Heritage is the government agency given the task of safeguarding the nation's natural environment. It is the main body undertaking research on the environment and produces a number of papers on the impact of development on the Scottish uplands. Many conservationists work for or with SNH. Therefore, SNH will reflect the views of those they employ, which will then further reinforce similar views in others.

We have to step back even further, looking at changes in capitalism itself, in order to understand why groups like the RSPB and SNH have so much political influence. As society is increasingly based on services and as income and education increase, leisure has become a major industry, manifested in the number of people taking up activities like birding and mountaineering. As they become involved in their hobby, many people begin to join relevant organisations and read associated publications. Therefore, the political power of organisations such as the RSPB, the WWF and the Mountaineering Councils rests on economic changes that have strengthened them financially. Scottish National Heritage represents what some have called an 'eco-cracy'. It is the growth in general concern about ecological issues that has forced the state to incorporate such organisations under its wing. These organisations have by no means replaced other powerful institutions, such as corporations, banks and private landowners. Nevertheless, the rise in the power of environmental organisations is an example of an outside group that has, in certain guises and with the discourse of sustainable development, been incorporated into the system (Poncelot: 2001). The above analysis shows the role power played in the creation of the distinct anti-funicular position. It works on a number of levels, each reinforcing the other such that the anti-funicular position becomes entrenched and solidified as a discourse that individuals have internalised (Foucault: 1986). This same process was at work with the pro-funicular position.

The local community is made up of a variety of individuals, arguably more disparate in their social make-up than the anti-funicular group. However, the need to make a living creates certain common elements to their sense of place. As a result, a discourse of social and economic development is common to many. This leaves people open to supporting projects that are presented as being economically beneficial. I will examine how support for the funicular came to be linked in the minds of many with the economic future of the area.

As mentioned above, the economic argument was popular. At the time of my fieldwork, many argued that the funicular would provide jobs in construction and maintenance. Though it was recognised that in the long-term few jobs would directly be provided, the local paper continued to stress the number of jobs that were 'underpinned' by the funicular.

For example, when work started on the funicular, an article with the headline, 'Mountain Staff Take on New Jobs', was published. The first paragraph reads:

> Some Cairn Gorm mountain staff whose seasonal work on the hill would now have come to an end have switched to working on the funicular railway. The new jobs for winter workers is just one of the spin-offs the local economy is reaping from the £14.8 million project which restarted last week (*Strathspey and Badenoch Herald*: 26 April 2001).

The owners of the construction companies have benefited most from the building of the funicular but it was hoped that there would still be jobs for others, many of whom were unemployed. This turned out to be the case for some. Anne and George have two sons who were for a time employed full-time for the mountain railway company. Previously, they had only been able to get odd jobs. Now they were in a financial position to buy houses, providing further economic benefits as they spend money on their new properties. In addition, the money to pay for the funicular came from the government (£23 million), giving the impression that there was nothing to lose and much to gain. The range of comments supporting the funicular showed a lack of understanding of the debate about the ski area and surrounding hills, unlike those who were against the funicular. In other words, mountaineers and conservationists who argued against the funicular focussed on what the funicular would do to the high ground on the mountain itself and were not familiar with the political and economic issues facing the low ground. Meanwhile, pro-funicular locals stressed the financial benefit to the low ground, where people live and work. This difference can be traced to the different senses of place, with a livelihood sense of place having an awareness that seems to end at the ski park entrance – where 'place' begins for others. As pointed out previously, many visitors remain within their own worlds. As one mountaineering visitor said: 'the only time I had any contact with local people was when I made my one trip to Tesco to stock up on food for the week'. Similarly, locals tend not to go beyond the areas surrounding the villages. Therefore, people who I met who were pro-funicular, tended to know little about the debates surrounding the Cairngorm plateau itself. Rather, they were concerned about the knock-on effects on local businesses.

Other arguments for the funicular come from the ski industry itself. The funicular had been proposed by the Chairlift Company because it seemed an excellent solution to the problem of getting people to the best skiing for beginners at the top of the mountain in windy weather. Similar to other activities, skiing gives rise to a sense of place, one in which technology, in the forms of lifts, buildings and snow fences, is part of the perception of what belongs on the hill. Peter Ord of Ski Scotland told me that at one time many people in organisations like SNH would have been happy to see skiing disappear altogether. But he maintained that: 'skiing is now accepted as an important part of the tourist industry'. The ski industry has a cherished history in the eyes of many locals. Though, as mentioned above, many locals have never been to the ski area, there is still a significant part of the local population that goes skiing regularly. Of course, this depends on one's economic and work situation. It was more often retired people or those with flexible work commitments that I saw during the week but when the weekend came, crowds formed long queues for the chairlift. I was able to buy an annual ski pass for a reasonable price for the time I was there; often it is retired people who are able to take full advantage of these, having the flexibility to go skiing when conditions are good. I had many good days during the week without the crowds and in sunny, windless conditions, all for research purposes, of course! Anne and I went up on the very first day the ski area opened and she recognised many people she knew. It was the development of skiing that attracted many current residents to the area – some to take up posts as instructors and others to work in the tourist infrastructure that supported the skiing. It was an exciting time and many would like to see this recreated. They hoped the funicular would do this.

MA, a member of the Strathspey Mountain Club, came up here from Edinburgh in 1963.

> I had long wanted to be a ski instructor. I got a job at the youth hostel in Loch Morlich, working as a ski instructor for them. It was a great time. We had to walk up to the Sheiling and then ski from there (half-way up the current ski area). There was a rope tow from there. We used to keep the tows open until seven p.m. in April. There was a great atmosphere – all the people attracted to Aviemore by the skiing in winter – with folk singers playing at Glenmore Lodge and in the hotels. Tom Patey, a famous Scottish mountaineer, came down with his accordion. The 'lefties' would all have been people we knew – many of them Creag Dubh climbers from Glasgow. It was all very informal and there was a lot of socialising. It was a time of optimism.

The unfolding of the conflict: the two sides do battle

Throughout my research as well as in the years that followed, the conflicts over the funicular and the National Park and their aftermath permeated both public and private discussions. So what happened to make it such a significant part of the area's economic and political life? Each side in the debate believed that they were right. This powerful belief held them in its grip, making it difficult to see or understand any perspective outside it. These interest groups had self-identified members who were active in campaigning as well as passive members who tended to identify with one side or the other. In Badenoch and Strathspey, two interest groups emerged out of the conflict over the funicular and have carried on a public existence in the debates about the National Park and more recently over the spread of housing developments. The sides can still be delineated by their contrasting senses of place – local livelihood versus outside conservation and recreation.

In the conflicts between these two groups, there appear to be incompatible positions. We must first examine how the funicular conflict unfolded, and then go on to consider how the debates around the National Park both resembled and differed from this, focussing on the ways in which each group attempts to achieve its aims. In both cases, it appears that the local livelihood, pro-development interests won. The funicular was built and was being claimed a success, even by many who originally had reservations. The National Park was established in 2003, with planning powers in the hands of only two local councils – Aberdeenshire and Highlands. Perthshire was not originally included in the Park (it since has been), which was a source of resentment by Mountaineering Scotland and Bill Wright of the Cairngorms Campaign. The pro-development interests thought the inclusion of Perthshire would introduce a 'southern' influence on decision-making. The vast majority of the first board members were local rather than feared outsiders. How did this happen? Why do many who were involved in or supported conservation and recreation organisations feel they were side-lined and their views ignored? The answer to this lies in the way in which key organisations pursued their campaigns.

In 1986 conservationists used the power of the courts to oppose the extension of the ski area into Lurchers' Gully. A similar strategy was followed in the case of the funicular. Armed with directives from the EU about the need to protect the environment, appeals were made to SNH to refuse the funicular proposal. The Cairngorms Campaign was set up by the WWF and others to lobby politicians and civil servants. This reliance on the courts and outside directives reinforced the views that locals were being ignored.

The Mountaineering Councils used their networks to encourage people to write letters opposing the funicular. General public opinion seemed to be against it on a national level. It was thought that the SNH would surely refuse to support it. They had the power to do so and are officially a conservation organisation. But the Chairlift Company cleverly found a way around the objections of the SNH by changing their proposal to include a 'closed system'. This meant that those using the funicular would not be allowed out at the top so that the funicular would not mean increased numbers on the adjacent fragile environment. The SNH withdrew its objections. Others held out. The RSPB considered taking the whole issue to the European Court but changed its mind, realising the difficulty of arguing the case.

The campaign relied to a large extent on state institutions. As mentioned above, Seamus Grant argues that outsiders have been imposing their vision of the Highlands on Highlanders for centuries and the anti-funicular lobby is just the most recent example. I interviewed Seamus at his home in Rothiemurchus. He himself had interesting stories to tell about how his family was able to get his house; it was the result of homeless soldiers returning to the area and squatting places that were empty. He could therefore make some claims to having the credentials of a native. He stressed the cultural power of those who come to the area for walking and climbing. He was particularly concerned that they 'have even taken over the names of the local hills'. Glenmore Lodge instructors pronounce the names of the mountains and corries in certain ways and these have now become the norm amongst walkers and climbers in general. Seamus was also very critical of conservation organisations. Their expertise gives them the 'power to declare how the land should be and who should have access to it'. He described at length the history of the glens and the factors that led to them being empty of people today. According to Seamus, there is something amiss when walkers find only ruined buildings and 'emptiness' rather than people living and working in the glens (see Chapter Four). For him, the funicular was just a modern version of Highlanders making a living out of the land. His view was confirmed to a certain extent in the way many funicular opponents presented their arguments, phrased in a language that implied that they know what is natural for the land. A funicular is 'inappropriate', will damage the 'proposed world heritage site' or 'does not belong' on a mountain. Such discourses have been very powerful in mobilising national opinion against the funicular.

Some residents, working either in outdoor recreation or conservation, attempted to win people over through local initiatives. Others spoke out on the radio or wrote letters to the local paper. They tended to use similar arguments to those mentioned above – claims to knowledge about what was appropriate and the importance of keeping people away from 'fragile' habitats. Roy and Gus of the BSCG wrote articulate, well-researched, persuasive letters. They were supported by the research work of Bill Wright of the Cairngorms Campaign and Mike Dales of Mountaineering Scotland who used economic arguments about how the funicular would be extremely costly as well as distributing any benefits unequally. They favoured a counter proposal, later put forwards by a consortium of organisations, including the RSPB and WWF, for a gondola up to the ski area from the valley and then a high-speed chairlift to the top (Save the Cairngorms Campaign and Scottish and Wildlife Countryside Link: 1996). They argued that this would be a lower cost solution to the upgrading of the ski area, leaving money available for other investment. A snowboard shop owner told me that the gondola would bring in more money to the valley itself. People would have to come into Aviemore to start their journey and therefore be more likely to spend money in the town. I asked him why this option had not been taken up. He replied that 'they had already made up their minds' and 'people didn't want to support anything that the RSPB proposed'. Other opponents even resorted to a protest demonstration. Two instructors from Glenmore Lodge, together with other instructors in the area, set up a group to just 'seek more information' which they felt was being hidden from them by the Chairlift Company. At one point they even held a protest at the ski area. Similar activities were advocated by some outside the area. A boycott of Aviemore was called for in the pages of a mountaineering 'hillzine', *The Angry Corrie*.

> Let's look at this thing and attack the opposition where it is going to cause them the most damage. We can hurt them now, but their unwanted white elephant isn't going to make them any money for another two years. By then the local economy could be in ruins. So, boycott everything and everyone that has anything to do with supporting or building the funicular. The Aviemore Chamber of Commerce is behind the thing, so don't buy anything from Aviemore.
>
> *Jimmy the Gael*
> *War on HIE (Highlands and Islands Enterprise)*
> *(Jan–Feb 2000)*

Though not officially, Mountaineering Scotland made it clear that they supported initiatives that showed the potential power of the mountaineering pound, something they felt in general was being ignored by the local tourist industry.

Opponents used a number of strategies in their struggle including state and international institutions, for example the law, the courts, politicians, the mass media, as well as expert knowledge and rational argument. However, it was not enough. The local livelihood strategy, relying on local political institutions and their own economic power, proved very effective. The business establishment was a central supporter of the funicular proposal. A number of local Highland developers, such as Morrison's construction, stood to gain from a funicular contract. A key member of the Highlands and Islands Enterprise, the body that approved the funicular, later left to join Morrison's construction. Support for the funicular was channelled through the various chambers of commerce. This strategy corresponded to the general government policy at the time, which was to include more business interests in the governance of the Highlands (MacKinnon: 2001). The argument was that the funicular would mean increased investment and therefore more business – and that what is good for business is good for everyone. These chambers of commerce were supported by local landowners. John and Philippa Grant, owners of Rothiemurchus, were key players in the local business associations. People told me that the Aviemore Chamber of Commerce was dominated by Rothiemurchus and the Chairlift Company. Certain individuals were able to use their economic influence, setting themselves up through the local business associations as representatives of the local community in general.

However, it is their use of the discourse of local versus outsider that proved to be one of the single most powerful weapons at the disposal of funicular supporters. I showed how this discourse came into play on a small scale in Chapter Five. In the funicular debate, it played a pivotal role in determining the outcome. By associating opponents of the funicular with outside interests, supporters effectively discredited their arguments. Many of the people who spoke out publicly against the funicular were vilified. A local councillor told a Glenmore Lodge instructor that he did not have the 'right to speak' on the issue as he was an incomer. A ranger told me that he was against the funicular but did not dare 'put his head above the parapet', a phrase also used by many including a business owner who told me that she had been against the funicular but didn't want anyone to know. One man told me of the 'Aviemore Mafia' – certain local developers and landowners who 'run everything'; he said 'they make it impossible to speak out, especially if you are English'. Bill Wright, when taking up his post as head of the Cairngorms Campaign, decided to live in Perthshire rather than Badenoch and Strathspey out of fear for 'harassment' of his family. Mike Dales backed these findings in a later interview. I asked him why the anti-funicular group had not made more of an effort to win the arguments amongst the locals themselves. He replied that:

> We did not get the active, vocal support of local people because of the Highland/Inverness Mafia. One councillor told me that they had been put under pressure by Strathspey councillors to vote for the funicular development or else they wouldn't ever support development in his area. The same in Aviemore. The Highland and Islands Enterprise and allies put pressure on people within the Chamber of Commerce not to dissent or they will be made to feel anti-business, anti-local. They whip up anti-conservationist, anti-birds, anti-Central Belt, anti-English feeling amongst locals when there is no need.

Despite the considerable economic and political power of the opponents, as well as their well-researched arguments, they lost the battle. Their voice had been made to seem illegitimate. Local opponents of the funicular were labelled incomers and therefore associated with outside interests. Even the ability to be articulate was questioned as the local livelihood interests accused them of being 'know-it-alls', thinking they were above the locals. The legacy of this conflict was felt in the debates about the National Park as the two sides prepared to do battle again, this time with the local livelihood group fresh from victory and the recreation and conservationists on the defensive, having to rethink their strategy.

National Park

The National Park debate, taking place in the aftermath of the funicular conflict, reflects similar divisions and discourses. The key differentiating issue became whether or not planning powers should remain with the Highland Council or be transferred to the new Park Board. Supporters of the status quo worried that the Park Board would stifle economic development whereas others argued that the council would not adequately protect the natural heritage. The basic disagreement concerned the purpose of the Park: promoting local social and economic development, protecting the natural environment or facilitating quiet outdoor recreation. All three aims are contained in the remit of the Park, thus creating fertile ground for conflict.

Towards the beginning of 2000, the build-up to the Cairngorms becoming Scotland's second National Park began. In October 2003, the Park was officially opened. During the consultation process, different interest groups busily manoeuvred for influence. I attended a number of meetings, in addition to conducting interviews and documenting how different groups, broadly similar to those around the funicular debate, sought to make their priorities the priorities of the National Park. Though there are many similarities with the funicular conflict, the National Park debate did not reach the same level of antagonism. This is partly because the areas for disagreement were less clear-cut and because of the way the consultation process was managed by the Cairngorms Partnership. This organisation was initially set up by the Conservatives as an alternative to a National Park. Following devolution, its brief became to pave the way for the Cairngorms to become a National Park. Many different stakeholder groups were formed, including business, landowners, farmers, local community and recreation, based on the idea that these stakeholders would represent different interests in the area and thus ensure that all views were taken into consideration. The consultation process was therefore largely orchestrated by this body with the aim of avoiding the acrimony of the funicular.

I initially had difficulty finding any signs of the public consultation. Neither the Cairngorms Partnership nor the local paper advertised any meetings. I finally tracked down a meeting through word of mouth – the Newtonmore Business Association. This meeting reveals the various discourses and alliances that formed in course of the build-up to the National Park. The meeting was opened by the Vice President of the newly formed Cairngorms Chamber of Commerce. This turned out to be, surprisingly, Sally, the English owner of Speyside Wildlife (see Chapter Three). The new Chamber of Commerce was supposed to represent businesses in the entire area, rather than having different villages all give their views separately. She was accompanied by another member of the Chamber of Commerce, an employee of Rothiemurchus. Sally's role in this meeting was indicative of certain changes that have emerged post-funicular. Her husband was a passionate birder. Her presence at this meeting, with the representative of a prominent landowner, suggested that green tourism was beginning to challenge the predominance of the traditional tourist business interests.

The meeting opened with a presentation by Stewart Fulton of the Cairngorm Partnership. Stewart was a civil service appointee. As a representative of the Scottish government, the tone of his presentation was surprising. He was very critical of the legislation. He stressed that the bill would 'exclude Community Councils' and that 'only 50 per cent of the board would be regional councillors'. 'Local people may not be a majority on the Park Board.' He also said, 'another worrying feature would be that in any conflict, nature conservation would take precedence over other interests, even in the development zone'.

Such an introduction provoked strong reactions in his audience. Some questioned why there should be a National Park at all, asking, 'what is in it for us?' One person said it was just 'jobs for civil servants'. Another said it was the 'price to be paid' to attract business, but someone else said that control over 'their ability to develop jobs, homes, businesses, careers would run rampant' in the hands of the Park Board. Several expressed great concern that the park would not be 'community-led' and that most of the people on the board could be 'conservationists from outwith the area'. References were made to National Parks south of the border where 'communities felt they had no control'. 'We don't want another quango'. One of the most impassioned interventions was made by the owner of Waltzing Waters, a popular attraction for coach parties. He said 'we don't want all those conservationists parachuting in from down south and telling us what to do'. Stewart Fulton, himself a civil servant representing one of these hated quangos, was then asked advice about what the association could do. He compared the situation to the funicular. 'Local business wanted it but many national bodies were opposed. But local people were vociferous and it succeeded'. Someone said that all people dependent on tourism in the valley were in favour of the funicular but with the National Park 'we don't know what we are fighting for'. He told them to campaign for representation on the Park Board. This was to be the main aim – to keep outsiders, especially conservationists, from having too much power. In this exchange, the arguments resembled those of the funicular supporters. However, the fact that Sally and Stewart were now included in this locals group was a significant change. Both seemed to be arguing the case of the local community against outside conservation and recreation interests.

The meeting then went on to discuss the new Wildcat Centre for walkers and the Woodlands Trust. The speaker was an incomer to the area and had not contributed to the debate on the National Park. Given the projects he was discussing, he might fit into the category of incomer who is allied with recreation and conservation interests. He couched his argument in terms of the economic value of these two projects to the local community. Also present at the meeting was Dick Balharry. I knew that he did not agree with the sentiments expressed but he too did not contribute to the debate. The fact that these two people, both very active in the community, did not give dissenting views at this meeting suggests that the local-versus-incomer discourse was still very powerful.

This meeting turned out to be one of the only public meetings held at this stage of the consultation. The main representation to the Scottish Executive was then made through the Cairngorms Chamber of Commerce. The fact that the business community had become the main forum for the local community to express its views was resented by Dick and others I knew in the John Muir Trust and BSCG. The domination of the business interest became increasingly apparent as the different phases of the consultation progressed. What was new, however, was that the composition of this business interest was changing.

One of the main areas to be affected by Park status is Glenmore, the main route of access into the core area of the Park. The Rothiemurchus and Glenmore Community Association was set up in order to ensure that an organised voice was heard. I attended the inaugural meeting, which aimed to establish the organisational structure. A debate took place around the relative positions of residents and business. Someone pointed out that people might have a business in the area but not live here, arguing for businesses to be included. A resident then complained that it is the residents, not businesses that are not represented. This opinion was echoed several days later by a resident who said that he hadn't even been informed of the meeting. He said last year there were bigger meetings but now it seems 'they are doing things without consulting people, or consulting only some people'. He said that 'they (the business community) has it all sewn up'.

John and Philippa Grant of Rothiemurchus were signifi- cantly present. John Grant made his views clearly known. 'There is a job to do that has never been done before, actually repre- sent people who live and work in the area, untainted by those from the outside'. I asked one resident what she thought and she said this was his way of saying that he did not want any of the conservation organisations having any say in what went on. Another resident later told me that John Grant is used to 'getting his way' in the area. Rothiemurchus is a major estate, and Grant was worried that he would not be able to develop his estate as he wants if the National Park Board had planning powers. He currently has several plans in the pipeline for major housing developments on his land. According to one Rothiemurchus resident whose mother had almost been evicted by Grant, 'He says he is all in favour of keeping locals in the area but then he sells his houses at prices that are only affordable to incomers'. Another resident told me that the issue of these housing developments is the main issue for residents who are worried about increased traffic and the change in character of the area. This was not raised at all at the meeting. She said she had 'not dared raise it'. At this meeting, Grant portrays himself not as a powerful landowner who employs many of the people in the room or owns the houses in which they live, but as just another local that wants to keep these outside organisations from interfering in their lives and work. His comment is a thinly veiled reference to the funicular debate in which outsiders were accused of wanting to 'stop people making a living'. A management committee was elected and will be the main locus of power. Two of the committee members are Rothiemurchus employees. A resident told me afterwards that it looked like the committee would be 'dominated by Rothiemurchus'. He was hoping for more of a residents' committee.

The Highland Council meeting on 2 March 2000 had a special item on the agenda so as to discuss the National Park Bill. Similar concerns were expressed by the councillors as in the local meetings about the lack of local representation. Most comments supported the proposal for '50 per cent, plus one', for local representation on the Park Board. One of the Strathspey councillors said this was the feeling in all the meetings he attended. Using the now very common discourse I had been hearing, he queried where the government appointees on the board would come from: 'Would they be parachuted in from the south of England?' Another councillor went even further, arguing against the whole concept of a National Park – 'too much bureaucracy, central government should be excluded', he said. Instead, he would like to have people who live and work in the area run things, and 'stop the Highlands becoming the recreational area for our cousins in the Central Belt'. I talked to another councillor afterwards and he reiterated some of the points that came out in the meeting. He is worried that turning the Highlands into a National Park would make it difficult for Highlanders to 'pursue their local development goals'. He doesn't want the Highlands to become 'a playground for outsiders, heedless of the needs of the local community who live and work there'. Basil Dunlop, however, a Strathspey councillor, was not so scathing about outsiders. He recognised that it is the 'natural beauty of the Cairngorms that drives the economy'. But he continued to argue that the local community was quite capable of 'safeguarding', as well as making the most of that 'economic asset'. It seemed that the Highland Council was unanimous in its views. However, I couldn't know for sure whether all of its members were in agreement with the general views expressed publicly or whether they felt pressured to identify with Highland development.

The local livelihood side of the debate had the power of the local state and business interests. They had also managed to make their views hegemonic – the idea of the Highlands being dominated by outside interests was very unpopular, especially given its history. The fight to control the National Parks was presented as yet another example of Highlanders having to struggle against the oppression of southerners. This side of the debate also had the power of organisation. The Cairngorm Chamber of Commerce put together a detailed document stating their views as part of the consultation. The Highland Council had their usual lobbying connections with central government.

Later in this stage of the consultation, the recreation and conservation interests became more prominent in the discussions.

Outside organisations continued to argue for a National Park that had planning powers. Mountaineering Scotland, the RSPB and the WWF put the power of their institutions to work in the same way as they had in the funicular debate. In fact, the funicular was used as an example to show why the local communities should not have planning powers – 'they cannot be trusted'. One member of the local conservation group said that 'people like those in Newtonmore could not see past their own noses to the wider issues'. Bill Wright from the Cairngorms Campaign, criticised the Scottish Executive's inclusion of sustainable development in the context of the National Park, writing in *Climber*:

> Witness past and recent so-called 'sustainable developments' that planning authorities and environment agencies have allowed across the Scottish Highlands. Bull-dozed roads that scrape, scratch, and scar; deer, sheep and forest management practices that have spread across the surface of mountains like cancer across skin; out of place tourist developments like tumours (that is, the funicular); and starving footpath maintenance work. (April, 2000: 96).

However, this time local recreation and conservation interests decided that they could not rely on winning from outside, using the power of the state. Several people told me that they were not going to make the 'mistakes' of the anti-funicular campaign. Their cause was helped to a certain extent by the existence of the Cairngorm Partnership, which encouraged the involvement of stakeholders. Recreation interests had already been organised into the Recreation Forum. The loose association of self-identified conservationists in the local area decided that if they were to have any influence, they also needed to have such a group. They asked Stewart Fulton, the Cairngorm Partnership representative who had so effectively stirred up anti-conservationist sentiment at the Newtonmore Business Association meeting, to organise a meeting of the conservation interests at the Cairngorm

Partnership offices. I attended this meeting as well as the meeting of the Recreation Forum held to debate the National Park. Both meetings give insights into how each group mobilised power for their cause.

Meeting of conservation group

This meeting was attended by Dick Balharry, Alan and George, members of the John Muir Trust group and the Strathspey Mountain Club, the Badenoch and Strathspey Conservation Group, some hoteliers who advertise as part of green tourism, an owner of a cycle business and Bill Wright from the Cairngorms Campaign. Stewart Fulton opened the meeting by giving a less partisan presentation of the background to the National Park debate than he had at the Newtonmore meeting. He told them how many others in the community feel, that they are worried about being controlled by outsiders. He said Sarah Boyack herself, the minister in charge, was also concerned to make sure that the National Park would be 'inclusive'. He reminded the group of the problems over the funicular and how the community had been polarised. He stressed that 'everyone needs to go forward together' and work through the community councils.

Stewart's position was challenged. The point of disagreement revolves around what the priorities of the Park should be. Dick raised a criticism of the Cairngorm Partnership (CP). He argued that the CP work was originally more environmental but 'I get the idea that now the economic and social is driving the whole thing, perhaps because of the funicular'. Two others raised the question of how representative community councils are. Roy has lived in Nethy Bridge for twenty-eight years and there has never been an election. Laura, the organiser of a recycling network, agreed and said that people don't come forward with their views because 'they are afraid of putting their head above the parapet' (this was a very common phrase used by many locals in my research). She resented the fact that the 'business interests are seen as more important than any other views'. She pointed out that only a small proportion of the community was in the chambers of commerce. The general feeling was that certain interests have more power to have their voice heard by the Cairngorm Partnership, SNH and the government. They felt that the funicular conflict had made people wary of challenging the local development discourse. It is interesting to note how their perspective of who has power is very different from those who fear the interference of powerful outside conservation interests. Roy brought up the issue of who should decide what the aims of the Park should be. He said that the point of having a National Park is that 'it is there for the nation' whose priorities are 'nature conservation and landscape enhancement'. He said 'Benefits to the local community will come from this. The national interest should prevail'. Stewart replied that this argument would be 'unpopular' and advised thinking of other arguments.

The rest of the meeting focussed on developing a strategy. They were well aware that it is the local-livelihood-versus-outsider discourse that they needed to challenge if their views are to be heard. Stewart Fulton suggested that they needed to address the concerns of people about whether business would 'flourish' in a National Park context. This idea was taken up by the owner of a cycle hire business. He said that 'recreation brings in invisible earnings – people are not aware of how much'. Bill Wright said that there is a need to commission some work on the benefits of recreation to the economy, saying: 'The fundamental issue is about the values expressed by John Muir. But the debate has lost sight of this. People may not be interested in snow bunting, lichen or moss but they do talk about transport – something made possible to finance because of those who come here for recreation'. Roy agreed: 'There is the value of recreation to B-and-Bs and then the value to people nationally – to people in the urban areas, it keeps them sane. So there are two values – people from outwith the area who need wild areas and people from the communities who manage to hang on because of the people who come here'.

The meeting contributed to the creation of an alternative narrative, stressing the value of the natural heritage as the basis of local livelihood. The message was to be 'Environmental protection and nature conservation are good for business'. The cycle business owner said he had joined the Cairngorms Chamber of Commerce, which he said does not generally represent 'people like us even though we are in business', to ensure that this alternative discourse was heard. At the moment it is dominated by 'Aviemore interests that push development, development'. Roy was encouraged to get involved in the Community Council. One member summarised the final outcome of the meeting for me the next day.

> We agreed to have a meeting, first with the conservation groups and then with the landowners, community councils and business groups. There will be a few arguments, even violent ones, but there could be some common ground so that Stewart Fulton could take something through to the National Park consultation. Environmentalists need to have their voice heard and they haven't really done this before. I am joining the Chamber of Commerce to do this. There are a lot of people – businesses – who bring money into the area but they are invisible. These people need to be heard because they are bringing in the conservation or environmental tourists. It is businesses like Sally's (Vice Chair of Chamber of Commerce – Speyside Wildlife) that are the way forward. These aspects of the community need to be heard. The landowners are a problem. In Norway things are more community-run, but here the landowners are out to get things for themselves. Johnny Grant is like this – how can he get the most money for himself. A lot of the business community is like that as well. They just think of their own profits.

This meeting illustrates the process by which those with a conservation sense of place were beginning to form themselves more coherently into an organised interest group at the local level. Instead of relying on outside institutions and structures, they managed to become identified to some extent as stakeholders. They were able to do this because of wider structural changes. As the head of the local tourist board said in an interview: 'we never used to have these groups before'. But, as one business owner says, 'green tourism is becoming important economically'. More local businesses rely on walkers, climbers and mountain bikers than skiers. This is also the result of changing leisure and consumption patterns. The ski industry has been severely affected by the growth in skiing holidays abroad, as well as by global warming. A key person in the development agency for Aviemore told me that despite popular conceptions, the area could easily 'survive the demise of the ski industry', but it is no longer important. It would be green tourism that would be the basis of any regeneration. These economic changes meant that local conservationists and recreationists, who had been afraid to speak out before, were now feeling more confident. And many of these people have considerable cultural capital to draw upon. They are, for the most part, university-educated, articulate and astute. Dick has national connections, together with a reputation for being extremely knowledgeable. And he could not be accused of being an outsider because he was Scottish and gained his experience by training as a stalker and gamekeeper. He lived in the area for many years. Sally from Speyside Wildlife has shown what can be done by using the dominant discourses of local livelihood and by daring to enter the domain of the anti-outsiders. She has been amazingly successful considering that she is English and owns a company that depends on conservation tourists. She and her husband were able to set up in business because of the large differential in house prices – another example of how the wider economic structure affects the way power operates in a local conflict. But her hard-working and competent approach, plus the fact that she stressed what she has in common with the others – a need to have a successful business – was so effective

214

that she was appointed to be on the new National Park Board. The result of the National Park debate was the creation of a rival power group to the power of the ski industry, coach-party tourism and development interests. Recent research found that this group is now referred to as the Green Mafia (Kathy Rettie: unpublished thesis), an obvious reference to the rival power of the Aviemore Mafia.

Meeting of the recreation forum

The meeting was attended by some people from the local area whom I had already met, including Nigel from Glenmore Lodge, a canoeist from Lagganlia and Dick (now with his Ramblers hat on). Others were representatives of national organisations: Alan Blackshaw, noted mountaineer and expert on land law and access issues; Colin, a representative from the British Association of Shooting and Conservation and Bill Wright (representing in this case Mountaineering Scotland). Peter Ord, a factor at Balmoral Estate, came as the representative of the national organisation Ski Scotland. A representative of the Hang-gliding Association was also present.

It was at this meeting that the differences between the recreation and conservation interests became more explicit. In the funicular debate, they had been allies, but in the National Park discussions cracks in the alliance began to appear. Within this forum, people who had been at loggerheads over other issues (walkers versus shooting, skiing versus mountaineering), joined together to make a common cause. This time it was Murray Ferguson of Scottish Natural Heritage who presented to the group. The conservation group thought that SNH favoured economic development whereas this group accused the SNH of putting too much stress on conservation of the natural heritage and ignoring the recreation interest. The SNH uses the phrase 'enjoying and understanding' in its their policy documents. The group took issue with this wording. Nigel pointed out that this is not what recreation is about. He says the purpose of recreation is 'to recreate' yourself and this 'implies engagement with the hills'. The representative of the Hang-gliding Association agreed. He repeatedly used the term 'antiseptic' to refer to the SNH and general conservation approach – that the hills are something to be 'gazed at from the outside' and not used.

The outcome of the meeting was that, like the conservation group, they planned to lobby politicians to make sure that recreation was included as the one of the main aims of the Park. Even though they seemed to see themselves as distinct from the conservation group, they shared two members and also stressed the importance of showing how central the outdoor industry was to the local economy. However, within this group the focus was not so much on how they could win the argument with the local community as with how they could use their power to influence events on a national level.

*

The conflict between the local livelihood and conservation/ recreation shows how groups are formed not only into interest groups, as in the last chapter, but into sides that mask the variety of views and positions within them. People become pigeonholed as either local livelihood or outside conservation/recreation. Once formed, the discourse of local versus outsider reinforces the divisions and even locals are divided between those who belong and incomers who don't. Boundaries have been created, partly as a result of lived experience (Barth. 2000) and sense of place, causing people to have particular values, but also because of the way in which the conflict itself unfolded. Once people have acquired an identity in these conflict situations, they 'invest huge values' (Cohen: 2000: 5) in the resulting boundaries that come in between these identities. The stakeholder model reinforces this tendency for people to identify themselves in a certain way. It is this model that was used by the Cairngorm Partnership (CP),

Looking for hazelglove with Ross

Andrew looking for dotterel

Cairngorms from Loch Morlich
Photo by Dorothy Carse

Bringing the stag into the larder

Peter presents the
Donald award

Out with Alastair on Kinveachy

Heather burning

Keepers' day

Billy training his dog

Skiing
Photo by Dorothy Carse

Above: Mary Yule

Left: Robert Waterson

Learning to paddle

Peaceful fishing on the Spey

Lionel giving some instruction to his guests

Above: Looking at deer fences with
Dick Balharry

Left: Cairngorm and the funicular

Aviemore from Craigellachie nature reserve
Photo by Dorothy Carse

Petal Power Mountain Biking Group
Photo by Dorothy Carse

Strathspey Mountain Club in 2020

which had been instrumental in shaping how the debates were conducted. In an interview with an employee of the CP, I was told that their remit was to 'facilitate communication between interest groups'. In their literature, 'stakeholder' is the common way to refer to these interest groups. This model can only operate when clear-cut interest groups are established that are defined by having distinct aims from other stakeholders. The mere identification of the groups serves to reinforce their identity and views. This was seen in the way the people, whilst meeting under the banner of Recreation Forum, seemed to distance themselves from the conservation group even though two of them were members of both.

The model then works on the idea that there will be some attempt to compromise on the entrenched positions. However, there are other levels of power that have been hidden. Who decides who the stakeholders are? There are of course many different groups in society with different senses of place. But to move from having a sense of place to being part of an interest group, which is then recognised as a stakeholder, is not straightforward. Not only are certain interest groups chosen above others, some are taken more seriously than others. In September 2004, I asked Alan Blackshaw, the former Chairman of the Recreation Forum, about his feelings regarding the first year of the Park. He was very angry that after all the build-up and the lengthy consultation process there was no one from outdoor recreation on the Park Board. The local conservation interest had only been belatedly recognised as a stakeholder in the local area, but through their newfound identity as part of the business community and income-generator, they increased their power to the point that they could be considered a stakeholder to some extent. At first the conservation group did not count but because of a conscious strategy and efforts to organise themselves, they now had more influence. This could be seen in the increase in the number of articles in the local paper about things like the RSPB ospreys and local initiatives, and the Recycling and Composting

Network. The paper regularly quoted the local conservation group as well as just printing letters.

Though the conservation and recreation interests felt themselves marginalised, others were excluded altogether from decision-making. One person told me that the Cairngorm Partnership is 'consulting the people that count'. This view was reinforced by an interview with a CP employee. He said that in the next consultation period SNH 'only plan on consulting key interest groups'. He said he was concerned about the groups that are excluded: 'young people and women with children at home'. The stakeholder model confers varying degrees of power on certain groups and, within those groups, on certain people who are selected as being representative. In the Cairngorms, new clusters have influence as a result of the role they played in the National Park debate. All had some link to the Cairngorm Partnership.

Another problem with the stakeholder model is that it may resolve conflicts, but in many ways it actually causes the conflicts to begin with and ensures that conflicts unfold in a predictable manner. As Roy Dennis said in Chapter Five – the conflict is not about the beaver but about who has the power to decide. This was confirmed by the CP employee: 'The funicular debate got very entrenched – it was difficult for there to be any communication. But in fact, both the pros and the antis had a variety of positions. The conflict was more about – it's my right to make this decision!'

Meanwhile the conflicts continue to take place, over different but nevertheless similar issues. Since the setting up of the National Park, major debates have emerged around the building of housing estates. One side argues that there is a need for housing for local people and that the conservationists put 'butterflies and trees' before people. The local conservation group argues that the new developments are not suitable within a National Park. They are then accused of being anti-development incomers. The sides are still the same and most people continue to be excluded. Letters

in the local paper continue to be abusive towards conservationists and incomers. Local conservationists continue to portray
the locals as ignorant of the obvious facts. Groups continue to
police their own boundaries and cling to certain discourses of
truth, fighting to assert their interests over others within the
framework established for consultations. Other options need
to be considered. If the veil is lifted on these power games then
the identity of people may become less rigid and fixed interest
groups may disappear. And where they do exist, the boundaries
will be less distinct and the respective aims less clear such that a
fresh eye may be cast on the whole situation. Conflicts will inevitably occur, but they may then take place in a more creative and
productive framework, rather than unfolding as a battle between
two entrenched, polarised sides. The next chapter will examine
what possibilities exist for creating these spaces.

CHAPTER SEVEN

Travelling Between Places and Finding Common Ground

The conflicts between various groups show the depth of feeling people have for both place and their activities in that place. Those who fish, paddle, climb, help to restore the forest, ski, watch birds or work in a hotel all have strong views on how to make the area better. At a public level, with different interest groups mobilising power in order to advance their perspective over others, the situation can become fraught and divisive. As I had spent time with people with a range of views, getting to know them on the ground rather than just in the public domain, the situation was disturbing and I hoped that I would find signs of people coming together. This would require leaving the public arena and moving behind the scenes, back to individual and private conversations with people in the course of their activities.

I believe one of the causes of the amplification of conflict is the stakeholder model of decision-making. It helps to create and reinforce any tendency for distinct positions and sides to develop. In this model, different social groups, who have been identified with specific material and ideological interests, are assumed to have particular positions on land use that set them apart from other stakeholders. The Cairngorm Partnership used this model for consultation and had different forums for different stakeholders, for example farmers and recreation. Different groups use specific discourses and representations of land, and people's relation to it, to argue their case. One of the key features of this power struggle is the local-versus-outsider/incomer discourse in which people's position on issues such as the funicular or the National Park is linked to their relationship to place. Many of the views discussed in the preceding two chapters were expressed either in the public arena, in letters, in interviews, or in circumstances which counterpoised two positions. In other words, certain circumstances encourage people to create boundaries between themselves and others (Barth: 2000). Recognising that these boundaries and identities, 'are contingent on the circumstances and relative positions of significant others' (Cohen: 2000: 3), this chapter will return to the individual and the private in order to explore circumstances in which these boundaries are either blurred or non-existent. Societies can be seen as collections of social groups or communities. However, these communities and interest groups are not homogeneous. Though at times they may act as one or be represented as a unit, they do so only in certain contexts (Amit and Rapport: 2002). I have shown how the context of public conflict brings out this tendency to form clearly defined communities of interest; in this chapter I show how my research has unearthed other layers of these conflicts. By examining the data gathered more informally, in the context of doing activities, interviewing people on unrelated matters or in casual conversation, the boundaries between positions are less clear. As my fieldwork progressed and I became more immersed in the area and got to know more people in many different contexts, the complexity of views was increasingly revealed. From this anthropological vantage point, the cards are reshuffled and people are no longer 'holding the same hand'.

Complexity is revealed in a variety of ways. Firstly, what may appear to be a dominant viewpoint is interpreted by people in different ways. People may hold particular positions but these may change or be modified in different situations. This is illustrated by the following extract from my field notes describing an incident from the Newtonmore Business Association meeting discussed in the previous chapter.

A man from a local tourist attraction had launched into a torrent of abuse against those who would be 'parachuted in from the south to dominate the Park Board'. The main enemies were conservationists from organisations like the RSPB and the WWF. Many others had similar comments but he was the most vehement. I was sitting next to him and when the meeting was over, I took the opportunity of asking for clarification on his views. We chatted awhile and then he pointed out someone well known for his interest in conservation and opposition to the funicular. He spoke favourably about him, saying how much he had done for the area. I pointed out what I saw was a contradiction in his views. I thought you didn't like conservationists. He had a ready explanation: this man was OK, as was the RSPB Warden at Insh Marshes. They were different. They cared about the local community.

In the above case, although the man appeared to be reinforcing the local-livelihood-versus-outside-conservation conflict in the context of the public meeting, when speaking privately and informally he wasn't really anti-conservationist or anti-incomer. His position was in fact much more nuanced. The issue for him was the person's relationship and commitment to the community. The question is why in certain circumstances, and not others, people choose to express only one aspect of their views.

Secondly, the dominant discourse is not as widely shared as appears in the public domain. In opposition to the 'centralising force', in which people seem to merge together around one dominant view, there is also the process of heteroglossia. This is a concept developed by Bakhtin (1981) to describe the process in which a monolithic position fragments into multiple views of the world. The following extract from my research diary is based on a conversation I had with a man who was cleaning up the village hall after a Community Council meeting, which he himself had not attended.

He is third generation Aviemore. His grandfather was a timber man, his father worked for a hotel and now he works for the railway. He did work for the Chairlift Company. He thinks the ski area is badly run and is totally opposed to the funicular. He says a lot of people who work for the Chairlift Company are against it. 'It is a real disaster.' He said Aviemore was 'brilliant' when he was a kid. A lot of times they made their own entertainment but there were also swimming clubs at the pool and he played ice hockey. Now these things are gone. 'Developers are just interested in making money. They build stuff and don't maintain it. They are just greedy. Local people have become lethargic and apathetic.' He berates them for not getting involved, not wanting to do anything, but at the same time he understands because 'their voice has not been listened to for so long that they have given up.' But he still loves it here and would not want to live anywhere else. 'I went down to London and couldn't orientate myself, there were no hills, no natural points of reference. It was difficult to tell which way the sun was going.'

It is only certain voices that are heard in public – the voices of those with the power to make themselves heard. But there are many more voices, as Bakhtin explains in his analysis of Dostoevsky:

> He heard both the loud, recognised, reigning voices of the epoch, that is the reigning dominant ideas (official and unofficial), as well as voices still weak, ideas not yet fully emerged, latent ideas heard as yet by no one but himself, and ideas which were just beginning to ripen, embryos of future world views (Bakhtin: 1984: p. 100)

It is the task of the anthropologist to make these other voices and ideas as widely heard as the 'reigning ideas.' The man quoted above does not accept the reigning ideas. His local credentials are impeccable, yet he does not support the funicular and is suspicious of those advocating development. He also appreciates the natural beauty of the area. His is a voice that was not heard in the public discussions.

Thirdly, there are a number of people who appear as anomalies, people who don't seem to fit with the stakeholder model. They are involved in a number of activities that mean they do not just occupy one place but several. They exist in a 'creative border zone' (Morris: 1994, Mageo: 2002), where new senses of place are being created. Ross, the trainee warden at RSPB Insh Marshes, and the son of a farm manager on Jamie Williamson's Alvie Estate is an example of such an anomaly. He explained to me the problems this creates:

> When I drive the RSPB Land Rover around the area I feel hostility from some members of the community. The work I do for the RSPB is similar to what they do on the sporting estate but many don't see it.

The existence of alternative voices opens up the possibility for new, creative ways of approaching conflicts over land use. The key is to somehow free people from the dominant discourse that sees every conflict in terms of local livelihood against outside conservation/recreation. According to Bakhtin (1981) this will happen when 'a variety of alien voices enter into the struggle for influence with an individual's consciousness (just as they struggle with one another in surrounding social reality)' (p. 70). Once people are aware of the relativistic nature of particular positions, it opens them up to new ways of perceiving. In other words, people have to become aware of other viewpoints – viewpoints of people who in many cases are their friends or people they know and respect.

Which circumstances are most likely to give rise to such an awareness? It can only come as a result of actually mixing with a range of people in the context of different activities and environments. As a result of these interactions new meanings can be created. There may be centralising forces at work to reinforce the status quo, but there are also forces at work in every interaction for the possibility of change. However, some interactions are more fertile than others and these are the creative border zones, contexts in which different ideas and experiences meet.

There are a number of individuals in the Cairngorms who evoked these border zones where different places merge. Though it could be argued that everyone has the potential to be part of these zones, certain individuals stand out as being especially conscious of their anomalous position. They are aware that they do not fit neatly to any group but instead carry within their consciousness the ideas and experiences of many different approaches to land use. This makes them more aware of the variety of possible positions and opens them up to creating ways of thinking and acting. Ross is such an example. His experience of many different ideas and activities made him an anomaly, such that he was able to free himself from the dominant discourses and become a creator of new ways of thinking about land, something he is acutely conscious of. 'I know I'm different. I wear many hats. I like hill-walking, was raised on a sporting estate and work for the RSPB'. In addition, the existence of a conflict situation can on one hand lead to the entrenchment of views but, paradoxically, can also provide the context of interaction that could lead to greater awareness of different ideas. Ross told me that he became more aware of the different positions because of the public nature of the debates.

Whether new ideas, meanings and worldviews are created is not just a matter of subjective experience. The historical conditions are also significant in affecting whether someone will be able to come across new ideas and be open to them (Lave and Holland: 2001). In the specific historical context of Badenoch and Strathspey, a number of sociocultural changes had been taking place. The fact that conservation organisations are in a financial situation to buy land, created the conditions for Ross to obtain a training post at Insh Marshes.

Different interpretations of dominant discourses:
I'm not a conservationist, but…

Walley (2004) found in her study of the Marine Park in East Africa that locals did not express a concern for nature as an abstract concept. The label 'conservationist' was reserved for the WWF representatives. However, in the course of their day-to-day lives, she discovered many examples of people appreciating things like wildlife and views. This is similar to what I found in the Cairngorms. John, head keeper at Kinveachy, would regularly denounce conservationists and he himself would be denounced for being anti-conservation. I discussed in previous chapters that those who see land as productive and those who see land as something to be conserved for its own sake, express different values that have the potential to clash. What does this mean in practice? Ross believes that what he did for the RSPB in terms of everyday land management is very similar to the work done on the sporting estate. My time spent on both the RSPB reserve at Insh Marshes and at Kinveachy supported this. When out with John and the others at Kinveachy, there seemed little difference in their knowledge and appreciation of the natural world. What distinguished them were the outward trappings – the Tweeds they wore as a symbol of their belonging to a particular land-owner or the RSPB logo on the Land Rover. On the day I spent heather burning with John, I wrote in my field notes:

He showed me where they had burned the heather yesterday and explained to me what they were trying to achieve. The grouse moor needs to be a patchwork of different stages of heather – old, youngish and new. The old heather provides the cover from predators and the new, young, post-burned bits offer new shoots to eat. He showed me how a variety of plant forms exist – different grasses, mosses, berries and the three types of heather. He said: 'I'm not a botanist so I don't know the name for everything but I know which ones the grouse eat.'

As previously mentioned, John was annoyed when the RSPB warden wrote the article on heather-burning for the official conservation column, further reinforcing for him the boundary between himself and conservationists.

When I was volunteering on Insh Marshes I was surprised at the kind of tasks I was assigned. I spent less time viewing wildlife than on Kinveachy, where I had seen deer and grouse of course, but also birds of prey and capercaillie. At Insh Marshes I chased escaped Highland cattle off the road and back into their field, I spent days building a fence to protect the aspen trees from rabbits, and conducted bird counts in the same way as the estate workers at Kinveachy do grouse and deer counts. At Insh Marshes I also met a trainee gamekeeper who had chosen to do his work experience for the RSPB. He said he noticed little difference in the kind of work undertaken at Insh compared to that in his training on a sporting estate. The only difference was that he said he enjoyed the part of the job that involves shooting 'pests' such as rabbits. Although rabbits are as much a menace on an RSPB reserve as on a sporting estate and Ross and the volunteer John agreed that it was part of their job as land managers, they prefer to enlist the services of a local farmer. Tom, the warden at Insh Marshes, confirmed my impressions. He stressed to me the importance of the grazing animals to the maintenance of the ecological system on the marshes. He said: 'When you actually get involved in working on a reserve you realise that you can't just let nature take its course. You have certain aims and to achieve these aims it needs to be managed.'

The conclusion to be drawn from this is that the difference between livelihood and conservation in this case has been much exaggerated and is more to do with general debates about land ownership, what counts as knowledge and what the overall purpose of the land should be. The dominant discourse, which highlights the differences rather than the similarities between those working on sporting estates and conservation reserves, is not only misleading but creates hostility, further fuelled by assigning them to distinct stakeholder positions.

The image of locals put forwards by some non-residents that they 'don't appreciate what they have' is also an oversimplification. Though very few locals may claim to be conservationists and many are quick to express anti-conservationist views, there is more to this picture. As Bill Wilkie, a retired railway worker and long-time resident of Aviemore, said about locals: 'Though they may not know a lot about conservation issues, they don't like it destroyed. There was a tremendous outcry when trees were cut down in front of the Aviemore Hotel.'

Locals are concerned about livelihood issues but this does not mean they are not sensitive to environmental issues. However, their interest manifests itself in different ways that are not often revealed at the public level. I have already noted that locals are less likely to have been on the high ground such as the Cairngorm plateau. Therefore, their interest in nature is exhibited in low ground issues like the cutting down of trees in the village rather than in concern for moss at 3,000 feet. There is a nature reserve just behind the village of Aviemore. I was told about it many times by locals who said it was a good place to go walking. Whenever I went walking there I encountered locals with families or with their dogs. In the spring, the reserve was a favourite destination for locals for other reasons. I first heard about the breeding frogs from a conversation between a woman working at the supermarket checkout and a local customer. She had seen the frogs and was letting the other woman know that this was the time to go and see them. I was later told about the frogs from a number of other locals including a restaurant owner who had expressed very vehement anti-conservation and pro-funicular views in a previous conversation.

Since leaving the field, there have been a number of campaigns initiated by a cross-section of locals that could be characterised as environmental. These include stopping mobile phone masts, rejecting new housing developments and organising a community buy-out of a local wood to stop it being cut down. Letters to the paper on these issues have come from both the conservation group and locals who had taken up different positions on the funicular and the National Park. This indicates that many people who would be identified by some as locals rather than incomers are not necessarily unappreciative of the natural world or unconcerned about the state of their environment. However, the focus of their concerns lies closer to home. Recently in the local paper, two letters were published supporting Cameron McNeish's (a local resident, President of the Scottish Ramblers Association and well-known for his anti-development views) critique of large-scale wind farms. These letters were written by two people who normally took anti-conservation and anti-McNeish stances. What makes this case different is that, in the opinion of the writers, large-scale wind farms would not only be an eyesore, but they would jeopardise the source of their livelihoods, that is, tourism. Similarly, the campaigns to save the local wood are relevant to everyone, whether they go there to look at moss and lichen or to walk the dog.

Aviemore Centre, not the funicular

Alternative conceptions of the livelihood approach also arose in discussions of the Aviemore Centre, which seemed of greater interest to local people than the funicular. I did not deliberately seek out people who could be identified with a specific position nor did I raise the issue of the funicular. In this way I allowed people to raise issues that were important to them. In many cases, the funicular was not even mentioned as a concern. For example, in the many months I spent with the stalkers and keepers on Kinveachy, and later with farmers, the funicular was not mentioned once. The main issue that was raised again and again was the question of the redevelopment of the Aviemore Centre. The Centre had been left to run down for many years. In the year of my research, apart from some tourist accommodation, everything had been closed including the ice rink,

Santa Claus Land and the cinema. Promises had been made for years about the redevelopment of the centre. There were even people employed to oversee and negotiate this redevelopment. But every time something seemed to be happening, it would fall through. The number of conversations I had and the number of articles in the local paper testify to the importance of this issue to local people. The redevelopment of the Aviemore Centre, more than anything, including the funicular, was seen as the key to the success of the area, not only because it would draw in tourists, but because the locals themselves want better facilities for their families. The closure of the ice rink in particular was resented as it was used by many local children.

Many pro-funicular views were articulated not so much in terms of the funicular itself, but in terms of the impact this investment would have on the Aviemore Centre. For example, one local business owner said that 'now that the funicular issue is settled, investment will be attracted to the redevelopment of the Aviemore Centre'. Other sources confirmed that the main aim is the redevelopment of the centre and the funicular was supported because it would lead to the achievement of the primary goal. These comments led me to believe that if the locals had been given the choice between a £14 million investment in the funicular and the same in the Aviemore Centre, they would have wholeheartedly supported the latter; but they were not given this option. And, if the proposal had been for the redevelopment of the centre, there would have been no opposition. Visitors and the outdoor recreation organisations have consistently argued for more wet weather facilities available for all to use. My research suggests that the general concerns and fears of locals, both long-term residents and incomers, over the decline in tourism and the effects on livelihood, were transformed, in the mouths of those engaged in the public debate, into complete support for the funicular, when in fact, their views should be interpreted very differently. As Roseberry (1994) puts it in the case of Mexican peasants in their relationship to state discourses:

Each case reveals ways in which the state, which never stops talking, has no audience, or rather has a number of audiences who hear different things, and who in repeating what the state says to still other audiences, change the words, tones, inflections and meanings. Hardly, it would seem a common discursive framework (p. 365).

Unfortunately, though large amounts of money were put into the Aviemore Centre, it has not lived up to expectations. Though a cinema was built, several people told me they never use it. Others referred to the 'Berlin Wall' that had been built (now removed) between the Centre and the rest of the village, which had made it seem something separate, for tourists. And the promised swimming pool is a continual source of controversy. It is frequently closed as MacDonald Hotels renegotiates the fee they get for opening it to local residents. According to one source, the council is being 'held to ransom'.

The other part of the discourse – the anti-incomer and anti-outsider sentiments, are equally problematic and do not represent a common way of framing the issues or the complexity of local feelings. I did come across many anti-southern (south of the Highland border) and anti-incomer sentiments. However, as the quote at the beginning of this chapter indicates, these views are considerably modified in practice, outside the public arena. It is not that people resent conservationists or incomers as such. There is more of a concern as to the way in which they relate to the community. As the man quoted above from the Newtonmore Business Association meeting says 'they're alright, they care about the community'. One local resident differentiated between two kinds of incomer. The first is 'happy to integrate into the community' whereas the second 'would only be here five minutes and find things not good enough and want to change things'. Tom, the English warden of Insh Marshes confirmed this. He said that he has had much more success in relating to locals because he made a point of trying to integrate his work on Insh Marshes with the community. He initiated a special project in local schools in which pupils built boxes for the rare golden-eye bird to nest in. He worked closely with local farmers on the birds and grain project, which gives financial encouragement to farmers to plant more grain, considered to be good for birds. The farmer Alistair MacLennan has worked closely with Tom and, though a slightly atypical farmer (see Chapter Three), told me: 'I couldn't believe how well we got on. He came over for dinner – a conservationist and a vegetarian! But we got on great. I have a lot of respect for him'. One person commented that Tom has had considerably more success in being accepted by the local community than the wardens at Abernethy Reserve because they tend to 'cut themselves off from the community and only focus on the reserve itself'. They thus have gained a reputation for being 'aloof'. I heard similar views expressed from a wide variety of people. This reputation came as a shock to one Abernethy warden, when I informed him of what many people had said to me about his reserve. He had not experienced this resentment in his own life. His children went to the local school and his wife was a teacher. So even within conservation circles public reputations are not always realised in practice. As noted by researchers into the English experience in Scotland: 'There was thus often a tension and interplay between the English-in-general – and the English-as-individuals (McIntosh, I., Sim, D., and Robertson, D.: 2004: 49–50)'.

This is equally true for conservationists-in-general and conservationists-in-particular. In day-to-day life, it is not the origin of the person or their occupation, but their perceived commitment to the local community that matters. This point was reinforced for me by the main proponent of the preservation of the local Gaelic heritage, Johnny Campbell. He had moved up to the area from Lanarkshire but was quick to point out that he was a 'native' by origin. Being a native carries even more weight with some people than being a local. It is difficult to give an exact definition of being a local. It is not strictly related to the length of time one has lived in the area. The category can be applied to different people at different times, depending on the context (Edwards: 1998). For example, Sally of Speyside Wildlife had not only not been in the area long, but was also English. Yet, she was allowed to prepare the response to the National Park consultation because she had the 'right' views. But for Johnny, the status of native cannot be acquired; you have to be born to it, preferably over many generations. Though he had been born elsewhere, his grandmother had lived her whole life on a local estate and Johnny had spent many summers with her. It was from her that he learned Gaelic and got his passionate interest in Gaelic history and culture. He is very much part of what others have identified as a 'Gaelic renaissance' (see McCrone: 1992 and Macdonald: 1997), in which people are consciously rediscovering their identity. Johnny's views on whole range of issues are expressed in terms of the common Highlanders' oppression by outsiders – whether Lowland Scots or the English. I had many discussions with him about what is wrong with the English and how Highlanders are different. He said that Highlanders are reluctant to put themselves forward on committees and public consultations. This means that it is often incomers who get involved in the public arena. His views are confirmed by the letters in the local paper and membership of various community and business associations. One woman told me that she had to act as mediator in her local church because of the problems created by what was perceived to be an 'incomers' takeover' of the church. Someone else, though of Scottish origin herself, said that it was mainly the incomers who had the 'drive and ideas to participate in community affairs'.

However, it soon transpired that it is not the English themselves whom Johnny is against, nor does he support all Highlanders without reservation. He hates the local landowners for their domination of the area even though some of them have 'pure' Highland backgrounds. And he has many English friends.

This last fact became apparent on a day I spent with Johnny. I had originally met him when I was working as a waitress in the café. He came in regularly for the £1.99 breakfast special. He had long been berating me about my lack of contact with real locals. I finally took up his offer and we arranged a day to drive around the area and 'meet the natives'. The first visit was to a ninety-year-old woman in a rest home in Nethy Bridge. She was one of the few remaining Gaelic speakers in the area. Hearing her stories of going down to London in service and then coming back to marry a keeper on the original Abernethy Estate was fascinating and certainly gave another perspective on the area. The stories of Seamus Grant had been similar – memories of an area that once had a Gaelic-speaking, rural population, with every aspect of their lives controlled by English and Lowland Scots landowners. There are not many of these people left in Badenoch and Strathspey and those who claim to be local today have only been in the area since the sixties when a tourist boom was caused by the opening up of the ski area. It is mainly the farming community and some people left from the railway and timber days who can claim to have been in the area for more than one generation. However, it soon became apparent that Johnny's hostility to 'southerners' is due to the role they played in Scottish history and is based more on class than on national identity. This impression was vindicated when we made our next visit. It was dark by now. Johnny had got lost driving around the forests surrounding Nethy Bridge. I caught a glimpse of many lovely houses through the forest, each with their own substantial grounds, giving an impression of idyllic rural living. Johnny told me that this is where a lot of incomers live, pointing out the house of Roy Turnbull, of the BSCG. I was surprised when we turned into one of these properties, the residence of Keith and Shirley, two members of his Gaelic language group. I was even more surprised to discover that they were English. They had come to the area twenty years previously for common reasons – to escape the urban life and make a living out of their favourite pastime – skiing. They now had a successful business that had managed to survive despite the downturn in skiing. Johnny and Keith communicated briefly in Gaelic but it was soon obvious that Keith was still a relative beginner. I had already heard of his wife Shirley because I listened to her programme on the local radio station. They were in many ways the classic incomer couple – they came up with money from the south of England, established a business, owned a lovely forest house in Nethy Bridge and were active in local affairs. They also have been critical of the funicular despite their association with the ski industry. So why did Johnny introduce me to them as the locals I needed to meet? When I asked him afterwards, he said that Shirley in particular was 'Scottish at heart'. She had the 'sensibilities of a Highlander'. So, despite the anti-incomer and anti-English talk that Johnny had been espousing to me for the past six months, these categories are filled flexibly in his everyday life. Again, what matters is the fact that this couple have demonstrated in practice that they are committed to and care about the community. And what matters to Johnny is that they are interested in the history and heritage of the area. When I asked him about the other members of the Gaelic language group, he admitted that they are also incomers, mostly English. Therefore, the discourse of anti-incomer/outsider that is used around public debates such as those on the funicular and the National Park does not encompass Johnny's approach. He is only anti-outsider when he feels they use their education, confidence and money to dominate and impose their way of doing things. But if the incomers are, in his eyes, genuinely committed to the area, show an interest in the history and culture and integrate sensitively into the public life of the community, they have effectively been redefined as a Highlander. Conversely, those who may be local by origin lose their claim to Highland identity if they are landowners or developers who only care about making money out of the area. Johnny himself believes strongly that private land owning should be abolished in the Scottish Highlands. What counts for Johnny is not so much national origin, but one's social class relationship to the community. His attitude towards landowners was shared by many other long-term residents over the course of my research. The example of Johnny illustrates how a variety of concerns may be concealed by a particular discourse. Only by spending time with people in the fieldwork context can such discrepancies be revealed. What first appeared to be a straightforward anti-incomer position, eventually emerged as a very complex and nuanced one.

My research has shown how, in many different ways, the local-livelihood-versus-outside-conservation-and-recreation way of thinking hides a complexity of interpretations. Though hostility towards incomers is not a myth, to regularly present issues in these terms over-simplifies a variety of positions held locally. It hides the fact that people are not really anti-conservationist at all but only against those that appear powerful and unconcerned with the community. It also hides the fact that people have as much resentment towards powerful locals that are pursuing their own interests at the expense of the community, such as land-owners and developers, as they do against the large conservation organisations. In addition, the impression is given that people are more divided than they actually are, leading to stakeholder models of conflict resolution that are inappropriate.

Resistance to the dominant discourses

In the previous sections I have shown that there are a number of people who did not fit neatly into particular groups, such as conservationist or pro-development, and who had much more nuanced views over land use than appeared in the public debates. There was a significant minority of people who not only did not go along with the dominant way of thinking but expressed views that directly challenged it. They can be differentiated, however, from those in the last chapter who took a more organised anti-funicular stand and whose views echoed quite closely those of the national conservation and recreation organisations. The people I will discuss here were based firmly in a local perspective and tend to share many criticisms that the pro-funicular people had made of outside organisations. This resistance was not monolithic and took different forms depending on the experiential and social context of the person. However, these other perspectives were often not heard because of factors that muffled these voices.

I had already encountered strongly pro-funicular views amongst those associated with the ski industry. However, as I got to know more people and spoke to them in different contexts I came to understand that these views were not unanimous. Though these people want to improve the ski area, many did not think the funicular was the answer. One long-term lift operator of the ski area told me that he was against the funicular but was not allowed to say anything. The main argument in favour of a funicular was that it could transport people to the top even in high winds. In reply to this argument the lift operator said: 'I don't understand why anyone would want to go up to the top in high winds'. An owner of a skiing business said that the funicular plan was 'flawed'. 'It won't underpin many jobs, the expertise will come from abroad, replacement parts will be expensive and there is potential for access to be restricted'. A snowboarding shop owner was extremely anti-funicular. He supported the ski lift operator's doubt that people would want to go up to the top in high winds. He had been in favour of a gondola up from Aviemore that would stop at the base of the mountain. In his view this would attract more visitors to Aviemore itself, rather than driving 'straight past Aviemore up to the car park'. He said: 'The Chairlift Company is very self-centred and they don't know what they are doing'. Another local skier thought that: 'The only people in favour of it are the Chairlift Company'. Such views were confirmed by other local residents. One person said: 'The ski area is very badly managed. I'm against the funicular and so are a lot of people who work for the Chairlift Company. It is a disaster. There will be deaths because people will go up to the top in bad conditions and they won't be able to cope. Anyone can say they're experienced and just go up.'

These voices belong to a variety of people. Some might be described as incomers, but in most cases they have been in the area for ten years or more, have businesses and families, and are committed to stay in the area. Others would count as locals in even the strictest definition, having grown up in the area. All of them remained unheard or at least unacknowledged in the public arena. Though many people had expressed pro-funicular views, when I met people in less public contexts, it became apparent that the local community was divided on the issue. But instead of having a full debate, only one side had been heard, the side that corresponded to the one with the most political and economic power. In the previous chapter, I argued that the pro-funicular group had won because they had managed to mobilise the power of the outsider-versus-local rhetoric. Those who had opposed the funicular publicly were either national conservation and recreation organisations or locals who were identified as incomers. However, the picture is actually more complicated because there were many locals who could never be accused of being incomers, in addition to people associated with the skiing industry itself, who had not supported the funicular. So why didn't they speak out? Why weren't their voices heard?

One major reason, as one person told me, is that people were too 'scared'. As one employee of the Chairlift Company said: 'It is very difficult to be publicly against the funicular. Letters in the local paper that were against it got so slated that people don't dare say anything.' The main reason they were 'slated' was for being 'anti-local community'. Though many people may consider themselves local, the definition of local varies according to the context. The vast majority of people in the area are in fact incomers. As one outdoor instructor said, 'So many people come from outside anyway. Just because they've lived here ten years, they start excluding people'. Conversely, a ninety-year-old who had come to the area in his twenties said that he still was not a native. But people get branded as incomers if they express views that do not fit the dominant discourse of those in power. This can be seen in a number of contexts. The Danish landowner of Glenfeshie is supported by other Scottish landowners as long as he maintains the tradition of the sporting estate. Another foreign landowner, on the other hand, had been criticised by others because she is against killing animals and doesn't want to have a sporting estate. With the funicular debate, anyone whose pedigree was in doubt could be publicly vilified. The owner of the snowboarding business had been in the area eleven years and had a business that contributes to the community. He saw himself as a local, indicated to me by the way he criticised 'outsiders' like the SSPB and Magnus Magnusson for not understanding the local situation. But when he went on local radio to question the funicular, he became a target. 'I am now seen as the enemy'.

Two outdoor instructors, who had been in the area for many years and plan to stay, found out what could happen if they dared get involved. They were all in favour of modernising the ski area and were critical of Mountaineering Scotland and the Cairngorms Campaign because the individuals involved 'don't know the area very well' and 'don't sit down and talk to people here'. But they had major criticisms about how they felt the funicular had been pushed through and how they were treated for raising any doubts. One said that there had been no general meeting to discuss what could be done for the ski area and they had just been 'presented with the funicular by the Chairlift Company, so they deliberately polarised people into pro-funicular and jobs/money in the local area and those that were against'.

Another told me what happened when a few of them went to a meeting called by the Chairlift Company because they had heard that a protest was planned at the ski area.

'We were faced with seventeen people – it was all very formal. All the local councillors appeared to listen but then one made a comment about me being English, the implication being that if you were a local then you would be in favour of the funicular because it meant jobs.'

These instructors soon became reluctant to speak out, as did the owner of the snowboarding business, largely because of the way were treated as anti-local, English incomers. There were others who had said nothing at all for this reason. One English business owner deliberately made no public statement though he had been personally against it. He therefore escaped the vilification and has survived to become a leading participant in community politics, well regarded by even the most anti-incomer advocate. This shows how being an incomer is not a problem as long as one does not challenge the power structure. Achieving the status of local and therefore belonging has particular significance because this status confers the right to participate in decision-making (Edwards: 1998). People like the outdoor instructors would not have suffered financially as a result of their stand. But others, like business owners and those employed by the Chairlift Company faced potential financial implications if they were seen to be publicly against. Therefore, there are a number of pressures on people to conform.

The case of the funicular reveals significant points about who belongs in the sense of having a right to decide, showing why some voices are not heard. Many locals, both long-term and more recent, would not even consider speaking out because they do not feel part of the decision-making structure. The more recently arrived locals are afraid of being branded as 'anti-community incomers' and the longer-term locals, like the lift operator, are afraid for their jobs or else do not have the confidence to speak out in the public arena. I suggested in the preceding chapter that the stakeholder model excludes the majority of people from public life. This is further supported in this chapter by the existence of different interpretations and outright resistance to the dominant discourse on the part of many people who do not fit conveniently into any of the categories for consultation. Anti-funicular views were invariably linked to a critique of the economic and political power relations. One business owner said that: 'The local area is politically and economically controlled by five people who own all the land'. A local teenager told me that:

> *The councillors are always consulting but never acting upon it, like with the funicular. That is a total waste of money. Money should be spent on things like a leisure centre. The Chairlift Company doesn't pay any attention to what the locals want.*

But it is these people, the landowners, leading business owners, politicians and other 'community representatives' who are called upon to speak for the local community. The way that consultation operated around the National Park illustrates the problem of lack of involvement of most people in decision-making. The Cairngorm Partnership (CP) is typical of the partnership approach to managing potential conflict over land use. In this model, key interest groups and their representatives are brought together in order to try and reach agreement. Such partnerships tend to be dominated by organisations and institutions that already have a certain degree of power and influence (Poncelot: 2001). The purpose had been to gather together, according to Ross, 'the people who matter', so that the transfer to National Park status could proceed with a minimum of conflict. Forums included Highland Councillors, landowners, farmers, recreation and Community Councils. Some of the forums were built around existing power structures but the existence of a recreation, farming and Community Council forum should theoretically have allowed for participation of a much wider variety of local opinion. However, even these proved to be problematic in their representation. The recreation forum consisted largely of national representatives of different sports, not local representatives. So, for example, the representative for skiing and snowboarding was the head of Snowsports Scotland. He is a skier of long standing, a supporter of the funicular and he also happens to be the factor (overall manager) of Balmoral Estate. When I mentioned this to the snowboard shop owner he said that he couldn't see this man representing 'the views of the young snow-boarders who hang around outside Chevy's (a pub in Aviemore)'. The farming stakeholders included a Highland Councillor and a farmer who was a controversial figure amongst the other farmers I had met.

In theory, the Community Councils should be the most likely to represent the local community. However, despite the dedicated and hard-working people involved, their claim to speak for the whole community was open to question. One of the reasons for this is because of the diverse nature of the community as already discussed. There was no one community view and gathering one representative for each community across the Cairngorm area could not be expected to communicate such diversity. But there were other reasons, largely to do with political, economic and social inequalities, that meant that such a group could never be relied on to speak for the community. Community Councils are local organisations that consist largely of volunteers because there are usually not enough candidates to warrant an election. The kind of people who volunteer to represent the commu-nity therefore tended to be those who have at least some spare time and have a certain amount of 'cultural capital', such as self-confidence, and who possibly see being on the council as furthering their economic ambition. Most Community Council-lors will therefore be those who already have a certain amount of social standing in the community. The representative for the southern Cairngorms was the factor from the Invercauld Estate. Others owned businesses. The problems with using the Commu-nity Councils as stakeholders is illustrated in my experience with Aviemore Community Council. My encounter with the local democratic process is described in my field notes.

Prior to the period of consultation for the National Park, I heard no discussions about the Community Council and what they were doing, except for the occasional reference in the local paper. No one I had met ever referred to them. When I learned from the paper that there were to be consultations about the National Park, I tried to find some local meetings to go to. As I had never been to a Community Council meeting, I needed to find out where and when they met. I started my search by contacting Highland Council offices but they couldn't tell me anything. I looked again through the local papers, to no avail. In the end, someone mentioned someone that they thought was on the council and I found her phone number and asked when the next meeting was. When I went to the meeting, which was an AGM, there were only seven people there, including the reporter from the paper. No one asked me who I was or welcomed me in any way. If I had been a genuine local I would not have felt very encouraged; no one seemed to care whether I was there or not. At no point at the meeting was there any indication that anyone had asked for anyone else's opinion on an issue. Views were expressed that just represented the people speaking. There was a short presentation from the new person in charge of the Glenmore Corridor but there was no discussion of the National Park, which I thought was to have been the main point of the meeting. Most of the discussion was spent on the problem with the flower boxes on the high street. I came away extremely frustrated. I certainly didn't feel that I had learned anything about what locals thought. The meeting was held in the village hall and next door there were at least three times as many people taking part in a keep fit class. As I was packing up my things to leave, a man came in to do the tidying up. I started talking to him and didn't get home for another hour and a half! That conversation proved to be one of the most interesting I had. I was clearly talking to someone with an immense knowledge and concern in the area. Yet, here he was cleaning up the village hall after the representatives of the community had had the major meeting of the year as if it was a complete irrelevancy. Yet, one of these Community Councillors I would later meet at a Cairngorms Partnership meeting of the community representatives. Their views were then presented to the government as being the views of the locals together with the business owners, Highland councillors, larger farmers and landowners.

The dominant discourse of outside-recreation/conservation-versus-local-livelihood has been exploited by certain groups to further their own interests. It is very difficult for this to be challenged through the normal political channels especially when a deliberate attempt is made, using the stakeholder model, to consult local opinion. Using the stakeholder model that makes use of the existing power structures therefore can only reproduce, and therefore reinforce, them.

People who wear many hats

Changes in the economic, political and social structure of the area may be creating a space for new interactions between 'contradictory and differing voices' (Morris: 1994: 15), opening up opportunities for redefining what it means to be local and blurring distinctions between outside and inside. The effects of structural changes in global capitalism as well as cultural and demographic changes have had an impact on the economy and the social composition of the area, resulting in an influx of new people. These changes open the situation with new voices and new social networks. This new wave of residents has largely come because of an interest in the natural environment and has brought with it a variety of different experiences, views and practices. These 'alien voices enter into the struggle for influence with an individual's consciousness (just as they struggle with one another in surrounding social reality)' (Bahktin: 1981: 79). The regular letters from Gus Jones and Roy Turnbull have exposed many people to alternative views. As a representative of the Aviemore Tourist Board said to me in an interview: 'We didn't use to have these people here' when speaking of the Badenoch and Strathspey Conservation Group. The increased economic importance of recreation, walking, climbing and birding, and the decline of skiing, has had a major impact on the socio-economic composition of the area. An increasing number of businesses are based on these tourists rather than the skier or the coach party, making people more positively disposed to interests that they might not share themselves. For example, Speyside Wildlife bought up a steading near the estate of Glenfeshie. Pete, the birding guide, told me that when they employed a local building firm to do the renovations, the workers couldn't believe that anyone could make any money out of birdwatching. Jamie Williamson expressed a widely held view when he said that: 'The only business that can make money out of birdwatching is Raymond Revue's Bar in Soho'. But when the firm then got a contract from the RSPB to work on the new Osprey Centre as a result of recommendations from Speyside Wildlife, they began to take the money-making potential of wildlife tourism more seriously. Pete thought that this would play a part in changing attitudes towards people he described as conservationists.

Newcomers have also had an impact on many locals in terms of what activities they engage in and what interests they have. When exposed to different experiences and people – to new senses of place – they open themselves up to change. This process of transformation, through practical interaction, has been found elsewhere by anthropologists. Writing about conflicts over land use in Australia, Strang (2000) notes, 'battles over land, though invariably contentious and unequal, involve the explication and exchange of values, providing all parties with exposure to alternative conceptual frames and qualitatively different environmental relations (p. 93).'

In the course of my research I came across several such people who were local in that they were born in and grew up in the area but challenge the stereotype of what it means to be local and cannot be associated simply with a livelihood sense of place. As a result of coming into contact with new experiences, they have developed interests in conservation and/or walking and climbing.

In addition, there are newcomers who may once have felt antipathy towards the livelihood and development interests but have now integrated their interest in conservation and/or recreation into a concern for the material wellbeing of the area. Instead of being satisfied with a 'hand of one suit, these people hold various combinations of cards, and their existence stands as testimony to the limitations of the stakeholder model. As someone said to me when I was explaining my research and how I had classified activities into livelihood, conservation and recreation: 'There is another category of people – those that do everything'. What sets them apart from others is the fact that they are involved in a range of activities and have had a variety of different experiences with the land. Examining the process by which these people integrate a number of senses of place provides insights into how conflicts between conservation, recreation and livelihood might be reduced or avoided.

Ross

Ross's story shows how exposure to new people and experiences can cause someone to break out of the particular sense of place that they were raised in. He told me about one of his earliest memories that he claims had a big impact on him. He saw Dick Balharry on TV, talking about how he rescued a golden eagle, nursed it and let it back into the wild: 'I don't remember my exact reaction but my parents said I cried'. As Dick lived locally, Ross was later to meet him at his school when Dick came to give a talk giving a broader perspective on birds of prey.

Ross also developed an interest in hill-walking. As many local children have not been up to the ski car park, much less the top of the Cairngorm plateau, Ross is again unusual. He said he had been on the hills on the estate with his father and that gave him the taste for it but it was the Duke of Edinburgh programme at the school that got him going out 'for fun' into the hills. The teachers who set up this programme were technically incomers who had sought jobs in the area because of their own love of the outdoors. Ross now goes hill-walking with his binoculars. He likes the hills of Drumochter, south of the Cairngorms, because they are not that popular with many hill-walkers but they have a wealth of wildlife. He spent two years as a trainee warden at RSPB Insh Marshes and then got a job in Norfolk and then in Dorset. But after a year he was very happy to come back to Scotland and the hills. He was a warden at Abernethy, the RSPB reserve that has provoked so much hostility from locals. He was chosen to represent the area for the Youth Parliament and participated in the National Park Board. He has recently moved from the RSPB to work for the Woodland Trust, carrying on his dedication for conservation work in Scotland. I met up with him just prior to publishing this book and he took me on a walk in a property near Oban leased to the Woodland Trust. We searched, and found, a rare fungus called hazel's gloves. As always, his enthusiasm and interest in all aspects of the natural world, as well as his knowledge of land management issues, made for a great time.

Ailsa

Ailsa is the daughter of a local teacher. She did a degree in zoology at Aberdeen University. She was the volunteer coordinator at the Osprey Centre. At the time of my research, she was about to go off to Australia for a year to do some volunteer work on different nature reserves. She told me that she wanted to come back to this area. She had a lot of ideas about what she would like to do. One of them was to take kids from the city and show them the hills and about the flora and fauna. She thought going away to university in Aberdeen did her a lot of good as she met new people and expanded her horizons. But still she wanted to come back. She has many memories of drunken nights in bothies (basic huts out in the hills) and getting lost in the nearby forest on her mountain bike. Despite her conservation interests, she was very sympathetic to the concerns of keepers and stalkers and was sometimes critical of Abernethy RSPB. She said that she felt different from most people because she was 'in between'. Ailsa got a job when she came back from Australia in Nethy Bridge as a ranger at the Interpretive Centre. This was the beginning of her career, which she hoped would involve sharing her love of nature with others.

Meeting Ailsa again, twenty years later, she has managed to realise her aspirations. She has had an adventurous life, working in Somerset on a children-and-nature project and travelling to South America. She is now back in the area with her husband and children. Her current job is to promote walking and outdoor activities for local people – just the kind of work she had wanted to do.

Eric

Eric was an instructor at Glenmore Lodge at the time of research. He was one of the few Scottish instructors and the only one born in the area. He started in the hills, like Ross, through the Duke of Edinburgh programme. He and some friends decided to take it further and formed an informal club where they would go out and do more serious hill-walking. He was also one of the locals who learned to ski and that is his first love, though he now prefers ski touring because it combines skiing with getting out into the hills. He went away to college to train as an engineer but came back after finishing because of the family's electrician business. He was glad he did because he needs to be near the hills, but he thinks it is good for youngsters to leave the area because it helps them to appreciate what they have. He took the first step on the road to becoming an instructor with the Mountain Rescue Team. He was taken on as an apprentice and says it is a good way to get to know the hills and all the skills you need. He continued to work as an electrician but gradually worked his way through the mountaineering instructor qualifications, spending more time with the local mountaineering community. Eric stood out amongst the Glenmore Lodge instructors. He could talk about a range of land-related issues. I recorded my observations of Eric in my field notes:

Eric got all excited today because we saw a couple of mountain hares. He didn't want to eat lunch near them because we would disturb them. However, he says he has no qualms about shooting rabbits. There are just too many of them and they end up dying of myxomatosis. Also, he will shoot a hare or pheasant if it is 'for the pot'. He admitted to poaching before but now he owns his own land and also a farmer he knows lets him shoot on his land. 'It's something you do when you are brought up around here'. But he's not into shooting for the sake of it. He doesn't understand how people can do it for sport or raise animals to be shot. He was horrified when I told him about the mass shooting of hares on Kinveachy. He says that the kids from the estates he went to school with didn't tend to follow their fathers' footsteps – their parents want them to get 'better jobs'. But he didn't think estate jobs should be seen as 'inferior jobs'.

Eric's knowledge of the world of the sporting estate contrasts sharply with that of people like Alan who I had met grouse-beating. He had lived in the area for over thirty years and had never been on an estate, whereas Eric had grown up with the sons and daughters of keepers and stalkers. This gives him a greater understanding of the issues and also enables him to empathise with the situation of sporting estate employees. He clearly has an interest and love of wildlife but this is balanced with an understanding of how it fits in to people's livelihoods. In addition to shooting, he has considerable knowledge of the local mountain legends, likes taking his fishing rod with him into the hills and plays in a local folk band. Eric is spoken of with great respect by his fellow instructors and someone said he would make an excellent future head of Glenmore Lodge. Eric has now left the Lodge but I am sure that his example can inspire a new generation of local children to look to their own hills for both enjoyment and work.

Douglas, Isobel and Dorothy

Douglas, mentioned in Chapters Two and Four, works as an employee on a cattle farm. His father was also a farmer from Aberdeenshire but came to this area to work as farm manager on a local estate. Douglas and his friend Gordon, also a farmer, are two of the main members of the local hill-walking club. Alan, one of the founding members of the club said about this – 'We must be the only club in Scotland to have hill-walking farmers'. Douglas is well aware that he is an oddity. He is now on his fifth round of Munros and has recently developed an interest in mountain biking. We also did both rock and winter climbing together. I asked Douglas what caused him to take an interest in these pursuits. He said he had been a 'typical local', did his job and then spent his evenings and the few weekends when he was free, smoking and drinking down the pub. He then met Gordon at a Young Farmers meeting. Gordon invited him to go out walking with him to Creag Meagaidh, a major Munro down towards Fort William. Douglas said 'it was something new, so I went'. Douglas recalls that it was a beautiful day and said this might have had something to do with it, but the end result as that he got 'hooked'. His interest was reinforced by Ann Wakeling, once an incomer, now a long-term resident. They used to go away regularly to remote and challenging places like Skye and Knoydart. Once he had his first taste, he never looked back. The experience was had and that transformed his life. Now he spends every free weekend in the hills. His family think he is 'mad' and 'just don't understand it'. He remarked, whilst sleeping out on the top of the Cuillin Ridge in Skye: 'my family couldn't comprehend what I am doing this for'. He gets a certain satisfaction from his non-conformity.

Douglas is also knowledgeable about birds and is a keen photographer. I once came across him when I was with my birding friend, Andrew. We were watching an osprey nest and Douglas drove up in his car. He brought out his camera and tripod. He had just finished work and had come to photograph the osprey. Douglas's interest in hill-walking and wildlife doesn't contradict at all his devotion to farming. He speaks equally passionately about the importance of maintaining a healthy farming industry. When I suggested that with his extensive local knowledge he could set up a tourist business, taking visitors out walking, he was aghast. He is quite happy being a farmer and producing something of use. He knows that other farmers aren't like him. The farmer he works for 'wouldn't think of going hill-walking'. But then, unlike Douglas, most farmers have never tried it. Mary Yule told me that she would like to go sometime, but then says that she doesn't know anyone to take her and she is so busy with the farm. This case shows that experiences can transform perspectives, broadening a sense of place. Perspectives are merged to create something new.

Isobel, the daughter of a local farmer, tells a similar story. Her first experience was when she and some of her friends decided to do a sponsored hill-walk for the Mountain Rescue Team through the Lairig Ghru from Glenmore to Braemar in the southern Cairngorms. This kindled her interest, which was then further fuelled by Ann Wakeling, who took her up onto the Cairngorm plateau. Isobel particularly remembers looking down on Loch Avon, from the furthest side of the plateau, a view only a few locals will ever have seen. Like Douglas, she uses the word 'hooked' to describe her reaction to the experience. She was one of the main members of the walking club and continues to walk regularly.

Dorothy came to Carrbridge when she was eleven. She had always enjoyed the outdoors but mainly on horseback. Her interest in hill-walking was kindled by a friend, Julian Lines, who had some up to Carrbridge to stay with the Hayes family, owner of the Landmark Forest Adventure Park. When her horse was injured she was looking for something else to do and accepted Julian's invitation to go over the Lochnagar area on the other side of the Cairngorms. She took some photos of Julian and his friends climbing and then set off to do a Munro, and ended up knocking off three before coming back to the tent! Like Isobel and Douglas, she says the views are what hooked her and she never looked back. She soon joined Strathspey Mountain Club. She loves the hills but also loves going out camping in remote spots just to enjoy the beauty and solitude.

Douglas, Isobel and Dorothy have friends from a variety of backgrounds, combining long-term residents, even natives with incomers. The Strathspey Mountain Club, of which they are all members, includes former ski instructors, hotel and catering workers, a secretary in a local tourist attraction, self-employed business people, doctors and retired people. Douglas is also now a member of a new mountain bike club that boasts an equal variety of people, brought together by an interest in outdoor activities. Douglas, Isobel and Dorothy follow in the tradition of a number of other Highlanders who go to the hills for fun. The climbing partnership of the crofter John MacKenzie and the London chemistry professor Norman Collie is legendary. Together they explored the Cuillin Ridge on Skye, making first ascents of remote and challenging peaks. They now lie buried together in a church yard in a Skye village (Mill: 1987). Other mountaineering Highlanders are documented in Mitchell's (1988) detailed study of mountaineering before it officially began. Therefore, there is no cultural barrier preventing Highlanders from appreciating hill-walking and climbing as a form of recreation. It is more a question of experience and opportunity. In other words, some people have had certain interactions with both the social and physical environment that have caused them to break out of the mould.

Victoria

Victoria, having found herself living and working in Aviemore in the early 1990s, discovered the hills in a rather unusual way. She was offered a chance to go up in a hot-air balloon. Being of an adventurous nature, she eagerly volunteered to have a go. Off she went, wearing nothing but summer clothes and sandals. However, she ended up having a life-changing adventure when the balloon lost altitude and ended up landing on the lower slopes of the hills, far from Aviemore. She had to walk back, crossing the River Einich in spate after a very wet month of June; it was quite an ordeal with what she was wearing. However, rather than being put off, she decided to go and find where the balloon had come down – this time better equipped. This exploratory trip back into the hills was the inspiration for a completely new life.

Whilst she has continued to live and work in the area, with the hills being a huge part of her life, she is concerned like other locals about what is happening in the communities, with the lack of facilities and affordable housing.

Her hope for the future is that all those living in this beautiful part of Scotland will be able to remain in an area for all to share.

Tom

It is not only locals who have been affected by outside influences. People coming into the area, motivated by their interest in the natural environment, have also found themselves changing as they become more involved in the community. Tom was the warden at the RSPB at Insh Marshes and now works for the Butterfly Conservation Trust. He has an engineering background but soon left that line of work to pursue a career in his favourite pastime – birding. Before coming to Strathspey, he worked up in the Orkneys on the Isle of Hoy. He is one RSPB member that even normally hostile locals speak about favourably. After spending many months on Insh Marshes and talking to Tom, I could see why. He said he had learned on Hoy how important it was to be seen as part of the community. He would go out of his way to make sure he got to know people. He told me that the most important thing he did for the RSPB–local relations was when he picked his children up after school. He was friendly with the local farmers and is constantly talking about how land management is a joint effort between farmers and conservationists. He has initiated projects with the local schools and he also set up a local naturalist group that he hoped would gradually expand from its incomer core. He became interested in moths and butterflies. Tom's reputation is of someone who is a dedicated conservationist but who is also 'concerned about the local community'. His integration of a livelihood sense of place into his conservation one, has endeared him to many traditional locals and this fact has helped him to spread his conservation ideas.

Others had similar experiences. Anne and George became pro-funicular after watching their sons' struggle with unemployment. Ed became more sympathetic to the plight of farmers after meeting Douglas and visiting places in the Highlands that have been completely turned over to tourism. He said: 'Without farming, all you would have is souvenir shops. There has to be some other way of making a living apart from tourism'. An English woman who came to the area because of her interest in the outdoors said: 'You have to live up here. It's just education – you learn more about the different uses of the land – it's all part of the area'.

Mary Walker

Mary had been a great help during my research year. Together with her grandson Craig, she was able to provide much information about the locals' perspective. She had arrived in Aviemore in 1970, though never considered herself a local. I caught up with her twenty years later. I was able to contact her because her name appeared on a website of a local walking group. She is now retired and has taken up walking with enthusiasm. Many other people I knew had heard about how fit she was. She told me she got into walking because when she retired, she wanted to 'do something'. She had always been adventurous – I had heard from Craig during my research year about her abseiling down the tower of Ragmore Hospital in Inverness. Though she walked and cycled the strath, she had never walked up a hill. She did have a brother, however, who was a mountaineer in New Zealand. But she didn't understand his interest in going up hills when she was young. Thanks to a number of walking groups that had emerged over the years, when she decided to look for a new activity, she was able to find one to suit her. She remembers looking at her first hill and thinking: 'I'll never get up that'. The walk leader, though, encouraged her and told her to take twenty steps at a time and then to stop and look around.

*

All of the above cases illustrate what happens when people do not identify with one particular sense of place. They are not stuck in one place but move freely between places. For these people, the discourse of outside-recreation/conservation-versus-local-livelihood holds no fixed or shared meaning. This opens the possibility for new ways of approaching debates about land use. These debates will not miraculously disappear because some people are now aware of more than one perspective, but they could take place within a framework that doesn't polarise people to the same extent. A representative of one of the Community Councils in the southern Cairngorms was especially interested in the conclusions of my research. He agreed that the biggest problem for the area was that 'people could not put themselves in other people's shoes'. Change depends on reshuffling perspectives, groups and identities.

CHAPTER EIGHT

Beyond Livelihood,
Conservation and Recreation

I had met many people who didn't fit neatly into the sense of place boxes I had started out with. This gave me hope that the public conflicts I had witnessed over the funicular and the National Park were not inevitable. How might it be possible to reconcile apparently conflicting land uses: conservation of wild places for habitat and their intrinsic value, recreational activities for humans' personal enjoyment and fulfilment, and the meeting of people's economic needs? I found that my research suggested possibilities for how this process of reconciliation could be facilitated as well as identifying potential resistance to change. Because of my anthropological focus on one particular area, these possibilities revealed themselves at the local level in the interactions, experiences and initiatives of individuals and groups. However, as I have argued, local events and practices are embedded in a wider network of institutions, structures and discourses. Therefore, the implications of my research need to be examined in terms of the causes of conflicts and what they suggest for the possibilities for and obstacles to change, at both the level of the locality or community and the wider society. This begins with the level of the individual sense of place but will necessarily have to move outwards to the broader society.

Travelling in more than one place

Though one's position on land use issues cannot be reduced to one's sense of place, as I have shown, there is still a relationship between the two. As one contact said, 'no one has an overview, they just see their bit'. In other words, individuals are travelling in parallel places, all versions of the same place, but nevertheless separate. It is this narrowness of perception that is one of the reasons for conflict. However, there are those who travel in more than one of these places because of the range of activities they are engaged in. They do not identify strongly with any particular group and therefore are able to have more of an overview and see the issues from a number of different perspectives. So, a key issue is how to encourage this travelling such that one's sense of place is enriched and extended. I have shown that people develop a sense of place from embodied experience. Therefore, if the aim is to extend one's sense of place, people need to extend the range of those experiences, as I did during fieldwork. I came to the area primarily as a walker and climber, someone with a largely recreational approach to the environment. After a year of participating in a host of other activities, my sense of place changed. Instead of just seeing the place in terms of what it offers for climbing, I now notice birds, lichen and moss, patches where the heather has been burned for grouse, the number of points on a stags antlers and the potential for ski touring or mountain biking. In addition, I do not just focus on the high ground, but I also know where locals might go to walk the dog, why they get frustrated at the lack of an affordable swimming pool and I am aware of the controversy surrounding the new housing developments that have sprung up. I can take the new funicular up to the top and appreciate the facilities on offer and how it has increased the number of summer visitors, as well as sympathise with those who see it as a waste of money. The key to my new awareness is new experiences. One has to be able to relativise one's perspective, see it as one perspective amongst many, and this can only come about through contact with the new. I found that my conclusions were shared by those in the local area who have managed to broaden their own sense of place. Some of their initiatives and ideas are of interest to other areas of the world where similar conflicts over land use are taking place.

Many locals do use the land for recreation. However, this is often confined to the low ground, stimulating some people and organisations to initiate projects to develop an appreciation of the high hill environment. Caroline Sterritt of the Sports Development Unit expressed in an interview her concern that local young people had so little contact with the outdoor environment. She started a programme to provide the opportunity for primary school children to take skiing lessons. She also initiated a summer programme that included a range of activities such as walking, mountain biking and kayaking. She said that the key to getting the locals to value what they have in the high hill environment is to 'get them out in it'.

The Duke of Edinburgh Award has served as a vehicle for young people to get some experience of the outdoors. The teachers involved in the programme are committed to giving young people positive experiences and, as in the cases of Ross and Eric, this could be their first step to taking a more long-term interest. There are limitations with the Duke of Edinburgh Award, however. Many people told me that the programme tended to attract more middle-class young people who had been encouraged by their parents. I met several young people from working-class backgrounds who said that they had not felt comfortable at the meetings and had dropped out. However, Pauline, a youth worker, recently moved to the area from Liverpool, was employed to try and extend the programme to young people who may not fit in so well with the school environment or who have left school. Will Carey, a resident of Laggan who also worked at the Highland Wildlife Park, worked for several years with the John Muir Award (similar to the Duke of Edinburgh Award, but with a focus on conservation). His goal was also to get more disaffected young people involved. His approach was to attract their interest via exciting outdoor activities such as kayaking and mountain biking; he could then integrate conservation activities. The John Muir Award has been taken up by the National Park Board and has been a huge success. Glenmore Lodge has also taken initiatives to introduce local young people to the outdoors. They are involved in the schools programme and one instructor has set up a climbing club for local youths. Nigel Williams told me of their efforts to overcome some of the hostility between anglers and kayakers. He invited local ghillies to come kayaking for the day so they could see for themselves that kayaking, if done sensitively, need not pose any threats to fishing.

The existence of local walking clubs like the Strathspey Mountain Club also provides the opportunity for people to further cultivate and extend hill-walking interest. Isobel, who became interested as a result of being taken out by Ann Wakeling and going on the sponsored walk for the Mountain Rescue Team, joined the club and completed all the Munros. Douglas and Gordon also joined the club after their interest had been kindled elsewhere. Douglas is now doing his Munros for the fifth time and has also taken up mountain biking. Because of its unique combination of long-term residents and more recent arrivals, it is attractive to a wide variety of people. Mary Walker also benefitted from the variety of walking clubs that had been set up.

There have also been steps taken by conservationists to foster an appreciation of the flora and fauna of the area. As I have argued, it is not that local people have no appreciation, but that it is limited by opportunities to have a wider range of experiences. Tessa Jones was a ranger who worked closely with local schools. She took children out to explore and get to know their natural environment. She said that the sons and daughters of gamekeepers, stalkers and farmers were especially knowledgeable and appreciative. She tried to encourage this and build bridges between people like herself who are labelled conservationists and those who see themselves as being on a different side. She said one of the most popular activities with the children is using the magnifying glass to look at lichen and moss. If she could succeed in encouraging this interest, then it would be less likely to hear the comment I heard from one local – 'Why is one piece of moss more important than thousands of people's enjoyment'.

Tom Prescott also sought to involve people in conservation activities. He worked with a school liaison officer and with the local schools on projects such as building nesting boxes for goldeneyes and placing them on farms so that farmers could monitor them. He held regular open days and set up a local natu-ralist group that he hoped would attract others apart from those working in the conservation field. Ross developed his interest in conservation when volunteering at Insh Marshes for his Duke of Edinburgh Award. The impact of this work is difficult to quan-tify but can only help to broaden a person's sense of place and foster greater appreciation of the environment from multiple perspectives.

As discussed in previous chapters, the Badenoch and Strath-spey Conservation Group took every opportunity to highlight conservation issues, often provoking hostile reactions. This con-tinues over debates around housing issues. However, over the years since my fieldwork, I have noticed that they have begun to make use of the local paper as a means of forging common ground with those they are often in conflict with. They have done this by publicising initiatives that are aimed at developing an appreciation of both the intrinsic and extrinsic value of flora and fauna. The following article in the local paper is indicative of this.

Conservation group declares delight over orchid discovery
The surprise appearance of an unusual flower has delighted members of a local conservation group, who claim it is an ex-ample of how farming incentives can aid local biodiversity. Dr. Gus Jones of the Badenoch and Strathspey Conservation Group: 'Flower meadows make a colourful contribution to local biodiver-sity, and this success story shows how agricultural subsidies for

environmentally friendly management of our farmland can make
a difference.'

Strathspey and Badenoch Herald: 3 July 2003

This article manages to combine a variety of reasons for this
orchid: its beauty, its 'localness', the financial benefits to farmers
as well as its value for biodiversity, thereby giving everyone a
reason to 'delight'.

Most visitors to the area, because they come to enjoy the
outdoor environment, do not have a sense of the place as a
community in which people live and work. People coming for
birdwatching holidays or to climb in the Northern Corries will
have little contact with anyone except their guides or instructors and people providing tourist services. The funicular case
showed that the locals were criticised for 'not valuing what they
have' and not being 'trusted to run a National Park'. Others who
come to work in conservation often do not see the land as an
economic asset, as something that can produce an income, but
as something with intrinsic value that needs to be protected from
farmers, sporting estate workers and those who want to build
tourist attractions like the funicular. But it is not only visitors who
could be hostile to local development interests. Those who work
as outdoor instructors or for conservation agencies and organisations can be equally unaware of how others may perceive the
land. As I have shown, learning a sense of place involves both an
opening up and a closing off of perceptions.

The Cairngorm Partnership, by organising its stakeholder
groups, tried to bring people together so they could see each
other's perspective. The problem, however, was that the different
groups rarely met together. Each group just fed the results of
their meetings directly to those working for the Cairngorm
Partnership, most of whom were brought in from outside the
area. My research uncovered more fruitful developments on
the ground, influenced by the existence of key individuals who
combined a sensibility to all three approaches to the land.

Tom Prescott at Insh Marshes made a point of getting to know the farmers and establishing good relations with them, continually stressing the importance of the partnership between farming and conservation. His understanding and appreciation could then be fed to volunteers who came to work as well as to the public through tourist information and the guided walks. Ross went from Insh Marshes to Abernethy. The impact of employing a local young man, son of a sporting estate farm manager, who has grown up with an understanding of the importance of land as livelihood cannot be underestimated. He was in charge of volunteers when they came to the reserve and was responsible for organising guided walks. Those who visit the reserve will thus be able to meet someone who has a well-rounded knowledge of all aspects of the area, not just birds or the conservation issues of Abernethy itself.

Eric, the first local to work as an instructor at Glenmore Lodge, also had an instrumental role to play in raising the awareness of those who come for courses, most of whom are from outside the area. Clients spend a lot of time with their instructor, and on courses like the Mountain Leadership course they are expected to have a broad knowledge of the hill environment. Most of the instructors will know the hills very well, but Eric could also discuss other aspects of the area. This happened on the course I was on when we talked about stalking, the problem of deer fences and concerns of local farmers.

The Duke of Edinburgh Award provides a variety of possibilities for the intermingling of senses of place. One excellent example was when I volunteered to support a Duke of Edinburgh expedition that went through the land of Kinveachy Estate. John, the head keeper, was there at his house to meet the young people as they passed through. He could get to know the kind of young person who walks into the hills for fun rather than driving up the track in the Land Rover. Meanwhile, the youngsters could see John as a sort of guardian of the land. He gave them advice about the dangers of the river, told them something of the local history of the place where they were going to camp and told me that he would be on call if I needed him for an emergency. This type of relationship, between hill-walker and stalkers, keepers and shepherds was much more common in the early days of hill-walking when people were much more likely to live on the land.

The following project, as described by Ross, is an excellent current example of bringing people together and helping the public to understand a variety of land issues whilst having fun in the outdoors:

At Woodland Trust Scotland's Ledmore and Migdale Wood, their most northerly property, and one of the most heavily designated (three SSSIs and an SAC), the management of the deer population is required for three reasons: to protect ancient woodland ground flora, tree regeneration and soils; to reduce the likelihood of deer–vehicle collisions along the main road running through part of the site; to reduce impacts on the economic interests of neighbours, particularly an organic, arable farm.

The population is managed collaboratively with the main neighbouring landowners, and done so through a Deer Management Group. The deer management itself is undertaken by local, well-known and well-respected professionals, with annual monitoring undertaken to prioritise locations and assess the requirements for the following year.

As this work has such a big impact on all other aspects of the woodland, it has been attempted to raise the profile of this work through events to promote the reasons for doing this, the ecological value of some deer in woodland demonstrating the importance of these animals managed at a sustainable level, and the value of the product – venison.

Through events called 'A Taste of the Wild' in 2019 members of the public could attend sessions discussing deer management in an open way, while learning how to build an underground oven and cook venison. This gave an opportunity to discuss responsible access, leave no trace, food mileage, benefits of venison, foraging

for berries and exploring the woods with their families. One of
these events took place overnight to experience the sounds of the
woodland environment in a different setting.

Outside organisations are aware of the importance of high-lighting any potential for common ground between those living and those working in the hill environment. For example, Bill Wright's series in *Climber*:

Mountain farmer, John Cameron
In the first of a new series contrasting the views of different individuals who have intimate contact with the mountains, Bill Wright interviews John Cameron. He is the tenant farmer who looks after sheep and cattle that graze upon the first Munro that most visitors are confronted with when driving north up the A9 into the Highlands.

Climber: November 2003

By writing such an article, Bill is helping to break down barriers between climbers and farmers. In addition, as this particular farmer took part in an alternative National Park opening ceremony (part of a protest against the official ceremony in the restaurant at the top of the funicular) he is also building up political alliances that are not based on divisions between locals and outsiders.

All of the above initiatives are part of a developmental process that will have the effect of broadening perceptions by bringing people into contact with perspectives and experiences that are new to them; an essential ingredient for bringing about change.

Fostering understanding or fuelling conflict:
the role of structures and institutions

My research has highlighted some of the social processes that have turned senses of place into parallel places that have then become fixed interest groups, exacerbating land-use conflicts. Because of this relationship between senses of place and the wider society, change will also have to be affected at the structural and institutional level.

Caroline Sterritt and Eric from Glenmore Lodge both stressed the financial constraints for young people getting more involved in outdoor activities. The high level of unemployment and low wages of many jobs prohibit families from introducing their children to skiing or hill-walking, even if the children have expressed an interest. Several youngsters had the impression that programmes like the Duke of Edinburgh Award were not for them. As one young man told me: 'It was for a certain kind of student'. Parents of youngsters in the programme confirmed this by saying that most tended to be from middle-class families whose parents had encouraged them. One girl on the D of E expedition that I assisted had borrowed her rucksack from the Director of Glenmore Lodge. Economic inequality also prevented participation in decision-making structures. Local political structures involved few people and tended to be dominated either by local elites such as the landowners and business owners, or by educated incomers, often retired and who had time on their hands.

Another issue brought to my attention from several sources was the lack of fit between the jobs and qualifications of young people. An economic development officer for the area said that the priority was to create well-paid jobs that would keep people in the community. The funicular created some jobs but most of them were low paid and seasonal. Jobs in the hotels are low paid and involve long working hours. And many of the well-paid jobs in recreation and conservation seem to be filled by people from outside the area. Local young people are not being trained or educated to the level that is deemed necessary to take up those jobs that are appearing in conservation and heritage management. All the Cairngorm Partnership posts, the employees of Scottish Natural Heritage and the RSPB reserve and most of the Highland Council rangers were from outside the area. This is not a criticism of the people themselves; they are enthusiastic and good at their jobs, but it is not a healthy situation for the community. Individual such as Ross with the RSPB, Ailsa as a local ranger and Eric at Glenmore Lodge were the exception. Businesses in outdoor and green tourism also tend to be run by incomers, because they have the capital to do so. The owners of Speyside Wildlife sold their house down south and this gave them the working capital to set up a business. Their story is similar to many others.

However, economic changes are beginning to create opportunities for livelihood, recreation and conservation to come together. The growth of green tourism and outdoor recreation has meant, either directly or indirectly, more jobs in this area. I discussed in Chapter Seven how more locals are becoming aware of the importance of such tourism and if local young people could get jobs in these areas, which is happening now to a very limited extent, then the three approaches would be more integrated. Significantly, those who were incomers at the time of my research have, over time, become more fully integrated into the community. Marriage, children, friendship and other connections with longer term residents have altered their status as incomers.

There is, however, an opposing tendency. Some locals have become financially successful as a direct result of increased development of the area, in opposition to conservation and recreation interests. Some farmers, rather than farming the land, are busy selling off parcels of land for housing developments or building holiday homes for which they receive diversification grants. One farm worker told me that the farmer he works for spends more time sorting out the buildings that he is going to sell or do up than he does actually helping with the cattle. A glance at the Scottish Tourist Board website lists a number of farmers with self-catering properties to let. It also shows how many who argue vehemently for more development and housing for locals have an interest in property, which they rent to tourists. It is understandable that people seek ways of improving their financial situation.

But this state of affairs highlights the problems created by the decline of farming and the sporting estate and the lack of alternative employment. Anyone who is in a position to buy a home to let, avails themselves of this option, sometimes renting to locals, but usually to holiday makers. The expansion of housing developments is at odds with the agenda of conservation and recreation and recently conflicts have taken place between those arguing for more housing developments, and conservationists, who stress the importance for biodiversity of maintaining woods and meadows. It is also in conflict with the needs of the majority of the population who cannot afford the houses being built.

The decline of farming, hastened by the outbreak of foot and mouth disease, is one of the key economic problems. Mary and Jimmy Yule did not want to become 'hobby farmers' but they are spoken of as the last of a 'dying breed'. They did not want their son to go into farming. What would happen if the farms were either sold to housing developers or turned into tourist attractions? Initiatives such as Tom Prescott's, to bring farming and conservation together, will not work unless there are institutional and structural supports. At the moment, economic and political policies are creating a situation in which there is more of an incentive for farmers to build houses than there is for them to develop environmentally friendly farming. The advent of the National Park has aggravated economic inequality. There has been a rush to buy property in the area, often by speculators who have not even seen it, because prices are predicted to rise. This is what has in fact happened and those who bought a second or even third property have become very well off. Meanwhile, the majority of locals, not having been in a financial position to take advantage of this opportunity, are finding themselves struggling to pay rents or to buy a house for themselves when their families expand. Many local shops had to close in Aviemore to be replaced by chain stores when the developer, a local man, put the rent up. There is much rhetoric about the need for affordable housing but most of the housing has been far from affordable. John Grant, the owner of Rothiemurchus, was criticised for building a housing development that ended up being very expensive and was sold to incomers, despite previous promises that some of the houses would be affordable housing for locals. One source recently told me that local developers are also sitting on land with planning permission for 3,000 houses as they wait for prices to rise before they build. Yet these same developers are putting pressure on authorities to allow more land to be turned over for housing because workers cannot find a place to live. Douglas, a farm worker living in a tied cottage, is one of many I met who say they will never be able to afford to buy a house. Meanwhile, they are surrounded by holiday properties, many of which are actually owned by the better-off locals. The debate over housing is going to be a major obstacle to any rapprochement between the livelihood, conservation and recreation approaches. Though it is only certain locals who benefit from development they are the ones with the political power to dominate decision-making and to maintain the anti-conservation/anti-incomer way of thinking. They carry on in this way despite making their money from the very people they are criticising. It is also ironic that many incomers who are moving to the area for the natural environment are in fact contributing to its demise by buying one of the many new houses. Locals remark on how well-off these incomers are and the effect their presence is having on the price of houses.

The structure of the economy complicates any attempts to break down barriers and extend people's sense of place. Economic imperatives will prevent people from being able to fully involve themselves or be open to conservation and recreation approaches. These economic forces are not just local phenomena but can be traced outwards to the local and global level as shown in Chapter Seven. Despite their image to the contrary, many locals value the environment. Perhaps they could have a different appreciation of the environment under more favourable economic conditions. Similar findings have been made in other parts of the world. Nygren (2003), in her study of rainforest conflicts in Central America found that those who were chopping down trees and coming into conflict with conservationists, had come to the area because they had been forced off their land elsewhere. Those who are struggling economically in Badenoch and Strathspey are similarly the victims of economic restructuring in other parts of Scotland.

These economic inequalities have a direct bearing on the process of decision-making. I have shown how politics is dominated by certain elites, consisting of landowners, developers, some business owners and politicians who benefit directly from the livelihood discourse. They are being challenged by a new elite, based on better-off incomers to the area, supported by conservation organisations such as the RSPB, who is also a major landowner. Most people have been left on the periphery of these political struggles but many locals will tend to side with the local elite rather than what they consider to be an outside elite. However, many are so busy or so disenchanted that they do not get involved at all. As noted above, those doing two jobs or single parents tied to the house will not have the time to get involved in local politics. The correspondence in the local paper illustrates this – debates go on for weeks between the same people. Community councils and stakeholder panels are not representative of the very diverse local community. This point is a key contribution of my research. Too often policy-makers treat the local community as either monolithic or consisting of a few distinct stakeholder groups. They can then claim to have consulted the local community when in fact they have barely scratched the surface, remaining ignorant of the 'multitude of voices' (Bakhtin: 1984). Even in my research, despite managing to talk to a very wide range of people, I inevitably missed out on those who do not do the activities I was able to do (my mountain biking efforts were dismal and therefore I didn't spend much time in those circles) or those who were marginalised from the day-to-day life of the area. All societies will have some degree of inequality and this has been a weakness of much research on land use conflict. Conflicts have been portrayed as being between the local community and Western environmentalists. But both groups are very diverse and it would be inaccurate to identify them with one outlook.

Political constraints are also national and global. Ross's experience with the gamekeeping students illustrates the problem. He gave talks to these students at Abernethy in order to encourage them to understand the RSPB perspective. But those students will not be open to what he is saying if their course is dominated by the anti-conservationist views of the landowners who will be their eventual employers. At a national level, political organisations like the Countryside Alliance, the British Association of Shooting and Conservation, Scottish Gamekeepers and the Scottish Landowners Federation are trying to ensure that the tradition of the Scottish sporting estate is maintained. The growth in land ownership by conservation organisations is a challenge to their power. Similarly, conservation organisations are mobilising their own forces, buying up land, using the legal system and EU directives and portraying keepers and stalkers as anti-conservation because of their deer management policies. Such political conflicts have left most people on the sidelines and will only hamper attempts to enlarge the base of political decision-making about land use.

One of the key problems that emerged from my research, in common with the findings of anthropologists working in developing countries, is the issue of what counts as knowledge (Walley: 2004, Ellen: 2000, Hobart: 1993). Many of the people I met lacked the confidence to speak out or get more involved in the public arena. Ross became a stakeholder and was consulted by researchers – he was the youth representative in a variety of forums. He was surprised by this and thought he would not actually get very far in his career because his doesn't have a college education. He commented on how 'intelligent' the various masters and PhD students are who come to Abernethy to do research. But at the same time, he questioned their knowledge.

He said: 'Someone comes to Abernethy for four months to do research on the black grouse and is then considered an expert. But Desmond has been studying black grouse for thirty years, but with no degree, and he is not respected in the same way'. Douglas felt the same. He said he could never get a job other than as an ordinary farm worker, despite all the knowledge he has, because he does not have any formal qualifications. This prioritising of academic knowledge over practical, local knowledge (discussed in Chapter Four) has created much resentment of conservation organisations and is therefore a major obstacle to overcoming hostility between the livelihood and conservation approach.

Though hostility to incomers is whipped up by local elites and largely ignored by ordinary locals, it is not completely an invented problem. Douglas mixed well with a range of people in the local walking club and the mountain biking group. Many of these people were incomers. But he did not feel comfortable with everyone. His view typifies others who do not usually buy into the anti-incomer discourse. Johnny Campbell, the local Gaelic heritage proponent was quite happy to work with English incomers in the Gaelic language group. But he also felt that incomers tend to 'take over' because they are educated and confident. He said, 'Highlanders are reticent; they do not like to push themselves forward'. Since incomers tend to be associated with an interest in recreation and/or conservation, such strained relations are an impediment to building bridges between the different approaches to land use and instead fuel the anti-incomer feelings in the public debates.

Despite very positive moves, there are a number of factors that are making it difficult to bring together the various approaches to land use. Change needs to come both through individual initiatives and changes in economic, political and social structures and institutions. This is also the conclusion reached by those who work around environmental justice issues (Guha and Martinez-Alier: 1997, Harvey: 1996, Pulido: 1996). They have found that many people are concerned about and appreciate the environment but that this is often expressed in ways that do not always concur with more dominant ideas. They have also found that the goals and discourses of traditional environmentalists are alien to many people struggling to survive. Their approach, though discussed mainly with reference to very poor groups in North America or the developing world, is relevant, if adapted, to the situation in the Scottish Highlands. The key is that environmentalism cannot be divorced from economic, political and social issues. (Harvey: 1996, Pulido: 1996, Anderson and Berglund: 2003, Brechin et. al.: 2003). These inequalities not only make it very difficult for people to have the experiences that will give them a broader, more integrated sense of place in the first instance but they also prevent people from participating and having their voice heard once they have developed this new sense of place, because it directly challenges the elites who benefit from the continued divisions.

Community: who 'belongs'?

The local-versus-incomer rhetoric has fuelled land use conflicts. Those who spoke out against the funicular were categorised as incomers who did not have the right to speak because they were anti-local development. The incomers were associated with outside organisations, which were portrayed as not being concerned about the local community and its future. This division made it very difficult for people to participate in the public arena and helped to ensure the exclusion of many voices and the continued polarisation of the different approaches to land use. Though there has been a problem across Scotland with incomers who, with their economic and cultural capital, may unintentionally antagonise the locals (Jedrej and Nuttal: 1996, Macdonald: 1997), my research has demonstrated that this resentment was exacerbated by the activities of certain groups operating within a particular decision-making structure, and was not necessarily inevitable. Incomers were welcomed if they appeared to commit themselves to the wellbeing of the community and integrated themselves sensitively into the community. Activity and friendship groups mixed people from a variety of origins, for example the Gaelic language group and the Strathspey Mountain Club. Even those who indulged in anti-incomer rhetoric retracted many of their more extreme statements when spoken to outside the public arena. Moreover, the concept of one local community is a myth. Some incomers integrated very well with some parts of the community and not with others. It was the groups that felt threatened in some way by the influence of these newcomers that were most likely to be hostile to them. For example, certain business and landowners felt that incomers with a conservation perspective challenged their key role in decision-making.

This raises the difficult question of who belongs in a community. In many ways, communities are invented. In other words, there is no natural community but rather a community that is continually evolving and changing (Lovel: 1998, Edwards: 1998, Cohen: 2000, Barth: 2000, Amit and Rapport: 2002). As people become more involved in the life of a place, they become part of that community. And even for those who would like to argue for a genetic link to place, such as Johnny Campbell, it is not so much where people come from but whether they seem to care about the community that carries weight. Those who participate and contribute, even if they are seen as different, such as Tom Prescott of Insh Marshes, will be accepted.

The reason for some of the hostility is the underlying differences in which aspects of the place people appreciate and value, and to have this appreciation requires knowledge. People hostile to Abernethy have had no experience of the dedicated, long-term work that RSPB wardens and volunteers have done to care for the land. Abernethy is internationally famous for its work, with many researchers and volunteers coming from all over the world. This is recognised by those parts of the community that have had contact with Abernethy. For example, David Hayes, owner of Landmark Forest Adventure Park, was full of admiration for the work they are doing. Alan and Robert from the Strathspey Mountain Club often suggested walks in Abernethy Forest because they admire and enjoy the way the forest has been managed for native tree generation. But this respect has not reached the wider community. Similarly, Glenmore Lodge, and their instructors' intimate knowledge of the Cairngorm plateau and climbing areas, seemed like an island, unknown to many locals but attracting people from all over the country to take their courses. Therefore, many locals had experience of neither the place – Abernethy or the Cairngorm plateau – nor the people who know and care for them. Both groups are part of the place, but without making the necessary links those who work in Abernethy and Glenmore Lodge could continue to be seen as not belonging, no matter how long they have been in the area.

Another related issue is the role of visitors and outside organisations in making decisions about land use. People from organisations like the RSPB and Mountaineering Scotland see the land in a national and even global context. Roy Dennis (see Chapter Five), who had been part of programmes to reintroduce birds to Scotland, questioned the 'localist' mentality. 'Why shouldn't I have a right to participate in decisions made about land on the other side of the world? If biodiversity is being threatened then it is everyone's business'. He challenged the idea of seeing land as belonging to one group of people who either happen to own it or live in proximity to it. The discussions about the National Park reflected the reluctance of many locals to give up control to those they saw as outsiders, whereas others argued that the Cairngorms should belong to the nation – after all, that is the ethos behind a National Park. The RSPB were managing their property primarily for the end of preserving birds – capercaillie, osprey and black grouse – but also for helping forest regeneration. This is why they did not feel beholden to local views. The same can be said of Mountaineering Scotland and the Ramblers. These organisations argued that the Cairngorms should not be a place that belongs to locals for their own economic benefit. It should be there for the nation, as a place in which people can enjoy quiet recreation. This view was argued strongly by those campaigning against the sale of the Cuillin Ridge in Skye, which the local laird wanted to sell in order to raise money for his new castle roof. The Cuillin Ridge is the domain of the serious mountaineer; uninhabitable, it is known only by those who have explored it over many years. As one mountaineer said, 'The Cuillin Ridge, if it belongs to anyone, belongs to those who have risked their lives on it'. However, some locals resented people having a say in their area because as one person said: 'Just because they have ruined where they live, they want us to remain undeveloped'. This view has been echoed elsewhere in the world where the creation of National Parks has been criticised as creating playgrounds for the rich (see, for example, Olwig: 1977, 1980, Neumann: 1998).

The John Muir Trust

The John Muir Trust (JMT) illustrates the possibility of integrating a livelihood, conservation and recreation approach as well as bringing together outsiders and locals into a common framework of decision-making. I found that the JMT aims to initiate change on several levels. On the one hand, the work on their properties brings together people who both live physically in a place and who care about a place but live elsewhere. This usually means that the Trust is balancing local livelihood and community interests with conservation and recreation concerns of the wider membership. On the other hand, they are involved at a national level with issues of land reform and rural development and inequality. The John Muir Trust is not without its critics, both outside and within. However, my research with the local JMT group as well as around Scotland on their property in Knoydart and Skye, found that their ethos and practices address some of the very issues that I was coming across in Badenoch and

Strathspey. This is because they recognise that the conservation goals can only be realised if one also takes seriously the economic issues that might lead to people being anti-conservation.

> By acquiring and managing key wild areas, the Trust sets out to show that the damage inflicted on the world over the centuries can be repaired: the land can be conserved on a sustainable basis for the human, animal and plant communities which share it; and the great spiritual qualities of wilderness, of tranquillity and solitude, can be preserved for those to come (*JMT Journal*: January 2004, statement of objectives).

> It is no longer enough for environmentalists to make the environment case convincingly we need the skill to make the economic arguments as well (*JMT Journal*: spring 2009; Environmental charities forced to debate economics by Helen McDade).

The JMT has incorporated into its statement of objectives the importance of integrating conservation, recreation and livelihood. Not only do they aim to provide a conservation model of land management that local residents can support but they have also tried to develop an interest in local culture and livelihood issues amongst those who join the Trust primarily because of its wild land objectives. Implementing these aims has not been without its problems. When the JMT organised an exhibition in the new visitors centre at the top of the newly Christened Cairngorm funicular, now referred to officially as the Mountain Railway, the Trust's magazine was inundated with letters expressing outrage at what appeared to be a betrayal of the Trust's basic ethos.

Internal conflicts have arisen between those who live on JMT's Skye properties and members who came from elsewhere for the occasion of the annual conference in 2000. The factor, Ian MacKinnon, told the conference that he preferred working with Ian Anderson (of Jethro Tull and former owner of the property).

This is because Ian had substantial capital to invest and let him take charge of the day-to-day running of the estate. With the JMT he is accountable to a large organisation. Moreover, the aims of the membership do not always coincide with the interests of what is essentially still a crofting community. Members join the Trust because of its publicity that stresses its conservation role – 'conserving wild places'. However, members do not often realise that the majority of Trust properties contain whole communities that have crofting rights. This means that they still have the right to graze sheep and farm the land. One member up from Newcastle for the conference was outraged that there were so many sheep on the property. He thought all the sheep should be removed in order to facilitate tree regeneration. Others were similarly critical of the policy of the forest manager who still manages non-native forests for timber. When I volunteered on Knoydart, a more remote property with no tenants, people questioned why the Trust did not just cull the deer rather than building deer fences.

However, what is noteworthy is that by inviting members to their properties, either for their national conferences or for volunteer work, they are able to let members see for themselves the problems of land management and engage them in debates about the best way forwards. The man who was anti-sheep was able to hear the crofters' side of the story and those who were anti-foreign trees were able to discuss the economic issues with the forestry manager. The people working at Knoydart heard from the manger about the problems they still had because they did not have shooting rights, as well as why the deer fences were not a problem because there were no grouse or capercaillie on the property to get caught. During both the conference and the conservation volunteer days, there was much discussion and debate. There was no clear agreement or resolution but all parties could at least try to understand the position of others. Everyone is made to feel as if it is their land. Anyone who lives on Trust land is automatically given free membership and allowed to participate in all decision-making. Local communities and JMT members who live elsewhere are, therefore, part of a common framework for managing the land. The volunteer programme encourages members from all over the country to come and contribute to the land. One woman had volunteered for several years on Knoydart. She arrived early this time because she wanted to check on the trees she planted in previous years. This volunteer work means that people do not just have an abstract commitment to 'wild land' but develop a more long-term interest in a particular piece of it. This can never be as intense as for those who actually live on the land but it can improve the level of understanding of land issues. And, by bringing the local people into contact with people from outwith the area, those who see the land as mainly something to make a living out of can gain an appreciation of why others appreciate the hills as a place to go walking or climbing.

The JMT is also active on a national level. They distinguish themselves from the RSPB and the SNH by stressing the way they work in partnership with communities. I was surprised by the attitude of the keepers and stalkers at Kinveachy towards the Trust. When the local JMT group suggested a visit to the estate in order to engage in a dialogue about land management issues, I heard very positive comments, very unlike what I heard about the RSPB. This was partly because it was seen as Scottish, but mainly because it has a reputation for not putting the conservation agenda above the livelihood concerns of the local people. This reputation means they are respected by a variety of people and they are often called upon to give their views on land issues. Though they themselves are buying properties and becoming landowners, they have initiated an internal debate about whether it should be the government that takes on the responsibility of managing land for the benefit of all. Several members expressed concern that perhaps the JMT was just reinforcing the whole concept of private property and hindering any attempts at land reform. They have also been part of debates on community buy-outs, seen by some as the way forwards. However, this approach tends to exclude anyone else from outside the area except through regulatory agencies such as SNH, which are then resented by the locals for interfering (MacAskill: 1999). The JMT approach involves outsiders in a less autocratic manner and seeks to build a relationship between local and national members.

*

Debates surrounding land are fraught with controversy, yet finding a way out of the conflicts is critical for the future of both humanity and the planet as a whole. As the JMT says, we need to find a way of ensuring that the land is 'sustainable for humans, animals and plants who share it'. My research has uncovered the origins of these conflicts and the social and cultural processes that are exacerbating them. It has also suggested possible ways to go beyond the straitjacket categories of livelihood, recreation and conservation, and local and outsider/incomer. Though people will always travel in parallel places to some extent, there could be more visiting and merging of these places. The Cairngorms, like many other places in the world, is a special place. There are many people, natives, incomers and visitors, who care very much what happens to the land. The experiences they have had and the stories they tell of epics and hard times, of joy and laughter with friends, and of wonder at the aesthetic beauty as well as the productive capacity of the land, have given them different senses of place and relationships with the land. These different senses of place, however, do not necessarily have to involve a struggle between competing approaches to land use. Instead, diversity, constructively engaged, can itself be the source of new relationships between humans and the land, relationships that are compatible with both environmentalism and social justice. This is not a straightforward task; there will continue to be competing interpretations of both environmentalism and social justice. Nevertheless, it is a goal worth pursuing.

Towards the end of my stay in the Cairngorms I attended a summer play written, produced and performed by the staff, parents, friends and pupils of the Carrbridge Primary School. It was performed in the open air and I attended with my friends Anne, George and Robert from the Strathspey Mountain Club and who live in Carrbridge. I was surprised by how many people I recognised in the audience and helping with the production. The livelihood sense of place was well represented by many of the staff from Kinveachy. The keepers John and Ian were there to watch their children perform. John's wife was active behind the scenes. Frank, the estate's sporting manager was helping his wife, a teacher at the school. David, the stalker, was also there, keen to see the costumes and set design that his girlfriend, the daughter of a local electrician, had helped the children design. In addition to the Strathspey Mountain Club, I also noticed several ski instructors as well as people from the cycling group based in Carrbridge. And I saw the conservationists, Gus and Tessa Jones, attending the event because their children were performing. There were also some visitors because the event had been advertised in the area's tourist offices. The message of the play itself was significant. It stressed the importance of maintaining a link to the past and the livelihood tradition, but also of valuing and preserving the area's natural beauty and biodiversity. In addition, it promoted a way of thinking, pitting a broader definition of local community against developers (who in this case are local). In other words, the community in all its diversity unites against those who want to use the land for profit rather than for the good of all.

Seeing all these people together, watching the new generation perform such a play about the future, was a fitting end to my research year, and a symbol of what could be.

Where to Now?

Anthropology has made a major contribution to understanding human beings and their relationship to each other and the world. Fieldwork takes place all over the world, from the homes of remote tribes to the centres of economic and political power in the West. It is this global context that provides the basis for understanding both the immense diversity as well the commonality of humanity. However, the global picture is not based on sweeping generalities but grounded in the concrete experience of individual human beings. The local provides the important detail that is vital for making sense of the wider picture. Such a combination of detailed ethnography, analysed with reference to global structures and processes, provides a firm basis for anthropology to enter the realm of policy, not just on a governmental level, but as an aid to anyone who seeks ideas and strategies for intervening positively and creatively in the world (for example Milton: 2002: 3).

I have tried to follow in this tradition. By studying a particular location, attentive to how this location links to wider cultural processes, social structures and the global economy, I hope to contribute to the work of finding solutions to the critical situation humans are now facing, including climate change and lack of economic and social justice. I have shown how in the Cairngorms this task has been hampered by the polarisation of conflicts over land use between economic development, conservation and recreation, similar to elsewhere in the world. Trump and his supporters in the resource industry used the argument of job creation to open up huge tracts of public land to fracking, logging and mining. Huge areas of forest in the Amazon have been cleared for mining, soybean production and logging. Again, the argument is the need for economic development. In Africa, species such as the elephant are in danger of extinction because their ivory is a source of much-needed income for locals. Such antagonisms mean that little progress can be made in realigning humanity's relationship with the land in such a way that both people and the rest of the planet can survive. Instead of looking for ways to ensure the wellbeing of both humans and the environment, discussions remain locked in polarised impasses, with the choice being *either* human wellbeing *or* the environment. My research, by revealing the genealogy of the opposing perspectives and documenting the process of their formation into divided, often intransigent, interest groups, provides a basis from which to consider ways out of those impasses.

Importance of people's lived, embodied experience

My research has detailed the very powerful forces at work in constructing an individual's sense of place. The engagement of the body and mind, cognitively and emotionally, in activity dramatically shapes the person's perceptions, both influencing what they perceive and what they do not perceive. Their experiences, thus imprinted on the person, both mind and body, will form a key part of their identity and their worldview. By taking activities such as mountain-walking or birding and applying the anthropological eye, we can see the infinite complexity, as well as the power and intensity, of humans' interaction with their social and physical environment. My work elaborates on the work of those who argue against a nature/culture dualism (Ingold: 2000, Ellen: 1996, Descola and Palsson: 1996) by showing ethnographically how humans' relationship with their environment is an active, developmental process that integrates dynamically their subjective perspective (culture) with an objective physical environment (nature). We may separate these two aspects of any activity conceptually, but in practice they merge into one. This was seen clearly in the experience of mountaineering. People bring to the hills various preconceptions, dreams and ambitions, but then engage in an activity which is inherently embedded in the physical hill environment, with its affordances and constraints. In the course of the activity, it is only possible to be aware of doing, when the subjective and the objective, the culture and the nature, become part of the same process.

My research goes beyond this work to show how people's embodied experience is influenced by and reflected in society outside the activity itself, significantly contributing to the position from which they interact with others in discussions and debates on issues that have an impact on land use. I have shown how structural forces (power of landowners, economic inequalities), discourses (local-versus-incomer, tradition), cultural practices (climbing magazines, the process of apprenticeship) and history (patterns of land use, ecological history) are interwoven with the embodied experience of the individual. The sense of place thus forms the basis for the development of conflict situations. If there were not different perspectives, arising out of different lived experiences, then conflicts would not occur. However, conflicts cannot be reduced to these different senses of place. The existence of different senses of place does not necessarily have to lead to conflict. After all, individuals each have their own sense of place and this does not usually lead to conflict. I have built on the understanding of how senses of place are formed to then show how, and under what circumstances, certain senses of place become formalised into interest groups, which then clash. I then explored the links between these different levels, the individual's relationship with the environment, which I call the sense of place, and the public conflict that could be observed between local livelihood and outside conservation and recreation interests.

This approach, beginning with the individual experience, but with an awareness of how that individual experience is embedded in social groups, structures and processes as well as a physical environment and history (historical ecology) is essential for understanding what is happening at a wider social level. Too often people are studied first as groups or communities, creating misleading generalisations. There are centralising forces at work within society that create such classes, social groups, identities and institutions but at the same time there is an opposing tendency that Bakhtin (1981) calls heteroglossia. This is when each individual has their own subjective experience and way of giving meaning to those centralising forces.

This does not mean generalisations cannot be made. Groups are formed through common experiences and practices. People relate to the land in particular ways through their work and leisure and this creates a tendency for them to form a common approach. By understanding the process at work beneath the surface, one becomes aware of the temporary nature of these groups that appear so fixed at the level of society. To understand how tendencies become entrenched positions is vitally important in learning how to deal with all conflict situations, not only the conflicts over land use discussed in this book.

Senses of place, interest groups, power and conflict

Before going to the field, I had heard of the Cairngorms because of the debate surrounding the funicular. I had read reports in climbing magazines and had discussed the issue with representatives of Scottish Natural Heritage and the Cairngorms Partnership at a conference in Oxford. I was advised to go to the Cairngorms for the very reason that there was so much conflict. It was thought that people's feelings and attitudes towards land use and the environment would be more readily apparent to the outside observer. At this stage, the conflict was portrayed in stark terms: locals were in favour of it because it would bring in money and jobs, and conservation organisations, with support from recreation groups, were against it because the funicular would increase the use of the fragile Cairngorm plateau and would appear a general eyesore that did not belong on the mountain.

In the first stages of fieldwork I did not intend to look for signs of this conflict. My main aim was to get a feel for how different people interacted with the land – in other words, to see how the activities in which they were engaged contributed to their sense of place. It soon became apparent that there were two contradictory tendencies. On the one hand, different activities seemed to foster different approaches to land use, as predicted by my pre-fieldwork encounters, debates at the political level and other literature on the subject. These could be broadly grouped into the livelihood, conservation and recreation approach to land use. The livelihood approach sees land, either directly or indirectly, as productive. The conservation approach aims to actually intervene to create wild land, valuing species for their own intrinsic worth. The recreation approach wants to ensure that land is available for the pursuit of whatever leisure activity its proponents participate in. These categories were not just my imposition. The people themselves would identify themselves with a specific approach, often in contrast to another one (Lund: nd: 9). Stalkers and keepers made it clear they did not like the 'conservationists' and also thought those who went 'walking for fun' were quite mad. Strong anti-conservationist views were expressed by a wide range of people who depended on the area as a source of livelihood. Meanwhile, I heard negative remarks about farmers and sporting estate workers from those working in conservation (see Chapters Four and Five). In addition, skiers would criticise walkers and vice versa, anglers are at odds with canoeists and walkers criticise conservationists for wanting to keep the land 'pristine', inaccessible to human enjoyment. It was obvious how these different approaches could lead to conflict over issues like the funicular.

On the other hand, these different approaches often remained unarticulated. When I merely noted what people actually did and spoke about whilst doing the activity, I began to notice the overlapping of supposed distinct approaches. When out with the stalkers and keepers early on in my fieldwork I was struck by their enjoyment of physical movement, skill in moving around the hills and appreciation of views and wildlife. At one stage I was alternating between going out with the stalkers and keepers on Kinveachy and volunteering at Insh Marshes, the RSPB reserve. My experiences were the same – they were just called something different. Ross, raised on a sporting estate, said that for him it was all 'land management' and he tries to explain this but many people are unable to separate the actual work he does from the label of conservation. The same is true of many locals who would never label themselves conservationists or walkers, yet they take their dogs for long walks, often up into the hills, make an effort to find the breeding frogs and say they would miss the background of the hills if they ever left. In addition to this overlap of approaches in practice, I also started coming across people who consciously did not identify with any approach (as in Chapter Seven). The experiences and activities they were involved in integrated all three approaches in a variety of ways.

As I began to focus more on the public arena, going to meetings, reading the local paper, interviewing those considered key people, I was once again faced with the articulation of distinct approaches. They were much more pronounced than in my encounters with people during the course of actually doing their work or leisure activity. At this level, I also became more aware that not only were there distinct approaches to land use, but the approaches were distinguished as belonging to either locals or outsiders/incomers. Those people who articulated such views in public often toned down the rhetoric in private. My research thus also explores the process by which the tendency to have a particular approach to land use manifests itself as a fixed, entrenched position, in particular circumstances, which then leads to acute conflict between different sides in the public arena. I found that whether one develops a broad approach into a fixed position on the environment depends on a number of factors. An individual may tend to favour one approach, but most people will be engaged in a number of activities or the activities that they are engaged in will have a number of facets, such that they cannot be pinned down. Those that have the broadest range of experiences (such as the anomalous cases discussed in Chapter Seven) will be impossible to fit into a general scheme, or even broadly into one approach. Depending on the intensity of involvement and the material stake one has in that approach to land use, a person will be more or less attached to one position.

The economic, social and economic context then brings these tendencies into clearly identified positions. Events in the wider culture, social structure and in the physical environment itself will put people in situations in which they are forced to take a position (Balee: 1998, Lave and Holland: 2001). The increased use of the river by recreational canoeists (itself the result of a number of developments in the wider society) has precipitated anglers into a fixed position vis-à-vis what they see as a threat to their sport. And they themselves are reacting this way because of the problems with salmon fishing and the lack of fish, the product of an interaction between a certain physical environment and set of economic practices.

When conflict becomes especially acute such as during the funicular debate, structural and discursive practices of dominant groups mould these temporary positions into fixed interest groups who then do battle with each other as opposing 'sides'. The anti-conservationist and anti-incomer discourses arose partially out of people's experience, but my research shows that this discourse appeared most predominantly at the public level, spoken by those with power in the community. As one informant said, 'These debates have nothing to do with conservation; they have to do with who has the power to decide'. The people who expressed anti-conservation views did not have any direct experience of conservationists. I only heard stories or rumours of what the RSPB had done or not done. And when probed, as I show in Chapter Seven, many of these statements are qualified and retracted. Ross experienced the effect of these discourses first-hand when he was sent on a one-week stalking course at a college in Thurso, a college known for training sons of stalkers and keepers to follow in their fathers' footsteps. At first he was fine, they were like him, there to learn about deer-stalking and doing similar work, but as soon as they found out he was from the RSPB, the trouble began. He said it was 'bullying' that he experienced, constant remarks and taunts. The worst was the last night when an outside speaker came and spent a large part of his talk 'telling lies' about RSPB Abernethy where Ross works. A Colonel from a countryside organisation that was involved in the course pointed out Ross to the speaker and called on Ross to defend Abernethy. Ross did not want to get involved in a debate with such a hostile audience. The Colonel used this as a pretext to argue that the speaker must have been right because Ross could not reply. The same process is at work on the other side. Many conservationists are scathing about keepers and stalkers, branding them as killers who have no interest in the environment. Similar criticism is directed towards farmers with their pesticides and sheep. These two groups, according to some, are uniquely responsible for the environmental devastation of the Highlands because keeping deer and sheep on the land is preventing tree regeneration.

From these examples, it is clear how people internalise certain discourses that are not actually based on any experience. These can only help either landowners in their power struggle with those who think the sporting estate is doing untold damage to the hill environment, or conservation organisations, also very powerful, in their fight for new regimes of land management. Since these discourses do not necessarily fit in with people's expe-riences, they will not always be present in everyday life, but are articulated in times of conflict when issues are being discussed in the public arena.

The genealogy of a conflict over land use is thus extremely complex. It stems from the fact that people are engaged in different activities with the land and therefore develop certain approaches to what they think the land should be used for. In certain contexts, their sense of place becomes a conscious position. The more intense and public the conflict, the greater the intervention of dominant groups, the more these approaches will develop into interest groups. This happens at the public level where power relations come into play. This is because to 'win' one's position, each side needs to mobilise power. This process is most developed with only some people, those that participate in debates in the public arena. Most people have not transformed their sense of place into a fixed position because this would require them to become part of an organised group and for various social and economic reasons this does not happen. Most do not have the social, economic or cultural capital to do so. Others, for various reasons outlined in Chapter Seven, do not buy into the terms of the dominant way of thinking. Therefore, most people remain outside or on the periphery of the debates. The stakeholder model reinforces this tendency for only certain people and groups to engage in the public debates. Ross is now often chosen to be a stakeholder. He says he is the 'token youth' but he admits that he can't really speak for all youth; he just happens to be the 'youth who always says yes'. He has recently joined what he calls 'the usual suspects – the Dick Balharrys, the Jamie Williamsons' – who are always called upon to speak on behalf of one section of the community. Such stakeholder panels encourage people to speak according to a fixed position and exaggerate differences.

The conclusion to be drawn from this analysis is that though there may be different approaches to how land should be used, depending on the activities that one is involved in and one's embodied lived experience, these only lead to conflict in certain contexts. And these conflicts are fuelled and exacerbated by economic, social and therefore political inequality, which gives power to the discourses of the dominant groups. These discourses, in the case of my research the local-livelihood-versus-outside-conservation/recreation discourse, create a polarised situation that is difficult to deal with constructively. The stakeholder model then reinforces this tendency by taking the different constructed interest groups as a reflection of the views of the community as a whole.

What can be done? My research shows that there are two tendencies at work. Firstly, there is the tendency for senses of place to develop into different approaches and, potentially, interest groups. Secondly, there exists the tendency for overlap and the creation of anomalies; a multitude of voices that are difficult to categorise (Bakhtin: 1984), in which there are only the activity and the perceptions, not the label given to them. As Nietzsche pointed out in *Beyond Good and Evil* (1999), oppositions (such as livelihood, conservation and recreation in this case) are human creations, 'logical fictions', that we mobilise at different times to serve different purposes. If we look at people's lived experience we find that these opposites are not so obvious. However, structural power and discursive practices ensure that the fictions continue to exist.

Moving beyond conflict

It is imperative to find a way to reconcile apparently conflicting land uses, including conservation of wild places for habitat and their intrinsic value, recreational activities for humans' personal enjoyment, and fulfilment and the meeting of people's economic needs. My research suggests possibilities for how this process of reconciliation could be facilitated, as well as identifying potential resistance to change. Because of my anthropological focus on a specific area, these possibilities have revealed themselves at the local level in the interactions, experiences and initiatives of individuals and groups. However, as I have argued, local events and practices are embedded in a wider network of institutions, structures and discourses. Therefore, the implications of my research need to be examined in terms of what they suggest for change at the level of the locality or community and the wider society.

Distinct senses of place have been identified as contributing to conflict situations in particular contexts. Therefore, it is important to consider how to broaden people's sense of place so that they begin to value a greater range of aspects of the land. Such fundamental changes in perception require long-term work and education, especially of young people. My research has stressed the importance of activity and practical engagement with the environment; thus, an educational programme would be more successful in expanding people's sense of place if it was based on a variety of active learning experiences in a wide range of locations. Such a programme would be important for both introducing those who live in the area to new environmental experiences but also for those from urban areas who may not appreciate the economic and social character of the areas they come to visit. The Duke of Edinburgh Award is one such initiative. More recently, the John Muir Award has been set up by the National Park and this has been a resounding success with hundreds of young people participating from the Cairngorms area itself.

Such a long-term programme necessarily requires co-operation between all those with an interest in the area and will therefore require appropriate structures and forums within which initiatives can develop. The Cairngorms Partnership, despite certain limitations, was such a forum in the sense that a range of people was brought together in order to foster a broad appreciation of the area. This has continued under the National Park. National organisations have a vital role to play in this project. The John Muir Trust and Mountaineering Scotland, and the British Mountaineering Council, have already introduced various initiatives through their members' magazines and locals and visitors forums in some areas. Projects that involve a variety of people with different senses of place, reflecting the wide range of views amongst locals, visitors and national organisations will also contribute to the undermining of the destructive local-versus-incomer/outsider discourse. Such projects and initiatives could contribute to the creation of a new perspective on who belongs and who has the right to decide about the future of a given area.

The power of the local-versus-incomer discourse in fuelling the conflict between different approaches must also be defused. In the case of the funicular, those who spoke out against the funicular were categorised as incomers who did not have the right to speak because they were anti-local development. Incomers are often portrayed as not being concerned about the local community and its future. This division makes it very difficult for people to participate in the public arena and will ensure the exclusion of many voices and the continued polarisation of the different approaches to land use. My research has shown that this is often unfair and at odds with reality. This hostility is whipped up by local elites for their own benefit. Communities are continually changing and the artificial division of those who live permanently in the area into incomer and local can be toxic. The main distinguishing feature should be between those who care about the community, the land and its future and those whose main interest is personal profit.

The different senses of place not only relate to how the land should be used but who should be involved in making decisions about it. The conflicts have been fuelled by local development wanting to exclude outsiders, and by the conservation and recreation approach that considers it legitimate for national and global interests to be part of the decision-making process. This is a difficult issue to resolve but given the interconnectedness of not only the ecological system but of society as well, it is difficult to see how anyone can continue to argue that one piece of the world is theirs exclusively (Kuehls: 1996). As one resident pointed out, those who want to exclude outsiders from decision-making are also those who are making their living from those same outsiders in the form of tourism. An economic development officer told me that they had to be careful not to have another situation like the funicular because those who opposed it from outside the area are the very people whom the area is trying to attract: the recreation and conservation visitor.

It may be useful to redefine community as a community of interests, in which everyone who is in some way is part of a place, no matter where they happen to live, can participate without at the same time completely drowning out those who physically live there. This issue is relevant for all areas of the world where local interests appear to conflict with global interests, for example in Amazonia where the destruction of the Amazon has an impact on people all over the world. The case of the Cairngorms also illustrates that neither global nor local interests are mono-lithic and that divisions may exist not only between locals and outsiders. Therefore, we need to be aware of a variety of perspec-tives when making decisions about land use: the impact on wider environmental issues and future generations, the interests of all those who have a link, often intensely emotional, to the area and the different parts of the local community.

Overcoming the social and cultural divisions amongst this community of interests will not be an easy task. Education, broadening people's senses of place, national and/or local ini-tiatives that encourage different groups to work together, and challenging cultural assumptions about who belongs and who decides, can only go so far within the current economic and political context. Despite very positive moves, there are a number of factors that are making it difficult to bring together the various approaches to land use. Change needs to come both through individual initiatives and changes in economic, political and social structures and institutions. This is also the conclusion reached by those who work around environmental justice issues (Guha and Martinez-Alier: 1997, Harvey: 1996, Pulido: 1996).

They have found that many people are concerned about and appreciate the environment but that it is often expressed in ways that do not always concur with more dominant ideas. They have also found that the goals and discourses of traditional environmentalists are alien to many people struggling to survive. Their approach, though discussed mainly with reference to very poor groups in North America or the developing world, is relevant, if adapted, to the situation in the Scottish Highlands. The key is that environmentalism cannot be divorced from economic, political and social issues (Harvey: 1996, Pulido: 1996, Anderson and Berglund: 2003, Brechin et. al.: 2003). This view is supported by the John Muir Trust, which has long been arguing that economic and social issues must be addressed if campaigns for wild land and conservation are to be successful. Economic, political and social inequalities make it very difficult for people to not only have the experiences that will give them a broader, more integrated sense of place in the first instance, but also to participate and have their voice heard once they have developed this new sense of place because it directly challenges the elites who benefit from the continued divisions.

These economic and social inequalities have a direct bearing on the process of decision-making. I have shown how politics is dominated by certain elites, consisting of landowners, developers, certain business owners and politicians who benefit directly from the livelihood discourse. They are being challenged by a new elite. Most people have been left on the periphery of these political struggles, but many locals will tend to side with the local elite rather than what they consider to be an outside elite. However, many are so busy or so disenchanted that they do not get involved at all. Those doing two jobs or single parents will not have the time to get involved in local politics. Though my research was based on living as an ordinary person and working in a restaurant used by locals and aiming to talk to as many people as possible, it will only have scratched the surface. That is why it is important to remember that there are many unheard voices. I have tended to focus on diversity of views within the community where I lived, but time spent with visitors also shows a diversity of perspectives.

Changing this political culture will be extremely difficult. Firstly, as noted above, it is based on economic and social inequality. Secondly, it is in the interests of the local elite to retain control of decision-making, in particular, the planning process. This is why such a big campaign was waged to retain planning powers with the Highland Council rather than the new National Park Authority (CNPA). However, there are more complex reasons why opening up the political process at the local level will be difficult. The local elites are supported through a network of regional and national interests. As noted by MacKinnon (2001), organisations such as the Highlands and Islands Enterprise were set up by the Conservatives in the 1990s in order to include more business interests in local decision-making. This has been seen in Badenoch and Strathspey with the way business associations, such as the Newtonmore Business Association, the Cairngorms Chamber of Commerce and the Economic Forum set up by the National Park Authority are used as representatives of the local community as a whole. The landowners are part of a national network that includes the Scottish Landowners Federation and other political organisations such as the Conservative Party, which seek to limit the current trend towards land reform and access rights. These networks are less visible to local people than the national networks with which local mountaineers or conservationists might be involved such as the Ramblers Association or the RSPB. Therefore, these organisations become targets for the local-versus-outsider discourse, even though the local development lobby is equally tied to outside national interests. If the political process is going to extend to a wider section of the community, then issues of land reform and the power of business interests over other interests will need to be addressed.

The National Park Authority is an organisation that seeks to be an alternative to the traditional political elites by involving a greater variety of people, both from the local community and from outside. There are a number of forums and advisory groups, divided along similar lines to those in the Cairngorm Partnership, dealing with, for example, outdoor access, nature, land management, deer, etc. I cannot comment on whether the Board has managed to overcome the weaknesses that I highlighted in the Cairngorm Partnership model. However, the structure, though including a greater range of interests than it did pre-National Park, still relies on the idea of interest groups and representatives of interest groups which can only reinforce the conflict model of decision-making. The alternative voices, who have emerged outside the traditional political structure of business associations, stakeholder forums, community councils and regional government, will most likely still be excluded as the model of decision-making and consultation remains the same.

*

What to do about the out-of-action mountain railway and the whole future of the ski area is still an important concern, however, housing is now a major source of controversy and illustrates the issues that still exist with decision-making and social and economic inequalities. There had been concern that the arrival of the National Park would mean the end of development and that planning permission would be more difficult to come by. However, this clearly has not been the case. One has only to drive through Aviemore to the north end of town where two massive housing developments have been built by local developers.

For the past decade, Kingussie has been a target for developers. Outline planning permission was given for 300 new homes in 2010. The way the debate was portrayed in the paper is typical of the way other conflicts have unfolded. The local community councillor had voiced objections but Cameron dismissed her as an incomer.

We know why the local representative would not answer all the questions today. Do you know why this is? She has not lived here long enough.

Strathspey and Badenoch Herald: 5 May 2010

The Badenoch and Strathspey Conservation Group was also mentioned as having objected because a biodiversity survey had not been done. Gus Jones wrote a lengthy letter to the paper slating the Park Authority: 'The decision reveals a catalogue of omissions by the planners and negligence by the board.' (*Strathspey and Badenoch Herald*: 5 May 2010).

The debate, as always, seems to be between those who are supposedly in tune with the local community, which needs jobs, and those who are more concerned with preserving the quality of the environment. However, there is some change in the arguments. This time, many of those who opposed the development were also using the local community livelihood discourse, arguing that such a large development will adversely affect the attractiveness of Kingussie and therefore be a problem for tourism. One of the developers replied that there are other jobs – those associated with the building industry – that will benefit. Recent figures show that tourism accounts for 43 per cent of employment in the area, and building and construction 6 per cent; it would seem that the tourist argument would be more persuasive. However, wages in the tourist sector are low and overall wages in the park are 30 per cent below the Scottish average, so there is a strong case for providing more jobs in construction (http://parkswatch-scotland.co.uk/2019/09/16/). Instead of the conflict being fully centred around outsider versus local, it is now framed more in terms of livelihood.

The other concern with housing is that it is not actually geared to the local market. Douglas and the children of low-paid workers would certainly benefit from access to truly affordable housing. However, as someone from the National Park board told me, the housing developments such as the one in Kingussie, are mainly individual three- and four-bedroomed houses on their own plots. He said this is not what the area needs but it is what the developers want to build. He said that the area needs more terraced houses and two- and three-story buildings with flats. It is mainly incomers who can afford the large houses, not locals. However, the housing needs will ultimately be determined by what the area is going to become. The area is now very popular both with those who work in Inverness and those who want a second home that is easily accessible from the Central Belt. This is the market that the developers are catering for. The end result could be the creation of a new urban area in the middle of the National Park.

This is supported by one resident of Kingussie who told me that around 60 per cent of these new houses are second homes or holiday lets. The problem is that the aim of house-building is to make a profit. According to Parkwatch, even though the Cairngorm National Park Authority wants more co-operation, it is not going to get it in the current system.

> For this to happen, capitalism as we know it – which is driven by profit and results in competition and people fighting for their own narrow interests, NOT the co-operation the CNPA desires – will miraculously have to cease. (http://parkswatchscotland.co.uk /2019/09/16/)

The continued existence of conflicts over land use show that there are many problems still to be resolved. Other models of decision-making are needed that involve more co-operation and consideration of the public good. But these can only work if there is more economic, social and political equality, an increased awareness and empathy for the experiences and views of others, as well as an expansion of horizons to include a much wider sense of community and who belongs.

All three senses of place

All three sense of place have value. Everyone should see the land as something that provides them with a living and a home, a place of beauty and source of adventure, and the habitat of many other species. If this was the case then it would be much easier to manage land for the benefit of people, including future generations, and the rest of the planet. I have already discussed ways to encourage people to develop and extend their experiences and awareness of land. In the Cairngorm region, as elsewhere around the world, there are numerous individuals and groups who are bringing about change through their activities, projects and initiatives. However, there need to be changes on a more fundamental level if we are to deal with the immediate challenge of ecological disaster both in terms of climate change and loss of biodiversity.

Though most, apart from the most extreme climate change deniers, would agree that we are facing an unprecedented crisis, there is enormous resistance to doing something about it. This resistance comes mainly from those who see land as an economic resource. Those who own most of the world's land and resources do not want to do anything that affects their profits. And most people are dependent on these same land- and resource owners for their own livelihood and therefore are also understandably wary of changing the status quo. Therefore, we will only be able to address the challenges facing humanity when we deal with the problem of those whose livelihoods will be affected.

Firstly, we need to ensure that the use of land is for the public good. Some will say this is possible with the current system of land ownership as long as subsidies, tax systems, etc. are there to ensure that the landowner can continue to make a living. An example of this can be found in Scotland with Povlsen – now the largest landowner in Scotland and a known conservationist. Another example is in Sussex where the owners of the Knepp Estate embarked on an ambitious transformation from an estate based on farming, which was making a loss, to a showpiece of biodiversity that provides jobs and income. Not only is the estate the darling of conservationists but also, it still produces food. However, in the early years of the project it was met with much hostility by other farmers. 'It was an affront to the efforts of every self-respecting farmer, an immoral waste of land, an assault on Britishness itself.' (Tree 2019, p. 98). Nevertheless, the owners felt that they were doing something productive. 'We went about the task like farmers but, for the first time, we were thinking like conservationists.' (p. 45) This is exactly what Ross said about his work for Abernethy and Insh Marshes – he is a land manager – it is just with a different aim in mind.

Some might argue, however, that choices about what to do with the land should not be in the hands of owners. When the land of Povlsen and Knepp passes into the hands of their children, there is no guarantee that they will continue to manage it in the same way.

> As private landowners we were concerned about the finances… We wanted our children and grandchildren to be free to make their own decisions about the land according to the circumstances in their lifetime – which might conceivably involve a return to agriculture if, for some unimaginable reason, farming on our clay was to become viable again (p. 76).

It may therefore be necessary to challenge the inequality of land ownership if there is to be a democratisation of discussions about how land is to be used. Parkwatch argues that this is crucial to ensure that social and economic issues are addressed. Referring to the National Park Economic Strategy (2017–2022), they argue:

> While average wages in the National Park are very low, a consequence of most jobs in the area being in tourism, agriculture and forestry, much of the land is owned by the very rich, the 0.1 per

cent, from Middle Eastern and European billionaires to the British Royal Family. No analysis is provided of inequality in the National Park, though it's possibly one of the most unequal places in Scotland and the rest of the UK. No analysis is undertaken either about how the thinking and actions of this very small group of people is the largest single influence over what economic activity takes place in the National Park.

It is not just the landowners themselves who are the problem. though they have the most to lose from any change; it is those who work for them, whose living is tied to the current system of land ownership and use, who must be convinced that changes would mean an improvement in their lives. My experience in the Cairngorms suggests that many land workers would be willing to make changes. One farm worker raises high quality beef on an estate owned by a foreign investor who shows no interest in what he is doing. For this he works long hours for a low wage. Wouldn't it be better if that land was put into the hands of those who work it so they can actually reap the benefits? And these farmers could focus on raising quality food rather than factory production. The estate workers on Kinveachy had little attachment to the landowner or the guests. They also worked very hard for little reward. Again, let them form a co-operative to manage the land for conservation purposes rather than as a sporting estate. This would meet with resistance but then as at Knepp, they would soon find that the work they are doing is very similar to their work on the sporting estate – they could treat the land as a garden, even though they would be promoting biodiversity. And shooting could continue but it should be of a different kind. The keepers and stalkers already believe that walked-up shooting is preferable to driven grouse. They had nothing but contempt for the rich guest who has to have everything laid on a plate for them. So, instead they could keep some deer and grouse – a much lower number so as not to necessitate such drastic measures such as hare-culling – and then have guests who are willing to do walked-up shooting. Is there that much support for keeping the historical tradition of the aristocratic landowner and his subservient estate workers? Ending the current dominance of aristocratic and rich businessmen would open up all sorts of possibilities. The end of the traditional sporting estate would be the death of one kind of way of life but the beginning of one that would be not only better for the environment but also better to all those who currently work hard for low wages, offering more opportunities rather than fewer.

Discussions about land use need to be more holistic and they need to engage everyone. Another obstacle to this is the nature of the planning system. We need a planning system that actually integrates the values, concerns and interests of all senses of place. Otherwise decisions will be made to address one issue, for example expanding renewable energy, which then negate other policy aims such as retaining peat bogs and preserving wild land. The John Muir Trust, again, is aware of the need to reform planning policy. According to Helen McDade in 'Time to Join the Dots' in *JMT Journal*, spring 2018:

> But rural land use affects everyone and is too important to be left entirely to private choices. We all need water, food, timber, energy and the other material benefits we derive from rural land. And we need the carbon sequestration properties provided by peatlands, woodlands and the sediment in our rivers. Then there are the cultural benefits we derive from the land, from recreational activities to aesthetic and even spiritual experiences. As John Muir himself put it, 'we all need beauty as well as bread'. So, surely, what is required is a holistic overview of land use, including planning policy, which does not artificially divide issues of public interest into those that are deemed as planning matters with others segregated into individual sectors such as agriculture, forestry, deer management, grouse-shooting or whatever. Ultimately, we need innovative ways of considering planning and other land uses together.

Conflicts over land use are an obstacle to resolving the urgent problems we are facing: ecological, social and economic. Dealing with land ownership, planning and control, as well as the issue of how to create communities in which all members have a voice, will be key to overcoming these conflicts. However, changes in individuals are also important. More people need to develop an appreciation of the land in all its uses. Though policy changes at a national and global level will be necessary, it is only by people themselves taking charge of their futures and coming together to think of new ideas for their communities that long-lasting changes will be affected. What happens between people and the land in actual places, is where the future will be decided.

The Why and the How

First spark

My interest in land use conflicts can be traced back several decades to the early 1990s, to my own experience as a mountaineer, a trekking holiday to Nepal and mountaineering literature. Though I had been drawn to mountains since my first sight of the Canadian Rockies as a child of nine years old, discovering the world of mountaineering in 1991 was a life-changing event. However, I could not understand how something without an obvious social value could become such an obsession. The title of Lionel Terray's book *Conquistadors of the Useless* (1963) is an appropriate alternative name for mountaineer. I had not intended to become so interested – I had taken a climbing course to keep a friend company – but the experience itself took hold and mountaineering continues, thirty years later, to be a major part of my life. As a result of my reluctant conversion, I began to wonder whether there was something innate in humans that made climbing and a love of being in the hills a universal need. If not, then where did this interest come from?

The experience of trekking in Nepal in 1993 in the company of Sherpas brought an extra dimension to the question. I was well aware that my views on the Himalayas were to a certain extent imagined, the result of years of being exposed to images and heroic tales. This meant that I had a very different perspective on what I was experiencing compared to that of the Sherpas. As Kahn (2011: 3) wrote in her ethnography about Tahiti, Tahitians see their island as a place for daily living and for tourists it was a paradise. For the Sherpas, the experience of being in what are, in my view, extraordinary mountains, is part of their day-to-day life. And trekking and climbing is their job, not a recreational activity thay pay to do. But is there that much difference in how these two distinct groups, trekkers and Sherpas, experience the mountains? The personal physical difficulties involved in the trek itself as well as language barriers, prevented me from asking all the questions I wanted to ask. What do the Sherpas think about the mountains? What do they think of us? Are our cultures so different that we relate to the mountains in completely different ways?

One of the most moving books I had read was by Kurt Diemburger. It is the story of his climbing partnership with Julie Tullis, which ended so tragically when she was killed on K2 in 1986. But it was his daughter's book that turned my mind to anthropology. Hilda Diemburger was an Austrian anthropologist who did her research amongst Tibetans. She wrote that she found there were many similarities between her father's views of mountains and those of the Tibetans she was studying – the mountains were special; they were sacred. This led me to anthropology and the decision to undertake a PhD as a way of giving structure to the search for answers.

The Highlands of Scotland

It may seem a long way from the Himalayas to Scotland. However, along with being a much more convenient and practical choice as a research site, Scotland has mountains and land-use conflicts. But where in Scotland?

In December 1997, I attended a conference on mountains at the University of Oxford. Participants included not only academics from a number of disciplines and countries, but the conference also attracted 'practitioners', people working in the field of conservation, hazard management and general policy towards mountain regions. The Cairngorms region of Scotland was well represented, largely due to the ongoing controversy over the building of a funicular railway as part of the redevelopment of the ski area. The conflict was presented by a number of poster presentations as one in which local people were lined up against conservation and recreation interests. It was widely accepted by those presenting that the funicular would have a negative impact on the environment and therefore was something that should be opposed. This motivated me to investigate anthropological work on environmental conflict.

Anthropologists, unlike the presenters at the Oxford mountain conference, had been questioning whether the views of environmentalists can be taken uncritically. A number of scholars have uncovered the culturally specific aspect of environmentalism (for example Olwig: 1977, 1980; Grove-White: 1993; Cronon: 1995; Berglund: 1998; Guha and Martinez-Alier: 1997; Proctor: 1995; Strang: 1997; McCarthy: 1998). Studies have taken place in both in the south (for example Guha and Martinez-Alier: 1997; Neumann: 1998; Strang: 1997) and in the north (for example Proctor: 1995; McCarthy: 1998) What they all have in common is a tendency to give voice to the local communities who find themselves in opposition to the agenda of the environmentalists. Therefore, in my research context, I would expect them to take sides with the local people.

Environmentalists and conservationists are associated with 'northern colonial' or urban interests and there is both implicit and explicit criticism of the way these groups have imposed or dominated debates around land use with a particular concept or discourse of nature. In developing countries, anthropologists have exposed the ethnocentric assumptions behind the establishing of National Parks. These studies span several decades and continents (for example Olwig: 1977, 1980; Baviskar: 2000; Macleod: 2001; Walley: 2004; Dowie: 2009). Neumann (1998) titled his book on National Parks in East Africa *Imposing Wilderness*. This title accurately represents the analysis of many of these anthropologists: National Parks are a form of colonialism, opposed by the local people. Meanwhile, in the metropolitan countries, environmentalists are portrayed as romantic and naïve and having a 'totalising discourse' similar to that of religion (Berglund: 2000 and 2001). This view is typified by the following comment from an informant of McCarthy from his work on the Wise Use Movement in the US.

> The environmental extremists' vision of the west is of a land nearly devoid of people and economic activity…everything from the 100th meridian to the Cascade Range becomes a vast park through which they drive, drinking their Perrier and munching on organic chips, staying occasionally in the bed-and-breakfast operations into which the homes of westerners have been turned, with those westerners who remain fluffing up duvets and pouring cappuccino (1998: p. 140).

In the south, Guha and Martinez-Alier stress the way conservation interests such as 'Save the Tiger' are at odds with concerns for social justice. They quote Eric Hobsbawm:

> It is no accident that the main support for ecological policies comes from the rich countries and from the comfortable rich and middle classes (except for the businessmen who hope to make money by polluting activity). The poor, multiplying and underemployed, wanted more 'development', not less (1997: p. xv).

Both north and south, there is conflict very similar to that in the Cairngorms. Local people need development and conservationists and recreation visitors value the wild qualities of the land. Different attitudes could be read from distinct economic positions as well as from different culturally based discourses of nature. As the title of Guha and Martinez-Alier's book suggests, there are 'varieties of environmentalism', or in other words, different priorities of how the land should be used.

'No Humanity without Nature', the epitaph of the northern environmentalist, is here answered by the equally compelling slogan 'No Nature without Social Justice' (Guha and Martinez-Alier: 1997: 21).

Environmentalism, then, rather than being based on any facts about nature, was just a point of view. As Proctor says, in his study of the conflict between loggers and environmentalists around old growth forests in Oregon:

> How, then, can we be sure that the environmentalists hold the moral high ground in their ancient forest campaign? It could be argued that there exists an infinite possible number of environmentalisms, each with its own nature to save (1995: 273).

If environmentalism is nothing but a Western, elite cultural product, then efforts to protect the environment are no more valid than any other position, and in some cases could actually be undermining social justice concerns. An impasse seemed to have been reached. Whilst the importance of the environmentalists' fight to save a 'real nature' cannot be questioned, the evidence against the role of environmentalists in neglecting social justice issues is compelling. There does not seem to be any way to resolve such conflicts where different groups have such fixed positions, cemented by their culturally induced outlook and economic interests. It appeared to be the same in the Cairngorms. The people I talked to at the conference and the articles in the mountaineering journals suggested that the only way to 'save' the Cairngorms was to impose a judicial decision on the locals, which would stop them from going ahead with the planned funicular.

The focus on conflict between different cultural groups is partially the result of the constructionist theoretical perspective. Research has tended to start with a particular interest or group, which has a clearly formulated public position based on their beliefs and values, that can be sharply distinguished from another group's position. For example, white Australians are contrasted with Aborigines (Strang: 1997), loggers with environmentalists (Proctor: 1995 and later Satterfield: 2002), farmers with conservationists (Neumann: 1998) and local islanders with the 'save the turtle' lobby from mainland Greece (Theodossopoulos: 2000). Whilst recognising the significance of this work in helping us to understand environmental conflicts, it has, nevertheless, unwittingly promoted a pessimistic picture, making it appear that conflict between the different environmentalisms is inevitable.

Other scholars have recognised the problems inherent in promoting such sharp dichotomies and in representing conflict in terms of interest groups (Grove-White: 1993). A number of studies paint a more nuanced picture, revealing divisions in the local community itself, providing evidence of local support for the environmentalist agenda or presenting the arguments of environmentalists as sympathetically as the local opposition. In one of the first studies of National Parks, Olwig (1977, 1980) stresses that not all locals were against the creation of the Park and that not only did some people benefit, some also admitted that the existence of the Park taught them to appreciate the beauty of the natural environment. Satterfield (2002), though focussing on distinct groups, does not privilege one view over the other, but uses the conflict situation to examine how each group sees each other. Walley (2004) has shown how unusual alliances were formed during the creation of a Marine Park off the coast of Tanzania, between an Australian working for the World Wildlife Fund and local fisherman, against other locals, the national government and the WWF itself.

Milton (2002) and Brechin et. al (2003), though not questioning the value of the work being done, argue that research should help promote environmental values.

> The most useful contribution anthropology can make is to improve our understanding of why we are as we are, of what makes us think, feel and act the way we do, in the hope that such understanding will provide a basis for informed change (Milton: 2002: 3).

Both Brechin et al. (2003) and Tsing (2001) challenge anthropologists to engage in 'new research trajectories' that explore collaborations rather than conflict.

> Anthropologists are used to a discussion of the divergent perspectives of groups that, endowed with long-standing and well-formulated differences in identity and interest, battle each other over political issues: villagers versus the state; frontiersmen versus natives; activists versus corporations. The new research I am interested in looks instead at how alliances rather than enmities are formed amongst dissimilar groups: indigenous people and urban environmentalists, southern nationalists and northern research foundations, fishermen and marine mammals (Tsing: 2001: 15).

Strang's (2004) work on conflicts over water is an example of an ethnography that aims explicitly to find ways of making sure that policies 'cohere – rather than conflict – with the meaning of water' (p. 3). She uses anthropology as a vehicle for providing the deeper understanding of people's relationships, views, and cultural meanings of water in order to challenge official policy-making processes and policies. In this way, Strang's ethnography, and I hope my own, are not only helping to 'reach an understanding of the kinds of beings we humans are' (Ingold, quoted in Milton: 2002:1), but also helping to understand what kinds of people we *could be* and what our relationship with the environment *could be like*.

Development of a new approach:
theoretical and conceptual framework

Reading the anthropological literature and increasing my knowledge of the situation in the Cairngorms, in particular Badenoch and Strathspey, enabled me to develop my research strategy.

Environmental conflicts have been framed in terms of distinct groups that have different economic, social and political interests as well as different beliefs and values. Without denying the existence of such groups and the reality of the conflicts, I wanted to explore how both the groups and conflicts come into being. What is the process by which individuals come to hold the views they do? What factors contribute to the forming of interest groups out of individuals who may hold only roughly the same views? And what are the processes at work that create situations where the interest groups come into conflict?

Answering these questions requires a different focus of research. Rather than beginning at the level of the group with the decontextualized, pre-identified interest groups, I began with the individual and the individual's sense of place, which is based on activity and lived experience. The concepts of activity and sense of place are useful analytical and methodological tools from which to develop a research project that does not pre-divide the field into interest groups in conflict. Beginning from the perspective of people and their concrete activity in a place, I hoped to reveal other aspects of the conflict situation, aspects that are often hidden behind the public debates. To do this, I participated in as many activities as possible rather than targeting specific groups in the public arena. That does not mean that I neglected people who had clearly defined positions on the funicular or other issues. However, the difference is that my starting point was with different activities rather than different people. In that way, I did not immediately categorise people into one group or another. What was important was the activity that they were involved in and how they actually related to their environment, rather than what they said their position was, or who they identified with. This turned out to be very effective and productive, in terms of both the data-gathering process itself and the kind of data I was able to obtain. As these concepts are pivotal in the research process, they require some further explanation.

Sense of Place

This concept is 'prior to' the formation of an interest group and is critical in understanding the processes by which individuals come to identify with a fixed interest. 'Place' is, therefore, not just a setting or backdrop for the 'play' of human action. Without place, things would not only fail to be located; they would not even be things; they would have no place to be the things they are (Casey: 1998: 71).

It is also broader, and includes many aspects of a person's relationship to the environment that may not be reflected in the concept of interest group. It is a concept that can refer to more than just the natural environment and conveys the idea of the integration of all aspects of an environment, defined by Milton (2002) as 'all that surrounds'. Whilst recognising that there is a physical reality (both natural processes and human-transformed) that people are engaged with, 'place' reinforces the idea that this engagement is inseparable from social relations and culture. Places are social constructions that emerge out of a particular physical environment and this process itself is based on activity – a dynamic interaction between the physical environment and people's actions, relationships and meanings.

Basso and Feld's (1996) work on the Apache made an important contribution to the development of the concept sense of place. They argue that anthropologists have not paid enough attention to 'one of the most basic dimensions of human experience – that close companion of heart and mind, often subdued, yet potentially overwhelming, that is known as *sense of place*' (1996: 54). Basso, in his chapter 'Wisdom Sits in Places', examines the factors that cause people to develop a certain sense of place. He concludes that this depends on the type of engagement that the person has with place. For example, the person who has more of an emotional experience with a place will develop a different sense of place than someone who has just passed through.

It is on these occasions of focussed thought and quickened

emotion that places are encountered most directly, experienced most robustly, and (in Heidegger's view) most fully brought into being. Sensing places, men and women become sharply aware of the complex attachments that link them to features of the physical world (1996: 55).

Places also have histories and power. When Basso's informants go back to a place, it has the power to evoke memories and to teach moral lessons as a result of the events that took place there before. To have a sense of place, therefore, involves sensual perceptions, feelings, memories, knowledge, attitudes and beliefs. These have emerged as a result of physical and social activity within a specific place that itself has power to evoke meaning, being both perceived and interpreted. This is very similar to Kahn's first experience of place in Papua New Guinea.

People would anchor personal narratives and communal histories to physical forms in the landscape – such as a breadfruit tree, a hill, a rock, a tree stump or a banana garden. (Kahn: 2011: 7).

In addition, places do not exist in isolation from the wider context. Places are formed through an interaction of the local and the global. Holland and Lave refer to this interaction between individuals and global structures as 'history in person' (2001). Therefore, the place people experience may have a specific geographical location, but it has been shaped by a broad range of historical and sociocultural forces (Olwig: 2003). Similarly, people's sense of place emerges out of both the experiences they have in a locality, and the contrast they make between other places they have experienced. Similarly, a sense of place may develop out of images they have been presented with before they come. Tourists in Tahiti formulate their sense of place from the images of blue lagoons and white sand beaches (Kahn: 2011: 3) that form part of the contrast they make between that and the 'ordinariness' of the place their own home.

Activity

The concept of activity is a necessary complement to the concept of sense of place because it is through activity, doing something in a particular locality, that a sense of place is developed. This concept developed out of the work of Tim Ingold, but has a much older genealogy. Ingold is one of the first anthropologists to develop a critique of the social constructionist approach to nature and culture. As early as 1986 he argued for a synthesis of the biological and the anthropological approach to evolution, 'flawed neither by biological reductionism nor by anthropocentric delusions of grandeur and ascendancy' (1986: pp. 34–35). He later uses the concept of 'dwelling', borrowed from Heidegger, to develop this perspective. Instead of starting with culture and seeing how it represents nature, we should start with the human condition, which involves 'being immersed from the start, like all other creatures, in an active, practical and perceptual engagement with constituents of the dwelt-in-world' (1996: 120–121). He stresses that the domain of nature is not separate from the domain in which people live as persons. Moreover, there is no distinction between 'Western' and 'non-Western' peoples. By making this point, he supports the growing body of literature that argues that to associate non-Western people with either more harmonious or more integrated relations with the environment is a myth (Kellert: 1995, Milton: 1998).

For hunter-gatherers, as for the rest of us, life is given in engagement, not in disengagement, and in that very engagement, the real world ceases to be nature and is revealed to us as an environment for people. Environments are constituted in life, not just thought, and it is only because we live in an environment that we can think at all (1996: 150–151).

'Active engagement' is a central concept of Ingold's perspective. With some adaptations, I make the concept of activity a foundational concept for my research. The term succinctly encompasses the notion of practical engaged experience within environments.

314

The use of activity as an explanatory concept is not common in the social sciences but it is nevertheless associated with the work of some key thinkers. In the work of Karl Marx activity could be considered one of the central foundational concepts of his theoretical system.

That is to say, we do not set out from what men say, imagine, conceive, nor from men as narrated, thought-of, imagined, conceived, in order to arrive at men in the flesh. We set out from real, active men, and on the basis of their real life-process we demonstrate the development of the ideological reflexes and echoes of this life-process (1974: 47).

In the early twentieth century, the Soviet psychologists developed 'activity theory', based on the work of Lev Vygotsky. A number of researchers from a variety of disciplines have been influenced by this work, including the anthropologists Lave and Wenger (1991). In their work on education they define learning as a 'situated activity'. The concept has also now become popular with those writing under the umbrella of 'performance' and 'performativity' (for example Szerszynski, Heim and Waterton: 2003).

Activity is necessarily embodied. However, in this instance, the body is not an object of study (Ingold: 2000: 170), but an integral part of the person, who cannot help but use his or her body to do the activity. Similarly, the mind, considered to be the domain of psychology, is part of activity because 'such processes as thinking, perceiving, remembering and learning have to be studied within the ecological contexts of people's interrelations with their environments' (Ingold: 2000: 171). By focussing on activity my research is undertaken within the framework for anthropology set out by Ingold (2000).

And the discipline that will be called into being to study these processes, whatever we choose to call it, will be the study of how people perceive, act, think, know, learn, and remember within the settings of their mutual-practical involvement in the lived-in world (p. 171).

Significantly, a similar approach, called non-representational theory, has been developed in geography. Lorimer (2004) describes it:

> The focus falls on how life takes shape and gains expression in shared experiences, everyday routines, fleeting encounters, embodied movements, pre-cognitive triggers, practical skills, affective intensities, enduring urges, unexceptional interactions and sensuous dispositions. Attention to these kinds of expression, it is contended, offers an escape from the established academic habit of striving to uncover meanings and values that apparently await our discovery, interpretation, judgement and ultimate representation. In short, so much ordinary action gives no advance notice of what it will become. Yet, it still makes critical differences to our experiences of space and place (p. 4).

Activity, Sense of Place and Conflict

Lefebvre's work, as used by Kahn (2011), shows the way in which the two concepts can be usefully combined. Though some of the terminology is different to that which I am using, the meaning is essentially the same. He identified a conceptual division that had been made unnecessarily between the mental, social and physical spheres. He argued that the concepts of 'space perceived' (physical space) and 'space conceived' (mentally, influenced by culture and social relations) have been artificially divided. What unites these two is a third space which he refers to as 'lived space'. It is within the lived space, or in my terminology, the activity, that a sense of place is created that is the product of both the physical environment and the social and cultural processes at work. Kahn calls this 'the dynamic space of everyday experience' and 'these places are filled with a 'multitude of interactions' (p. 19).

It is within this 'dynamic space' – one in which individuals are engaged in activities in a place – that the source of conflict will be found. The process by which different senses of place are transformed into conflict is best explored through the anthropological study of people engaged in activities in a locality. I use the ethnographic data to illustrate how senses of place are created and then how these become mobilised within interest groups to form the conflicts that are seen at the public level. My starting point is the acceptance that there are key interest groups that have been identified in the public debates in Scotland: livelihood, recreation and conversation. However, in order to understand how these interest groups have been formed, I focus on the individuals that are associated with these interest groups, usually 'unofficially'. In other words, the individuals who are the subject of my research are not the ones who will officially represent the interest at the public level or the people who express the discourses of the interest group. Rather they are those who are involved in the activities that are associated with that interest. In other words, in order to gain an understanding of a sense of place, it is more important to explore what people actually do in relation to that place as supposed to the rhetoric or discourse of a spokesperson or stakeholder for a particular interest. In other words, it is not through listening to what people say about the meanings they give to place or the views they have on relevant issues, but in engaging in the same activities that they do. This does not mean that listening to what people say is not important, but in keeping with the anthropological tradition of immersing oneself in the life of those who are being studied, it is critical to immerse oneself in the activities they are engaged in. The key concepts of sense of place and activity thus also influenced the methodology which will be explained in the next section.

Research methodology

Ingold (2000) suggests that research should be undertaken along the lines of the radical empiricism outlined by Jackson (1989).

There is much overlap between Ingold and Jackson, though they use different vocabularies. Jackson objects to the 'dissolving of people's lived experience of the subject into the anonymous field of discourse' (1989: 1). For both Ingold and Jackson, as with Latz and Csordas (2003) and Lorimer (2004), what is important is to firmly situate the person in the world. Therefore, the researcher should also be part of that world, living similar experiences to the people they have been studying.

Anthropology fieldwork has always demanded a certain degree of immersion (Amit: 2000). Whether Jackson's radical empiricism is qualitatively different from many other anthropologists' fieldwork is open to question (for example Evans-Pritchards' (1976) study of the Azande or Susan Greenwood's (2000) study of British witchcraft). Nevertheless, it is important to recognise that the researcher's own lived experience is a major source of knowledge about the people being studied. Research on the environment, focussing as it has on people's concepts of nature or on different groups in conflict, has necessarily demanded a certain distance between researcher and those being researched. This results in a tendency to focus on attitudes, expressed publicly to the researcher. Pepper (1996) points out in his history of environmental ideas that such an approach can only reveal what key people have said about nature and can tell us nothing about how ordinary people live that relationship. Plumwood (2002) argues that what people say they think is very different from what they actually do, in terms of the care or not that they take of the environment around them. The tendency of social constructivist and representational theory to focus on cultural groups and how these groups represent the environment has a similar orientation, in that research is directed towards how culture is represented rather than lived (Katz and Csordas: 2003). This does not mean that such perspectives have not produced many valuable insights. Rather it is a case of not revealing the complete picture of people's relationship with their environment. Walley (2004) found this to be the case in her study of an East African

Marine Park. When she tried to get the local inhabitants to talk about their concept of nature, she encountered incomprehension. Rather than concluding that they did not value the natural environment, she concluded that she was asking the wrong questions and going about her research in an unproductive way. She decided to focus on what people do in the environment, their lived practice, and she obtained a much more revealing picture of human–environment relations.

An illustration of the limitations of a constructionist approach, relevant to my research in the Scottish hills, is Ortner's work on climbing Sherpas and Western mountaineers (1999) in Nepal. She portrays the two groups as distinct cultures that bring distinct sets of values, beliefs and practices to mountaineering. As a result, she argues, they will have very different experiences of the mountain. Despite the importance of this study, her approach leaves no room for finding points in common between the two groups, who in the course of day-to-day *activity* are often doing the same tasks and undergoing the same experiences. If she had mountaineering skills and had been able to participate alongside the Sherpas and the Westerners in their climbing, she might have found that in some respects they transcended their diverse cultural backgrounds through their common experiences on the mountain, creating an alternative climbing culture that exists in that lived moment.

Limitations of other methods, in terms of my own research aims, are also seen in the following two examples from sociology and geography. In their research on people's attitudes towards the Lake District, the sociologists MacNaughton and Urry conducted interviews (1998). Though their aim was to find out about social practices, such a method, performed out of the actual context itself, give a partial, one-dimensional picture. Crouch (2001), a geographer, in his study of caravanning, spent considerable time on the caravan site. However, he admits that despite participating by being on the site and doing certain of the day-to-day activities that caravanners have to do, he did not participate as a caravanner. He maintained his identity to both himself and his subjects of study as that of observer. He said he never felt like a caravanner and therefore had more difficulty in collecting the data he sought. Crouch recognises, though it is not always possible to do so, the importance of living the part of whatever is being studied, not just intellectually, but physically and emotionally. For example, a very successful example of radical empiricism (Jackson: 1989) or 'phenomenological ethnography' (Latz and Csordas: 2003) is Wacquant's (1995) study of boxing. His aim was to discover what people feel about boxing, their lived experience, rather than gathering data on social background and attitudes. In order to do this he had to do more than just be immersed in the boxing world; he deliberately set out to study boxing from the inside out, through his own body, by learning to box.

By adopting elements of a radical empiricist approach, similar to Wacquant, wherever practical, I hoped to supplement other research methods and therefore gain a better understanding not only of what people say about their relationship with the environment but also of the entirety of the lived experience or sense of place – physical, cognitive and emotional. My preferred method of research was to do, as far as possible, whatever activity the group I wanted to study was doing. For example, studying mountaineers in Scotland involved doing mountaineering.*

However, my research involved much more than my doing the activities with my informants. The activities provided the basis on which to engage people in conversation, to observe behaviour and to conduct interviews.

---

* A year after I completed my research, this was the method adopted by a research project organised by Tim Ingold on hill-walking in Scotland and carried out by Katrin Lund and Hayden Lorimer. The results of this research were published in 2003 as 'Performing Facts: Finding a Way over Scotland's Mountains'.

In the field

From the beginning, I participated in activities. Over the course of the year I beat grouse, went ice-climbing, navigated around the Cairngorm plateau in a blizzard at night, slept in a snow hole, burned heather, scared myself on white water, learned to build a rabbit fence, herded cows, spent hours waiting to see a sea eagle, sweated up hills on my mountain bike, took snowboard lessons and suffered a head injury falling on a black run on a ski mountaineering course. In addition, I also did the usual sorts of things that have always provided anthropologists with valuable data-collecting opportunities – shopping, taking yoga lessons, going to the doctor, sitting in the Jacuzzi after a day on the hills and having my hair done.

The reliance on the body will have biased the research in certain respects. If I had been unable to keep up with the beaters in what was a gruelling march up and down the heather moors, my data collection would have been severely hampered if not ended after the first day. My skill at mountaineering enabled me to gather large amounts of data compared to my data on mountain biking – a sport I found it quite difficult to get to grips with. Nevertheless, I found the method to have a number of advantages. I met a very wide range of people that I wouldn't have met otherwise, heard views that were not normally heard as well as having many of Jackson's 'lived experiences'.

By taking an organic approach to data collection, I was able to meet a wide range of people. Though I was aware of the interest groups that existed, I did not start by picking activities that were associated with interest groups. In other words, I did not decide to look at people doing recreation activities and then people doing conservation activities. Instead, I began with the activities that fitted my personal situation and the season and waited to see what happened as a result, rather than deliberately seeking out particular people to talk to. The process began immediately upon arrival.

The method helped me find out what people value most in the environment without directly asking them. I would be able to see for myself whether they stopped to admire the view, whether they got excited at the sight of an eagle or a deer or whether they were focussed on the challenge of navigating. For example, when out with people doing their Munros, I found it very significant the way they decided not to go to the top because one member of the party was having difficulty. They were disappointed that they had not got to the top, but they were not overly concerned. This action reinforced what they told me in future conversations – that doing Munros was a way of organising the hill-walking and was more important as a process than a goal. Another example was the anguish on the face of the stalker when he had to shoot an injured deer, which was worth more than hundreds of conversations about attitudes towards killing.

The informal conversations that took place also provided me with views on wider issues. I would never ask people to state their view on an issue but would wait to see what issues people raised. The environment itself provided the prompts. For example, when out walking with the local walking club for the first time, a lengthy conversation took place about deer fences because we had to climb over one. I also found out a lot about the keepers' and stalkers' attitudes towards their clients and the general management of a sporting estate when we had a problem with one of the guests who had wanted to shoot a better quality of deer than he was entitled to. A key part of my research findings is based on the contradiction between what people would say unsolicited in the course of their everyday lives and what they would say when asked officially or publicly.

The problem with this method is, of course, remembering what people have said. There is not a lot of opportunity for writing up one's diary in a snow hole! However, I found that I learned to listen in such a way that I could remember long enough to write up conversations later in the day. I would remember keywords or phrases that stood out. The more I did it the better I became.

Some anthropologists have also stressed the importance of physical involvement in activities. Basso (1996), in his work on senses of place amongst the Apache, found that his most revealing data was that which was gathered when he went on a horseback trip with one of his informants. Brody (2001), in his studies of the Inuit, remarked on how he really started to understand something about the culture when he went on a long dogsled trip and nearly lost his life. Taking part in activities is important for the context it provides to speak to informants, but it also gives the researcher a chance to see the world through the eyes as well as the body of the informants, not just in the metaphorical sense. I would have found it far more difficult to understand the attraction of deer-stalking or the obsessive side of birding if I had not done the activities myself. And not only was my mind learning, so was my body. I found myself instinctively looking for birds or remarking on the quality of heather burning. Learning became a key part of all of the research I did. I realised I could not just do an activity but it had to be learned through a process of apprenticeship (see Lave and Wenger: 1991). And, as I learned an activity, I could understand the process my informants had gone through, providing an insight into why they enjoyed what they did or why they saw and acted in the world the way they did. My understanding of the process by which people 'learn a place' was further extended through my own teaching. I made a point of introducing people to climbing. Watching them in the process of learning provided an interesting source of data about how people can learn to see a place from a different perspective. A sense of place is, therefore, not just a question of mental constructs or even stories (as in Basso), but is also a physical 'being in the world.'

This method also helped me when I came to do interviews. I chose people who became known to me from my informal conversations whilst doing activities. There were three main types of interview. Firstly, I would interview 'ordinary' people who had been recommended to me by others that I knew it would be difficult to meet in the normal course of my day. For example, I interviewed the grandmother of the boy I worked with who in turn recommended a retired railway worker. Secondly, I interviewed better known people whom my contacts spoke about frequently. For example, everyone mentioned David Hayes, the owner of the Landmark Forest Adventure Park, because of his break with the business community when he came out against the funicular. As I hadn't come across him in the course of my everyday activity, towards the end of my stay I made an appointment to interview him. He soon realised that I was already very well informed, which freed him to go into much more depth on the issues making the interview very productive and wide-ranging. Thirdly, I interviewed some of my everyday contacts, such as Ailsa, who I did not see often once she quit the waitressing job. I knew she would be a good source of information about conservation as well as about growing up in the area so I made an effort to seek her out and record her experiences in detail.

I also gathered data by attending public meetings. These increased in number during the initial phase of consultation for the National Park. My first public meeting towards the beginning of my stay was limited in usefulness because I did not really know that many people. But later, such meetings proved to be an invaluable source of information, not so much for what was said during the meeting but the conversations I had afterwards. My involvement in activities again helped the process of data gathering. For example, I attended an Aviemore Community Council meeting, which was more interesting for what it did not tell me than what it did. Afterwards, I was gathering up my things when a man arrived to clean the room. I started talking to him about fishing because I had been out with the salmon fishers during the day. It turned out that he was a keen angler and this was the opening for a two-hour discussion on a wide range of local community topics: a conversation much more informative than the meeting with the local community 'representatives'.

Knowing people through activities also meant I was invited to meetings that I normally wouldn't have known about such as the first meeting of the conservation group formed to lobby for their views in the National Park consultation. At other meetings, I found that I had already come across most of the people there in a variety of capacities, such as on the ski slopes or at the climbing wall.

*

The focus on activity, rather than on particular groups of people, not only provided me with an exceptional amount of data, it also affected my findings. Though I found evidence for different approaches to the environment – recreation, conservation and livelihood senses of place – that correspond to the interest groups that have been identified by other research, there is a crucial difference: people did not necessarily fit neatly into any of these approaches. Because I encountered people on the basis of wanting to find out what senses of place emerged from a specific activity, I believe I saw a different side of people than if I had said I had come to research the conflict. If I had said that, then people would have lived up to what they thought their public position should be. In addition, because I was focussing on sense of place and not conflict, I could discuss my work on the RSPB reserve with my friends on the sporting estate or my work on the farm with anti-farmer birding visitors. This enabled me to have more informative discussions as people replied to what I said were the arguments of others. I could honestly say that I did not have a definite side because I had got so involved in each activity that I really did see the value of everyone's perspective. (I still do not have a definitive view on the funicular, I love birdwatching, am sympathetic to the plight of farming and am willing to eat venison even though I am a vegetarian!) When I went out with the sporting estate people, I did not talk about the conflict with the RSPB over birds of prey. In the end they did raise this issue, but it ended up being much more nuanced then

I would have originally expected. When talking to local people, I did not raise the issue of the funicular, but waited to see what concerns they had in the course of their everyday life. By doing this I learned that what was going to happen to the Aviemore redevelopment plans was a more important issue to many local people than the funicular. Many did not even know much about the conflict. Therefore, I have evidence that the stereotypical battle between outside recreation and conservation versus local development is just that – a misleading stereotype that does not necessarily correspond to the complexities of a particular place and its people, which is the conclusion that I support through the presentation of my research findings, based on fieldwork.

Acknowledgements

A book such as this relies completely on the contributions of all of those who let me have a glimpse of their sense of place, talking to me about their views, beliefs and feelings and often involving me directly in their activities. I have tried to faithfully represent what people have said but ultimately the way I have organised the material and the conclusions I have drawn are my sole responsibility.

It is impossible for me to thank everyone who contributed because I talked to countless people in the course of my research year, as well as in subsequent years. Much of my information was gathered as I was out and about in the course of everyday life: shopping for food, buying skis or outdoor equipment, renting a flat, at the hairdresser, walking on the hills, going to meetings, travelling around Scotland with my mother and partner. So, a big thanks to everyone who shared their views and experiences with me.

I would like to single out a few members of the Strathspey Mountain Club for special thanks. Isobel first introduced me to the club and invited me on my first meet. Here I met people who became instrumental in subsequent research, both at the time of research and in later years. Alan, as a long-term resident, was able to offer me insights on both landscape and social issues and introduced me to the local John Muir Trust. Anne become a firm friend and we spent many memorable days in the hills, on the ski slopes and on rock climbs. MA, another long-term resident, involved in both skiing and mountaineering, provided useful background as well as views about what was going on at the time. Gordon who was a farmer as well as a hill-walker, helped me understand the farming side of things. Victoria, Dorothy, John and Angus have been regular companions on the hills from the time of research to today.

Strathspey club member Douglas Anderson, a local farm worker, multiple Munroist, daring mountain biker and naturalist, deserves particular mention. He wears many hats and is able to see things from a variety of perspectives, thus providing inspiration for my basic conclusion that in order to resolve conflict, different groups need to be aware of a range of ways of being in and using the land. We have shared many mountaineering adventures in the Cairngorms, as well as elsewhere, including the Cuillin Ridge and the Dolomites.

The staff of Kinveachy: Frank, John, Alastair, Alan, David, Peter, Lionel and Ian. They went out of their way to let me into the world of the sporting estate and showed me what it means to know and care for the land, even if they do not own it. They let me participate in many different activities from deer-stalking to heather burning and even let me drive the Argocat!

Ross, Tom and John from the Insh Marsh RSPB Reserve opened my eyes not only to the fascination of bird life but to the interrelationships between different parts of nature, including human beings. They not only let me work with them on the reserve but spent many hours discussing the issues and suggesting avenues to explore.

The farmers Jimmy and Mary Yule showed me the passion and love farmers can have for their animals and made me aware of their worries and concerns for the future.

The staff at Glenmore Lodge. I learnt a lot of different skills, for example winter navigation and climbing, ski mountaineering and kayaking, as well as being inspired by their love of the natural environment and their dedication to helping others to enjoy it safely and responsibly. Special thanks go to my instructors Steve, Eric, Shaun, Rosie and George.

Speyside Wildlife, Sally and Pete, who let me accompany one of their very high-standard birding trips to the north-west coast.

Thanks go to Harkai's fish restaurant, the Happy Haggis, where I worked for several months. I appreciate their patience with my rusty waitressing skills. Craig Docherty, my colleague, deserves special mention. Not only did he save me embarrassment on a number of occasions, he also gave me a unique perspective of a young person who grew up in the area. He introduced me to his grandmother Mary Walker who helped me get a longer-term view of life in Aviemore and the issues surrounding the Aviemore Centre. She also introduced me to one of Aviemore's oldest residents, the railway worker Bill Wilkie. Ailsa Campbell was also a brilliant co-worker and gave me insight into the life of a local who had ambitions to work in the area of conservation. We attended meetings, looked for hen harriers and enjoyed walking in the snow.

It was whilst working at Harkai's that I met Johnny Campbell, who helped me think about the differences between native, local and incomer and what it means to belong in a place. He went out of his way to introduce me to people who would have been difficult to meet.

Thanks also go to those who were visiting the area. Stuart Carter, now a mountaineering instructor and director of Climb 365 in the Lake District, was then only starting out on his career trajectory. He was keen to explore the area and acquire skills and this led to many exciting as well as anthropologically useful days on the hills. John Driver, Ed Wray and Andrew Peel were friends who were happy to act as research material. John is a keen mountaineer and loves Scotland in the winter and Ed is a passionate rock-climber. Andrew is a skilled and enthusiastic birder. Going out with them for winter or summer climbing or searching for the dotterel let me get close to people as they were engaged in these particular activities.

I would also like to thank some individuals who gave me interviews as a way of discussing the bigger picture. These include:

representatives of the Aviemore development group, David Hayes from the Landmark Forest Adventure Park, Roy Dennis, Andy from RSPB Abernethy, Seamus Grant, Mike Dales from the then Mountaineering Council of Scotland. Bill Wright from the Cairngorms Campaign, a representative from the Deer Commission, Colin Sheldon from the British Association of Shooting and Conservation Scotland, Peter Moore from Scottish Natural Heritage, Willie McKenna from Rothiemurchus Estate, Caroline Sterritt from Sport Development, Dorothy and Rod from the Laggan Forestry Trust, Yvonne Blackstock from the tourist board and Peter Kuvall from the British Association of Skiing Instructors (BASI).

I met a number of individuals as a result of going to meetings and participating in conferences. I would like to thank the staff and members of these organisations for allowing me to observe. The Cairngorm Partnership welcomed me to a number of meetings that were held as part of the preparation for National Park status. The local John Muir Trust group held meetings and organised trips. I also worked as a conservation volunteer on their Knoydart property. Thank you to the other volunteers, especially Richard from Sheffield, who spoke at length with me about the issues. The Badenoch and Strathspey Conservation Group had a high profile in the area and their letters were regularly included in the local paper. Their articulate expression of their views and willingness to debate with other local interests was a help in clarifying the issues.

I would like to give special thanks to the late Dick Balharry, who would joke about the way I kept turning up at events he was at. His passion for nature conservation and what he called the 'health of the land' was evident in all his activity in the Cairngorm region and elsewhere in Scotland.

I would also like to thank the staff at Goldsmiths, University of London, and my fellow PhD students who got me started in anthropology and supported me through the completion of my thesis. Special thanks to the late Steve Nugent, Brian Morris and my supervisor Rebecca Cassidy. I must also thank my thesis examiners, Kay Milton and Allen Abramson. I was very lucky to have them because they had a personal interest in the subject matter. Kay is a keen birder and Allen is a mountaineer.

This book would not have seen the light of day if it hadn't been for my editor, Natalie. She gave me the encouragement to undertake what was a massive task – turning a thesis into a book – and provided the necessary expertise to see the project through. I would also like to thank Nick Hayes for providing a stunning cover.

Finally, I would like to thank my partner Nick Heath who was a support and encouragement during the years I spent as a mature student and then writing this book.

Bibliography

Resources from organisations and websites

Assynt Foundation: www.assynt-foundation.co.uk/
Badenoch and Strathspey Conservation Group: www.bscg.org.uk/
British Association of Shooting and Conservation: www.basc.org.uk/
Cairngorms Campaign: www.cairngormscampaign.org.uk/
Cairngorm National Park Authority: www.cairngorms.co.uk/
Coalition for Grouse Moor Reform: www.revive.scot/
Community Land Scotland: www.communitylandscotland.org.uk/
John Muir Trust: www.johnmuirtrust.org/
Land Justice Network: www.landjustice.uk/
Mountaineering Scotland: www.mountaineering.scot/
National Farming Union Scotland: www.nfus.org.uk/
National Trust for Scotland: www.nts.org.uk/
Parkwatch Scotland: www.parkswatchscotland.co.uk
People's Land Policy: www.landjustice.uk/category/working-groups/
    policy/
Ramblers Scotland: www.ramblers.org.uk/scotland.aspx
Rewilding Britain: www.rewildingbritain.org.uk/
Royal Society for the Protection of Birds: www.rspb.org,uk
Seafield Estate, including Kinveachy: www.seafield-estate.co.uk/
    about_us
Scottish Anglers National Association: www.sana.org.uk/
Scottish Canoe Association: www.canoescotland.org
Scottish Environment Link: www.scotlink.org/
Scottish Gamekeepers: www.scottishgamekeepers.co.uk/
Scottish Land Commission: www.landcommission.gov.scot/
Scottish Land and Estates: www.scottishlandandestates.co.uk/

Scottish Landowners Association: www.caledonia.org.uk/
Scottish Natural Heritage: www.nature.scot/
Scottish Wild Land Group: www.swlg.org.uk/
Scottish Wildlife Trust: www.scottishwildlifetrust.org.uk/
Shooting and Countryside Sports: www.sacs.org.uk/
Strathspey Mountain Club: www.strathspey.btck.co.uk/
Trees for Life: www.treesforlife.org.uk/into-the-forest/
    the-caledonian-forest/
Wildland: www.wildland.scot/
Wild Land Research Institute: www.wildlandresearch.org/our-work/
    mapping/
Woodland Trust: www.woodlandtrust.org.uk/about-us/
    where-we-work/

Books and journals

Abramson, A. (2000) 'Mythical Land, Legal Boundaries' in Abramson
    and Theodossopoulos eds. *Land, Law and Environment: Mythic
    Land, Legal Boundaries*. London: Pluto Press.
Abramson, A. and Theodossopoulos, D. eds. (2000) *Land, Law and
    Environment: Mythic Land, Legal Boundaries*. London: Pluto Press.
Adams, V. (1996) *Tigers of the Snow*. Princeton: Princeton University
    Press.
Allan, E. (1995) *Burn on the Hill: The Story of the First Munroist*.
    Beauly: Bidean Books.
Alvarez, A. (1988) *Feeding the Rat*. London: Bloomsbury.
Ament, P. (1999) *Climbing Everest*. Camden, Maine: Ragged Mountain
    Press.
Amit, V. ed. (2000) *Constructing the Field*. London: Pluto Press.
Amit, V. and Rapport, N. (2002) *The Trouble with Community*. London:
    Pluto Press.
Anderson, D. and Berglund, E. eds. (2003) *Ethnographies of
    Conservation: Environmentalism and the Distribution of Privilege*.
    New York: Berghahn Books.
Anderson, L. (1991) *Sisters of the Earth*. New York: Vintage Books.
Archetti, E. (1998) 'The Potrero and the Pibe: Territory and belonging

in the mythical account of Argentinean football' in N. Lovell ed. *Locality and Belonging*. London: Routledge.

Arhem, K. (1998) '*The Powers of Place*' in N. Lovell ed. *Locality and Belonging*. London: Routledge.

Avery, M. (2015) *Conflict in the Uplands*. London: Bloomsbury.

Bakhtin, M. M. (1984) *Problems of Dostoevsky's Poetics*. (Translated C. Emerson and M. Holquist ed. M. Holquist.) Minneapolis: University of Minnesota Press.

Bakhtin, M. M. (1981) *The Dialogic Imagination: Four Essays*. (Translated C. Emerson and M. Holquist ed. M. Holquist.) Austin, Texas: University of Texas Press.

Balee, W. ed. (1998) *Advances in Historical Ecology*. New York: Columbia University Press.

Barth, F. (2000) 'Boundaries and Connections' in *Signifying Identities*. A. Cohen ed. London: Routledge.

Bartlett, P. (1993) *The Undiscovered Country*. The Ernest Press.

Basso, K. and Feld, S. eds. (1996) *Senses of Place*. Santa Fe: SAR Press.

Basso, K. (1996) 'Wisdom Sits in Places' in K. Basso and S. Feld eds. *Senses of Place*. Santa Fe: SAR Press.

Baviskar, A. (2000) 'Claims to Knowledge, Claims to Control: Environmental Conflict in the Great Himalayan National Park, India' in R. Ellen et al. eds. *Indigenous Knowledge and its Transformations*. Amsterdam: Harwood.

Bayer, K. (2004) 'Canadian tries to nail "myths" of Clearances' in *Scotland on Sunday*: 15 August.

Bell, Catherine (1992) *Ritual Theory, Ritual Practice*. Oxford: Oxford University Press.

Bell, J. H. B. (1988–1950) *Bell's Scottish Climbs*. Wigston: Magna Books.

Benanav, M. (2018) *Himalaya Bound*. Pegasus: New York.

Bender, B. ed. (1993) *Landscape: Politics and Perspectives*. Oxford: Berg.

Berglund, E. (1998) *Knowing Nature, Knowing Science*. Cambridge: White Horse Press.

Berglund, E. (2000) 'Forestry Expertise and National Narratives: Some Consequences for Old-Growth Conflicts in Finland' in *Worldviews*, Volume 4–1.

Berglund, E. (2001) 'Self-defeating Environmentalism?' in *Critique of Anthropology*, Volume 21–3.

Bloch, M. (1989) *Ritual, History and Power*. London: Athlone.

Bloch, M. (1995) 'People into Places' in E. Hirsch and M. O'Hanlon eds. *The Anthropology of Landscape*. Oxford: Clarendon.

Bloch, M. (1991) 'Language, Anthropology and Cognitive Science' in *Man*, New Series, Volume 26, Issue 2.

Borgmann, A. (1995) 'The Nature of Reality and the Reality of Nature' in M. Soule and G. Lease eds. *Reinventing Nature? Responses to Postmodernism Deconstruction*. Washington D.C.: Island Press.

Borthwick, A. (1983–1939) *Always a Little Further*. London: Diadem Books.

Bowker, G. and Leigh Star, S. (1999) *Sorting Things Out: Classification and its Consequences*. Cambridge, Massachusetts: MIT Press.

Boyle, D. (2003) *Authenticity: Brands, Fakes, Spin and the Lust for Real Life*. Flamingo, London.

Brady, E. (2003) *Aesthetics of the Natural Environment*. Edinburgh: Edinburgh University Press.

Braun, B. and Castree, N. eds. (1998) *Remaking Realities: Nature at the Millennium*. London: Routledge.

Brechin, S., Wilshusen, P., Fortwangler, C. and West, P. eds. (2003) *Contested Nature: Promoting International Biodiversity with Social Justice in the 21st Century*. Albany: State University of New York Press.

British Association of Shooting and Conservation (2000) *The Sport of over 100,000 People*. Trochy, by Dunkeld: BASC.

Brody, H. (2001) *The Other Side of Eden*. London: Faber and Faber.

Brosius, P. (1999) 'Anthropological Engagements with Environmentalism' in *Current Anthropology*, Volume 40: 3.

Brosius, P. (2001) 'The Politics of Ethnographic Presence: Sites and Topologies in the Study of Transnational Movements' in C. Crumley ed. *New Directions in Anthropology and Environment*. Walnut Creek, California: Altamira Press.

Brown, D. and Mitchell, I. (1987) *Mountain Days, Bothy Nights*. Edinburgh: Luath Press.

Buchaner, J. (1996) *The Lewis Land Struggle*. Stronaway: Acair.

Budiansky, S. (1995) *Nature's Keepers: The New Science of Nature Management*. London: Phoenix.

Burnham, P. (2000) 'Whose Forest? Whose Myth? Conceptualisations of Community Forest in Cameroon' in A. Abramson and D. Theodossopoulos eds. *Land, Law and Environment*. London: Pluto Press.

Callender, R. 1998 *How Scotland is Owned*. Edinburgh: Canongate.

Casey, E. (1998) *The Fate Of Place: A Philosophical History*. Berkeley: University of California Press.

Cave, S. (1998) *Applying Psychology to the Environment*. London: Hodder and Stoughton.

Castree, N. and Braun, B. eds. (2001) *Social Nature*. Oxford: Blackwell.

Chenevix-Trench, H. and Philip, L. (2001) 'Community and Conservation Land Ownership in Highland Scotland' in *Scottish Geographical Journal*, Volume 117: 2.

Clark, T. (Autumn 2016) 'Bringing Communities and Nature Together' in *John Muir Trust Journal*.

Cohen, A. ed. (2000) *Signifying Identities: Anthropological perspectives on boundaries and contested values*. London: Routledge.

Cocker, M. (2001) *Birders*. London: Jonathan Cape.

Cosgrove, D. and Daniels, S. eds. (1988) *The Iconography of Landscape*. Cambridge: Cambridge University Press.

Cramb, A. (1996) *Who Owns Scotland Now?* Edinburgh: Mainstream Publishing.

Cramb, A. (1998) *Fragile Land: Scotland's Environment*. Edinburgh: Polygon.

Croll, E. and Parkin, D. eds. (1992) *Bush Base: Forest Farm*. London: Routledge.

Cronon, W. ed. (1995) *Uncommon Ground*. New York: Norton.

Crouch, D. (2001) 'Spatialities and the Feeling of "Doing" in *Social and Cultural Geography*, Volume 2: 1.

Crumley, C. ed. (1994) *Historical Ecology: Cultural Knowledge and Changing Landscapes*. Santa Fe: School of American Research Press.

Crumley, C. ed. (2001) *New Directions in Anthropology and Environment*. Walnut Creek, California: Altamira Press.

Csikszentimihalyi, M. (1998) *Living Well: The Psychology of Everyday Life*. London: Phoenix.

Cullen, S. (1992) 'The Highland War' in *The Raven*, Volume 5:1.

Daniels, H. ed. (1996) *An Introduction to Vygotsky*. London: Routledge.

Daniels, S. (1993) *Fields of Vision*. Cambridge: Polity.

Descola, P. and Palsson, G. eds. (1996) *Nature and Society*. London: Routledge.

Dickens, P. (1992) *Society and Nature*. Hemel Hempstead: Harvester.

Dickens, P. (2004) *Society and Nature*. Cambridge: Polity.

De Botton, A. (2002) *The Art of Travel*. London: Penguin.

Durman, P. (2000) 'Tract: Locke, Heidegger and Scruffy Hippies in Trees'. in A. Abramson and D. Theodossopoulos eds. *Land, Law and Environment*. London: Pluto Press.

Edensor, T. (2000) 'Walking in the British Countryside: Reflexivity, embodied practices and ways to escape' in *Body and Society*, Volume 6 (3–4), pp. 81–106) London: Sage.

Edwards, J. (1998) 'The Need for a "Bit of History" in N. Lovell ed. *Locality and Belonging*. London: Routledge.

Einarsson, N. (1993) 'All animals are equal but some are cetaceans' in K. Milton ed. *Varieties of Environmentalism*. London: Routledge.

Ellen, R. and Fukui, K. eds. (1996) *Redefining Nature*. Oxford: Berg.

Ellen, R., Parkes, D. and Bicker, A. eds. (2000) *Indigenous Knowledge and its Transformations*. Amsterdam: Harwood.

Escobar, A. (1998) 'After Nature' in *Current Anthropology*, Volume 40–41.

Evans, R. (2003) 'Replacing the Countryside: Identity and the new English countryside'. Personal photocopy.

Evans-Pritchard, E. E. (1976) *Witchcraft, Oracles and Magic among the Azande*. Oxford: Clarendon Press.

Fiennes, W. (2002) *The Snow Geese*. London: Picador.

Fine, B. (1975) *Marx's Capital*. London: MacMillan Press.

Forestry Commission (1998) *Native Woodlands of Scotland*. Edinburgh: Forestry Commission.

Forsyth, William (1900, reprinted 1999) *In the Shadow of Cairngorm.* Aviemore: Lynwilg Press.

Foucault, M. (1986) 'Disciplinary Power and Subjugation' in S. Lukes ed. *Power.* New York: New York University Press.

Fowler, M. (1995) *Vertical Pleasures: The Secret Life of a Taxman.* London: Hodder and Stoughton.

Franklin, Adrian (1999) *Animals and Modern Cultures.* London: Sage.

Gallagher, W. (1993) *The Power of Place.* New York: Poseidon.

Gell, A. (1985) 'How to Read a Map: Remarks on the Practical Logic of Navigation' in *Man*, New Series, Volume 20, No. 2, June (271–286).

Gessner, D. (2015) *All the Wild that Remains.* New York: Norton.

Glen, A. (2002) *The Cairngorm Gateway.* Dalkeith: Scottish Cultural Press.

Gow, P. (1995) 'Land, People and Paper in Western Amazonia' in E. Hirsch and M. O'Hanlon eds. *The Anthropology of Landscape.* Oxford: Clarendon.

Graber, D. (1995) 'Resolute Biocentrism: The Dilemma of Nature in National Parks' in M. Soule and G. Lease eds. *Reinventing Nature? Responses to Postmodernism Deconstruction.* Washington D.C.: Island Press.

Greenwood, S. (2000) *Magic, Witchcraft and the Other World.* Oxford: Berg.

Grove-White, R. (1993) 'Environmentalism: A New Moral Discourse?' in K. Milton *Environmentalism.* London: Routledge.

Guha, R. and Martinez-Alier, J. (1997) *Varieties of Environmentalism.* London: Earthscan.

Hall, S. (1996) 'Introduction' in S. Hall and P. DeGuy eds. *Questions of Cultural Identity.* London: Sage.

Hann, C. ed. (1998) *Property Relations.* Cambridge: Cambridge University Press.

Harris, M. (1980) *Cultural Materialism.* New York: Vintage Books.

Harrison, P. (2000) 'Making Sense: Embodiment and the sensibilities of the everyday' in *Environment and Planning D: Society and Space*, Volume 18: pp. 497–517.

Harvey, D. (1996) *Justice, Nature and the Geography of Difference.* Oxford: Blackwell.

Hay, P. (2002) *Companion to Environmental Thought.* Edinburgh: Edinburgh University Press.

Hayes, N. K. (1995) 'Searching for Common Ground' in M. Soule and G. Lease eds. *Reinventing Nature? Responses to Postmodernism Deconstruction.* Washington D.C.: Island Press.

Hearne, V. (1982) *Adam's Task: Calling Animals by Name.* New York: Vintage Books.

Henderson, C. (1998) 'The Great Cow Explosion in Rajastan' in W. Balee ed. *Advances in Historical Ecology.* New York: Columbia University Press.

Hirsch, E. and O'Hanlon, M. eds. (1995) *The Anthropology of Landscape.* Oxford: Clarendon.

Hobart, M. ed. (1993) *An Anthropological Critique of Development: The Growth of Ignorance.* London: Routledge.

Hobsbawm, E. and Range, T. eds. (1983) *The Invention of Tradition.* Cambridge: Cambridge University Press.

Holland, D. and Lave, J. eds. (2001) *History in Person.* Santa Fe: SAR Press.

Hollander, J. (1995) 'Advancement of Learning' in A. Mack ed. *Humans and Other Animals.* Columbus: Ohio State University Press.

Horigan, S. (1988) *Nature and Culture in Western Discourse.* London: Routledge.

Hughes-Freedland, F. ed. (1998) *Ritual, Performance, Media.* London: Routledge.

Hume, D. (1972) *A Treatise on Human Nature.* London: Fontana/ Collins.

Humphrey, C. (1995) 'Chiefly and Shamanic Landscapes in Mongolia' in E. Hirsch and M. O'Hanlon eds. *The Anthropology of Landscape.* Oxford: Clarendon.

Hunter, J. (1976) *The Making of the Crofting Community.* Edinburgh: John Donald.

Hunter, J. (2012) *From the Low Tide of the Sea to the Highest Mountain Tops: Community Ownership of Land in the Highlands and Islands of Scotland.* Kershader, Isle of Lewis: The Island Book Trust.

Ilgner, A. (2003) *The Rock Warrior's Way: Mental Training for Climbers*. La Vergne, Tennessee: Desiderata Institute.

Ingold, T. (1992) 'Culture and the Perceptions of the Environment' in E. Croll and D. Parkin eds. (1992) *Bush Base: Forest Farm*. London: Routledge.

Ingold, T. (1995) 'Building, Dwelling, Living: How Animals and People Make Themselves at Home in the World' in M. Strathern ed. *Shifting Contexts*. London: Routledge.

Ingold, T. (1996) 'Hunting and Gathering as Ways of Perceiving the Environment' in P. Descola and G. Pallson eds. *Nature and Society*. London: Routledge.

Ingold, T. (2000) *Perceptions of the Environment*. London: Routledge.

Ingold, T. (2001) 'Evolving Skills' in H. Rose and S. Rose eds. *Alas Poor Darwin: Arguments Against Evolutionary Psychology*. London: Vintage.

Ingold, T. (2011) *Being Alive: Essays on Movement, Knowledge and Description*. London: Routledge.

Jackson, M. (1989) *Paths Towards a Clearing*. Bloomington and Indianapolis: Indiana University Press.

Jedrej, C. and Nuttall, M. (1996) *White Settlers: The Impact of Rural Repopulation in Scotland*. Luxembourg: Harwood.

Jenkins, R. (1992) *Bourdieu*. London: Routledge.

Jimmy the Gael (2000) 'Boycott in Aviemore' in *The Angry Corrie*, No. 44: Jan–Feb.

Johnson, M. (1987) *The Body in the Mind*. Chicago: University of Chicago Press.

Kahn, M. (2011) *Tahiti Beyond the Postcard: Power, Place and Everyday Life*. Seattle: University of Washington Press.

Katz, J. and T. Csordas (2003) 'Phenomenological ethnography in sociology and anthropology' in *Ethnography*. London and Thousand Oaks, California: Sage.

Kellert, S. and Wilson, E. eds. (1993) *The Biophilia Hypothesis*. Washington D.C.: Shearwater.

Kellert, S. (1995) 'Concepts of Nature East and West' in M. Soule and

G. Lease eds. *Reinventing Nature? Responses to Postmodernism Deconstruction*. Washington D.C.: Island Press.

Knight, J. ed. (2000) *Natural Enemies*. London: Routledge.

Kovel, J. (2002) *The Enemy of Nature*. London/New York: Zed Books.

Kozulin, A. (1996) 'The Concept of Activity in Soviet Psychology' in H. Daniels ed. *An Introduction to Vygotsky*. Routledge: London.

Kuehls, T. (1996) *Beyond Sovereign Territory*. Minneapolis: Minnesota Press.

Lambert, R. (2001) *Contested Mountains*. Cambridge: White Horse Press.

Lash, S., Szerszynski, B. and Wynne, B. eds. (1996) *Risk, Environment and Modernity*. London: Sage.

Latour, B. (2004) *Politics of Nature*. London: Harvard University Press.

Lave, J. and Wenger, E. (1991) *Situated Learning*. Cambridge: Cambridge University Press.

Law, J. and Lynch, M. (1990) 'Lists, field guides, and the descriptive organisation of seeing. Birdwatching as an exemplary observational activity' in M. Lynch and S. Woolgar eds. *Representation in Scientific Practice*. Cambridge, Massachusetts: MIT Press.

Leach, E. (1964) 'Anthropological aspects of language: animal categories and verbal abuse' in E. Lenneberg ed. *New Directions in the Study of Language*. Cambridge, Massachusetts: MIT Press.

Lease, G. (1995) 'Nature Under Fire' in M. Soule and G. Lease eds. *Reinventing Nature? Responses to Postmodernism Deconstruction*. Washington D.C.: Island Press.

Lewis, N. (2000) 'The Climbing Body, Nature and the Experience of Modernity' in *Body and Society*, Volume 6 (3–4).

Lien, E. (2004) 'Domestication 'Down Under': Atlantic Salmon Farming in Tasmania'. Conference paper.

Lister-Kaye, J. (1994) *Ill Fares the Land*. Battleby, Perth: SNH.

Lopez, B. (1986) *Arctic Dreams: Imagination and Desire in a Northern Landscape*. London: Picador.

Lorimer, H. (2000) 'De-bagging the Munros: The promotion and commodification of Scotland's mountains'. Paper presented at Leisure Studies Association Conference, Glasgow.

Lorimer, H. and Lund, K. (2003) 'Performing Facts: Finding a Way over

Scotland's Mountains' in B. Szerszynski, W. Heim and C. Waterton eds. *Nature Performed*. Oxford: Blackwell.

Lorimer, H. (2004) *The busyness of being 'more-than-representational': Some recent work in cultural geography*. Department of Geography and Geomatics, University of Glasgow at: http://web.geog.gla.ac.uk/olpapers/hlorimer03.pdf.

Lovell, N. ed. (1998) *Locality and Belonging*. London: Routledge.

Lovell, N. (1998) 'Wild Gods, Containing Wombs and Moving Pots' in *Locality and Belonging*. London: Routledge.

Luhrmann, T. (1989) *Persuasions of the Witch's Craft*. Cambridge, Massachusetts: Harvard University Press.

Lukes, S. (1986) *Power*. New York: New York University Press.

Lund, K. (nd) 'Finding place in nature: "Intellectual" and local knowledge in a Spanish Natural park', special edition: B. Campbell ed. *Conservation and Society: Re-placing Nature*.

Macaskill, J. (1999) *We Have Won the Land*. Stornaway: Acair.

McCall, I. (2002) 'Letter to the Editor' in *Scotsman*: 24 January.

McCarthy, J. (1998) 'Environmentalism, Wise Use and the Nature of Accumulation in the Rural West' in Braun and Castres ed. *Remaking Realities: Nature at the Millennium*. London: Routledge.

McCarthy, J. (1998) *An Inhabited Solitude: Scotland, Land and People*. Edinburgh: Luath Press.

MacCormack, C. and Strathern, M. (1980) *Nature, Culture and Gender*. Cambridge: Cambridge University Press.

McCrone, D. (1992) *Understanding Scotland: The Sociology of a Stateless Nation*. London: Routledge.

Macdonald, S. (1997) *Reimagining Culture*. Oxford: Berg.

Macfarlane, R. (2003) *Mountains of the Mind*. London: Granta.

Macfarlane, R. (2007) *The Wild Places*. London: Granta.

McIntosh, A. (2004) *Soil and Soul*. London: Aurum Press.

McIntosh, I., Sim, D. and Robertson, D. (2004) 'We hate the English, except for you, cos you're our pal.' in *Sociology* Vol. 3(1) pp. 49–50.

MacKinnon, D. (2001) 'Regulating Regional Spaces: State Agencies and the Production of Governance in the Scottish Highlands' in *Environment and Planning A.*, Volume 33: pp. 823–844.

Macleod, D. (2001) 'Parks or People? National Parks and the Case of
    Del Este, Dominican Republic' in *Progress in Development Studies*,
    Volume 1: 3.

Macnaghten, P. and Urry, J. (1998) *Contested Natures*. London: Sage.

Mageo, J. ed. (2002) *Power and the Self*. Cambridge: Cambridge
    University Press.

Magnusson, M. (2001) 'Forward' in Lambert, R. *Contested Mountains*.
    Cambridge: White Horse Press.

Marvin, G. (2000) 'The Problem of Foxes' in J. Knight ed. *Natural
    Enemies*. London: Routledge.

Marx, K. and Engels, F. (1974) *The German Ideology*. London: Lawrence
    and Wishat.

Maxwell, F. (2000) 'Time to Teach Townies the Facts' in *Scotsman*:
    17 November.

Maxwell, F. (2001) 'Country Folk on the Fightback Trail' in *Scotsman*:
    1 November.

Mels, T. (1999) *The Cultural Nature of Swedish National Parks*. Lund:
    Lund University Press.

Merchant, C. (1980) *The Death of Nature*. London: Wildwood House.

Merleau-Ponty, M. (1962) *Phenomenology of Perception*. London:
    Routledge.

Michael, M. (2000) 'These Boots are Made for Walking: Mundane
    Technology, the Body and Human–Environment Relations' in *Body
    and Society*, Volume 6 (3–4), pp. 58–80. London: Sage.

Mill, C. (1987) *Norman Collie*. Aberdeen: Aberdeen University Press.

Milton, K. ed. (1993) *Environmentalism: The View from Anthropology*.
    London: Routledge.

Milton, K. (1996) *Environmentalism and Cultural Theory*. London:
    Routledge.

Milton, K. (1998) 'Nature and the environment in traditional and
    indigenous cultures' in D. Cooper and J. Palmer eds. *Spirit of the
    Environment*. London: Routledge.

Milton, K. (2000) *Ducks out of Water: Nature Conservation as
    Boundary Maintenance* in J. Knight ed. *Natural Enemies*. London:
    Routledge.

Milton, K. (2002) *Loving Nature: Towards an Ecology of Nature.*
    London: Routledge.

Mitchell, I. R. (1988) *Scotland's Mountains before the Mountaineers.* Edinburgh: Luath Press.

Mitchell, R. (1983) *Mountain Experience: The Psychology and Sociology of Adventure.* Chicago: University of Chicago Press.

Monbiot, G. (2014) *Feral: Rewilding the Land, Sea and Human Life.* London: Penguin.

Moran, E. (1996) 'Nurturing the Forest: Strategies of Native Amazonians' in R. Ellen and K. Fukui eds. *Redefining Nature.* Oxford: Berg.

Moran, M. (1992) *Scotland's Winter Mountains.* Newton Abbott: David and Charles.

Morris, B. (1996) *Ecology and Anarchism.* Malvern Wells: Images Publishing.

Morris, B. (2012) *Pioneers of Ecological Humanism.* Brighton: The Book Guild Publishing.

Morris, B. (2014) *Anthropology, Ecology, and Anarchism: A Brian Morris Reader.* Oakland: PM Press.

Morris, P. ed. (1994) *The Bakhtin Reader.* London: Arnold.

Moss, R. (2000) 'Extinction of Capercaillie by Forest Fences' in Badenoch and Strathspey Newsletter: May.

Murray, W. H. (1992–1947) *Mountaineering in Scotland.* London: Diadem Books.

Nabhan, G. P. (1995) 'Cultural Parallax in Viewing North American Habitats' in M. Soule and G. Lease eds. *Reinventing Nature? Responses to Postmodernism Deconstruction.* Washington D.C.: Island Press.

Nabhan, G. P. (1997) *Cultures of Habitat.* Washington D.C.: Counterpoint.

National Trust for Scotland Council (2002) *Wild Land Policy.* NTS.

Neumann, R. (1998) *Imposing Wilderness.* Berkeley: University of California.

Nichol, R. (1999) 'Access Issues' in *Horizon*, Issue 5.

Nichols, B. (1992) 'Nature Conservation as Land Use' in *The Raven*, Volume 5:1.

Nietzsche, F. (1999) *Beyond Good and Evil.* Oxford: Oxford University Press.

Noyce, W. (1950) *Scholar Mountaineers*. London: Dennis Dobson.

Noyce, W. (1954) *Men and Mountains*. London: Geoffrey Bles.

Olwig, K. (1977) 'National Parks, tourism, and the culture of imperialism' in *Anthropological Society 2*: pp. 243–256.

Olwig, K. (1980) 'National Parks, Tourism and Local Development: a West Indian Case' in *Human Organisation*, Volume: 39: 1: pp. 22–31.

Olwig, K. F. (2003) 'Global Places and Place-Identities – Lessons from Caribbean Research' in T. Eriksen ed. *Globalisation: Studies in Anthropology*. London: Pluto Press.

Ortner, S. (1974) 'Is Female to Male as Nature is to Culture?' in M. Rosaldo and L. Lamphere eds. *Women, Culture and Society*. Stanford: Stanford University Press.

Ortner, S. (1999) *Life and Death on Mount Everest: Sherpas and Himalayan Mountaineering*. Princeton: Princeton University Press.

Patey, T. (1986–1971) *One Man's Mountains*. London: Victor Gollancz.

Perrin, J. (1997) 'Street Illegal' in T. Gifford ed. *The Climbers' Club Centenary Journal*. The Climbers' Club.

Pepper, D. (1996) *Modern Environmentalism*. London: Routledge.

Perrota, L. (2000) 'Politics, Confusion and Practice: Land Ownership and De-collectivisation in Ukraine' in A. Abramson and D. Theodossopoulos eds. *Land, Law and Environment*. London: Pluto Press.

Peterson, A. (2001) *Being Human: Ethics, Environment and Our Place in the World*. Berkeley: University of California Press.

Plumwood, V. (2002) *Environmental Culture: The ecological crisis of reason*. London: Routledge.

Poncelet, E. (2001) 'Environmental Partnerships' in Crumley, C. ed. *New Directions in Anthropology and Environment*. Walnut Creek, California: Altamira Press.

Power, T. (1996) *Environmental Protection and Economic Well-being*. Armonk, New York: M. E. Sharpe.

Power, T. and Barrett, R. (2001) *Post-Cowboy Economics*. Washington DC: Island Press.

Prebble, J. (1969) *The Highland Clearances*. London: Penguin.

Primozic, D. (2001) *On Merleau-Ponty*. Belmont, California: Wadsworth.

Proctor. J. (1995) 'Whose Nature? The Contested Moral Terrain of Ancient Forests' in W. Cronon ed. *Uncommon Ground*. New York: Norton.

Pulido, L. (1996) *Environmentalism and Economic Justice*. Tucson: University of Arizona Press.

Ramsey, P. (1996) *Revival of the Land*. Battleby, Perth: SNH.

Read, P. (2000) *Belonging: Australians, Place and Aboriginal Ownership*. Cambridge: Cambridge University Press.

Rebanks, J. (2016) *The Shepherd's Life: A Tale of the Lake District*. London: Penguin.

Rettie, K. (2006) 'At home in national parks: a study of power, knowledge and discourse in Banff National Park and Cairngorms National Park'. *Unpublished PhD thesis*. https://research-repository. st-andrews.ac.uk/handle/10023/2819

Reynolds, F. (2016) *The Fight for Beauty*. London: Oneworld Publications.

Richards, C. (2004) 'Grouse Shooting and its Landscape' in *Anthropology Today*, Volume 20: 4.

Rose, D. and Douglas, E. (1999) *Regions of the Heart: The Triumph and Tragedy of Alison Hargreaves*. London: Penguin.

Rose, N. (1999) *Powers of Freedom*. Cambridge: Cambridge University Press.

Roseberry, W. (1994) 'Hegemony and the Language of Contention' in G. Joseph and D. Nugent eds. *Everyday Forms of State Formation*. Durham and London: Duke University Press.

Sahlins, M. (1977) *Practical Reason*. Chicago: University of Chicago Press.

Saltman, M. ed. (2002) *Land and Territoriality*. Oxford: Berg.

Satterfield, T. (2002) *Anatomy of a Conflict*. Vancouver: UBC Press.

Save the Cairngorms Campaign and Scottish and Wildlife Countryside Link (March 1996) *The Northern Cairngorms: An alternative approach*. Inverness, Perth.

Schieffelin, E. (1985) 'Performance and Construction of Reality' in
    AE 12: 707–24.
Schieffelin, E. (1998) 'Problematizing Performance' in
    F. Hughes-Freedland ed. *Ritual, Performance and Media*. London:
    Routledge.
Schofield, B. (2000) 'Runaway Train' in *Trail*. February.
Scottish Natural Heritage (1994) *Red Deer and the Natural Heritage:
    Policy Paper*. Battleby: SNH.
Scottish Wild Land Group (2002) *Scotland's Wild Land – What Future?*
    Edinburgh: SWLG.
Sean the Relevator (1999) 'Funny peculiar: a brief guide to the
    funicular' in *The Angry Corrie*, No. 43: Oct–Nov.
Shepard, P. (1995) 'Virtually Hunting Reality in the Forests of Simulacra'
    in M. Soule and G. Lease eds. *Reinventing Nature? Responses to
    Postmodernism Deconstruction*. Washington D.C.: Island
    Press.
Shepherd, N. (2011) *The Living Mountain*. Edinburgh: Canongate.
Shipton, E. (1970) *The Untravelled World*. London: Hodder and
    Stoughton.
Shiva, V. (2001) *Protect or Plunder*. London: Zed Books.
Shoard, M. (1997) *This Land is Our Land*. London: Gaia.
Shoard, M. (1999) *A Right to Roam*, Oxford: Oxford University Press.
Short, J. A. R. (1991) *Imagined Country*. London: Routledge.
Shrubsole, G. (2019) *Who Owns England?* London: William Collins.
Simpson, J. (1994) *This Game of Ghosts*. London: Vintage.
Simpson, J. (1997) *Touching the Void*. London: Vintage.
Smout, C. (1992) *The Highlands and the Roots of Green Consciousness:
    1750–1990*. Battleby, Perth: SNH.
Solnit, R. (2001) *Wanderlust: A History of Walking*. London: Verso.
Soper, K. 1995 *What is Nature?* Oxford: Blackwell.
Soule, M. and Lease, G. eds. (1995) *Reinventing Nature? Responses to
    Postmodernism Deconstruction*. Washington D.C.: Island Press.
Soule, M. (1995) 'The Social Siege of Nature' in M. Soule and
    G. Lease eds. *Reinventing Nature? Responses to Postmodernism
    Deconstruction*. Washington D.C.: Island Press.
Storer, R. (1998–1994) *The Joy of Hill Walking*. Edinburgh: Luath.
Strang, V. (1997) *Uncommon Ground*. Oxford: Berg.

Strang, V. (2000) 'Not so Black and White: The Effects of Aboriginal Law on Australian Legislation' in A. Abramson and D. Theodossopoulos (eds). *Land, Law and Environment: Mythic Land, Legal Boundaries*. London: Pluto Press.

Szerszynski, B., Heim, W. and Waterton, C. eds. (2003) *Nature Performed*. Oxford: Blackwell.

Tenner, E. (1997) *When Things Bite Back*. London: Fourth Estate.

Theodossopoulos, D. (2000) 'The Land People Work and the Land People Want' in A. Abramson and D. Theodossopoulos eds. *Land, Law and Environment: Mythic Land, Legal Boundaries*. London: Pluto Press.

Thomas, K. (1983) *Man and the Natural World*. London/ Harmondsworth: Penguin.

Tree, I. (2018) *Wilding: The return to nature of a British Farm*. London: Picador.

Tsing, A. (2001) 'Nature in the Making' in C. Crumley ed. *New Directions in Anthropology*. Walnut Creek, California: Altamira Press.

Urry, J. (1990) *The Tourist Gaze*. London: Routledge.

Urry, J. (1995) *Consuming Places*. London: Routledge.

Van De Veer, D. and Pierce, C. eds. (1998) *The Environmental Ethics and Policy Book*. Belmont, California: Wadsworth Publishing.

Volosinov, V. N. (1986) *Marxism and the Philosophy of Language* (translated L. Matejka and I. R. Tutunik). Cambridge, Massachusetts: Harvard University Press.

Wacquant, L. (1995) 'The Pugilistic Point of View: How boxers think and feel about their trade' in *Theory and Society* 24–4, pp. 489–535.

Walley, C. (2004) *Rough Waters: Nature and Development in an East African Marine Park*. Princeton and Oxford: Princeton University Press.

Walley, C. (2004) 'Best Intentions' in *Boston Review*: December/January.

Watson, A. (1992) The Cairngorms. Scottish Mountaineering Club Trust.

White, L. (1967) 'The Historical Roots of our Ecological Crisis' in D. Van De Veer and C. Pierce eds. (1998) *The Environmental Ethics and Policy Book*. Belmont, California: Wadsworth Publishing.

Wigan, M. (1998) *The Scottish Highland Estate*. Shrewbury: Swan Hill Press.

Wightman, A. (1997) *Who Owns Scotland*. Edinburgh: Canongate.

Wightman, A. (1999) *Scotland: Land and Power*. Edinburgh: Luath Press.

Wightman, A. (2015) *The Poor Had No Lawyers: Who owns Scotland and how they got it*. Edinburgh: Birlinn Ltd.

Williams, R. (1973) *The Country and the City*. London: Chatto.

Williamson, J. (2004) 'Protest sparked by change at Deer Commission' in *Strathspey and Badenoch Herald*: 14 April.

Wilson, K. ed. (1996) *The Games Climbers Play*. London: Baton Wicks.

Wolch, J. and Emel, J. eds. (1998) *Animal Geographies*. London: Verso.

Wolf, E. (1999) *Envisioning Power*. Berkeley: University of California Press.

Worster, D. (1995) 'Nature and the Disorder of History' in M. Soule and G. Lease eds. *Reinventing Nature? Responses to Postmodernism Deconstruction*. Washington D.C.: Island Press.

Wright, B. (2000) 'A Walk in the Park' in *Climber*, April.

Yi-Fu Tuan (1974) *Topophilia*.

Index